D1349626

THATCHERISM AND TERRITORIAL POLITICS

To Holly

Thatcherism and Territorial Politics

A Welsh Case Study

DYLAN GRIFFITHS
Department of Politics
University of Newcastle upon Tyne

Avebury

Aldershot • Brookfield USA • Hong Kong • Singapore • Sydney

© D. Griffiths 1996

All rights reserved. No part of this publication may be reproduced, stored in a retrieval system, or transmitted in any form or by any means, electronic, mechanical, photocopying, recording or otherwise without the prior permission of the publisher.

Published by
Avebury
Ashgate Publishing Limited
Gower House
Croft Road
Aldershot
Hants GU11 3HR
England

Ashgate Publishing Company
Old Post Road
Brookfield
Vermont 05036
USA

British Library Cataloguing in Publication Data

Griffiths, Dylan
    Thatcherism and Territorial Politics:
    Welsh Case Study
    I. Title
    320.9429

    ISBN 1 85972 296 2

Library of Congress Catalog Card Number: 95-83052

Typeset by The Setting Studio, 121 Newbridge Street, Newcastle upon Tyne

Printed and bound by Athenaeum Press, Ltd.,
Gateshead, Tyne & Wear.

Contents

List of tables

Acknowledgements

I gratefully acknowledge the reward of a studentship from the Economic and Social Research Council which enabled me to conduct this research. I thank my supervisor, Professor Ian Budge at the University of Essex, for his numerous suggestions, comments and personal kindness. Also, I thank Dr J Barry Jones at Cardiff University of Wales who looked at and commented on earlier drafts of this work. Any errors within this work are obviously the sole responsibility of the author.

1 Theories of territorial politics

Introduction

> "To study 'territorial politics' is to raise the problem of what is being studied and how it is to be understood"

> (Rhodes and Wright 1987 p1)

Some thirty years ago a book on the government of a part of the United Kingdom would have seemed an oddity. This scepticism would have arisen for two reasons. Firstly, much of this scepticism would have been due to the notion of British political homogeneity and the consequent downgrading of ethnic, religious or territorial cleavages in British society. For A. H. Birch the British homogeneity thesis depicted the United Kingdom as "... a national society affected by class divisions but not by the regional, ethnic or cultural conflicts that scarred political life in less fortunate countries" (Birch 1977 p13). Secondly, Britain constitutionally is an unitary state (defined by Rokkan and Urwin as being "built up around one unambiguous political centre which enjoys economic dominance and pursues a more or less undeviating policy of administrative standardisation. All areas of the state are treated alike, and all institutions are directly under the control of the centre" (Rokkan and Urwin 1982 p11)) and this seemingly precluded any discussion of territorial differentiation in British administration. Rhodes's caricature of this conventional wisdom on the British constitution emphasises the power of central institutions and, by implication, claims that all other institutions are not worth studying, "The conventional picture of Britain is of a unitary state, with a single Parliament, government and civil service, deciding on policy for the whole country and applying it through the national territory...There are no local or other autonomous bodies which even compare in authority with national government" (Rhodes 1985 p33).

In this chapter, I will combat this scepticism by examining why territory has (re)emerged as a subject of interest to political scientists generally and British politics in particular, how political scientists have analysed the territorial dimension of politics and, lastly, what lessons their conclusions hold for a student of policy-making and politics in Wales.

Territory and political science

"Geography and politics have long been in search of each other"

(Gottman 1980 p11).

It would be equally true to say that, until comparatively recently, political science studiously avoided geography. For Rokkan and Urwin, "(A) territorial approach to politics which seemed to disappear from the academic lexicon after 1945 with the seeming discrediting of political geography acquired a new respectability in academic studies after 1960" (Rokkan and Urwin 1983 p1). Before examining why political science has until recently neglected the territorial dimension of politics it is as well to observe that political scientists had not always done so; the work of the Annales school showed that politics could be studied geographically, and earlier still, in Montesquieu's "Spirit of the Laws", for example, territory and topography were at the heart of an analysis of societies (Claval 1980).

One fundamental reason for a neglect of territory and geography in much of political science is its conception of itself as a science. Political science, following the positivist tradition, saw the role of science as making and testing generalised or universalised hypotheses. Geography is an obstacle for this project as "...the recognition of geography implies uniqueness rather than universality," (Sharpe 1987 p149) and, "No political scientist can fail to cast an envious eye at the sophistication of economics in which variation based on territoriality seems to have disappeared" (Sharpe 1987 p149). The methodology of the social sciences seemed to eschew an interest in territory as an element of social life. In its place were preferred sociological concepts that did not have a geographic component such as class, status groups, age or gender; or the placeless rational egoist of rational choice theory.

An aterritorial methodology has given rise to a political science that has worked with aterritorial concepts. Political science, in its quest for observations comparable across time and place from which generalisations and hypotheses

2

could be drawn, made this inevitable. Sharpe describes this state of mind thus: "There are Catholics, semi-skilled white collar workers, or socialist parties in a number of countries. They can therefore be treated as uniform categories irrespective of domicile. Comparison is possible and thus political science is possible" (Sharpe 1987 p149).

Where geographical variations in political behaviour are observed, for example in support given to a political party or to the level of voter turnout in different areas, these have been explained in terms of the spatial distribution of individuals exhibiting different traits and fitting into predefined national census categories. Composition effects accept that the characteristics of the inhabitants of an area might vary but deny that the history of that area (in relation to other areas perhaps) might also be significant. Agnew concludes that for many political scientists, "geography is epiphenomenal, it is merely the aggregate product of "individual" attributes that just happen to covary with location" (Agnew 1987 p4). Individuals and their characteristics are the variables preferred in political explanation.

However, Agnew has noted that some recent writings in politics, sociology and geography have been "sensitive to the fact that human activities take the form of concrete interactions in time-space" (Agnew 1987 p5). He observes that Foucault, Giddens and Pred "all argue, if in different ways, that in order to explain human behaviour, one must deal with the material continuity of everyday life, or the process of 'structuration' whereby the structural properties of social life are expressed through everyday practices which in turn produce and reproduce the micro- and macrolevel structural properties of the social groups in question" (Agnew 1983 p5). The behaviour of individuals has to be placed in its context to be properly understood or as Agnew states "Attention is thus directed to the settings and scenes of everyday life: to place" (Agnew 1987 p5).

The aterritoriality of much political science may also seem odd given the territorial component within so many of the concepts at the heart of political analysis. Gottman reminds us that the root of the word *region* is the same as the word *regulation* and that *police* and indeed *politics* both derive from the Greek *polis* – the city. (Gottman 1980 p12). The state, a fundamental political concept and one vital for an understanding of territorial politics (as I shall argue below) has a territorial base as the sociologist Max Weber well knew (Sharpe 1987 p150). Maybe, as Agnew suggests there may be normative grounds for preferring aterritorial concepts as well as methodological reasons. Place is seen as belonging to a dark past of rigid boundaries constrictive of individual opportunities and a source of conflict between populations. The future is seen in terms of universal categories and the breaking down of boundaries set by race, language or ethnicity. This is certainly how modernisation theories saw social progress in the 1950s and 1960s.

3

Modernisation was thought to unify and homogenise different groups, assimilate them into a common culture, and thus, erode territorial cleavages, replacing them with functional or class cleavages in society. The forces of modernity, industrialisation, greater social mobility and advances in communication were regarded as inevitably eroding the degree of difference between places (and the inhabitants of places) and thus eroding the political salience of places. Rokkan himself had expressed this belief writing: "The National Revolution forced ever widening circles of the territorial populations to choose sides in conflicts over values and cultural identities. The Industrial Revolution also triggered a variety of cultural counter movements, but in the longer run tended to cut across the value communities within the nation and to force the enfranchised citizenry to choose sides in terms of their economic interest, their share in the increased wealth generated through the spread of new technologies and the widening markets" (Rokkan and Lipset 1967 p18). Deutsch (Deutsch 1953) foresaw that developments in communications, transport and the market economy would homogenise societies, eroding and finally erasing territorial, regional or ethnic cleavages.

Marxism also tended to neglect territory, place and ethnicity. Marxism concurred with the liberal diagnosis that territorial cleavages belonged to a previous stage in history, a stage successfully negotiated in Western Europe at least. Communism, it was believed, would hasten the demise of territory and ethnicity as politically significant issues. In The Communist Manifesto Marx and Engels wrote: "National differences and antagonisms between peoples are daily more and more vanishing, owing to the development of the bourgeoisie, to freedom of commerce, to the world market, to uniformity in the mode of production and the conditions of life corresponding thereto. The supremacy of the proletariat will cause them to vanish still faster... In proportion as the exploitation of one individual by another is put an end to, the exploitation by one nation by another will also be put an end to. In proportion as the antagonism between classes within the nation vanishes, the hostility of one nation to another will come to an end" (Marx and Engels 1975 p57).

The United Kingdom as an archetypally modern state – the British homogeneity thesis

Nowhere was this process of modernisation thought to have progressed further than the United Kingdom. Urwin (1982 p19) noted that "Until the 1960s the United Kingdom was accepted as a textbook example of a homogeneous society where influences and characteristics were equally significant and effective throughout the whole territory". Almond and Verba (1963 p6) claimed that the "whole story of the emergence of the civic culture is told in British history".

4

Britain's nation-wide two party system (leaving Northern Ireland aside) allowed Pulzer (1967 p98) to declare that "class is the basis of British party politics ; all else is embellishment and detail".

The belief that Britain was socially uniform to an exceptional degree came to be characterised as the British homogeneity thesis. This thesis assumed that political behaviour in Britain was characterised almost exclusively by class conflict and that other social cleavages, religion, national or regional identities were unimportant in the British context. Budge and Urwin (1966 pp48-51) in their study of 'Scottish Political Behaviour' defined the four elements of the British homogeneity thesis as:

1) "that the whole British electorate is exposed to a common social environment and a common (mass) culture arising form centralisation in London of the channels of the mass media and all cultural agencies.
2) social class assumes such importance as the main divisive force in British politics in every area of the country that regional, religious or other variations in political behaviour which could exist independently of class must be comparatively unimportant and indeed perhaps can be ignored altogether.
3) that the class division forms the only general division to be found in the political opinions and attitudes of British electors. Only on social welfare and economic issues is any consistent division of support for opposing parties to be found among British electors. This division is linked to party and hence to class identification.
4) that the conclusions of the theory of homogeneity in respect of voting behaviour apply equally to all other types of political behaviour. That is to say, it is implied that most British political activity of any kind centres solely around class divisions"

Based on an analysis of a survey of voters in Glasgow, Budge and Urwin (1966 ch10) found the theory of British political homogeneity to be 'defective' as non-class based factors such as religion, Scottish issues and a sense of Scottish national identity influenced the political behaviour of the sample.

The British homogeneity thesis underwent further revision following Rose's study of the United Kingdom as a multi-national state. Studying the component nations of the United Kingdom, England, Scotland, Wales and Northern Ireland, Rose (1976) found that differences in terms of religion and national identity for example remained across the United Kingdom. The cultural differences that were supposed to have been eroded "by the consequences of industrialisation, personal mobility, mass communication and the increasing activities of the national government" (Birch 1977 p33) had endured remarkably well, even in the first industrialised nation. Cultural and territorial cleavages, significant in

Britain's political history, persisted in the latter half of the twentieth century. However, it could still be plausibly maintained that, for the most part, these differences were no longer politically salient in the twentieth century and what political significance they retained could be accommodated comfortably within the institutions of the unitary British state, by providing a measure of home rule in Northern Ireland (at Stormont castle from 1920 to 1972) or separate offices in Scotland and Wales to add a Scottish or Welsh stamp to United Kingdom policies.

The notion of the United Kingdom as an unitary state also came in for revision. The gradual and often violent creation of the United Kingdom was emphasised (Birch 1977 Chapter 2, Urwin 1982 pp22-31). Urwin noted that "There were several different paths... towards incorporation. The English inner periphery was annexed directly, ... Wales was absorbed in the face of limited and unco-ordinated opposition [militarily in 1282, politically in 1536]; the merger with Scotland [in 1707] from a treaty between two independent states; while the incorporation of Ireland [in 1801] was more a blunt political take-over that followed upon centuries of abortive military conflict and oppression" (Urwin 1982 p27). Evidence of this process of territorial acquisition could still be seen in the institutions of the United Kingdom centuries later. The Treaty of Union between Scotland and England preserved a separate Scottish established church, a different legal system and a separate education system. Distinctiveness was enhanced in 1885 when the Scottish Office was created to oversee the work of government in Scotland. The distinctiveness of Wales too was re-asserted in the twentieth century with the disestablishment of the Anglican Church in Wales and a process of administrative devolution that culminated in the creation of the Welsh Office in 1964. The assertion of Irish separateness was more protracted and violent than that of Wales and led in 1920 to the partition of Ireland into a southern Irish Free State which became the Irish Republic in 1937 and the Protestant dominated province of Northern Ireland under the British Crown but administered by its own assembly at Stormont until 1972.

These differences led Rokkan and Urwin to characterise the United Kingdom not as an unitary state but as an union state whereby "Incorporation of at least parts of its territory has been achieved through personal dynastic union, for example by treaty... Integration is less than perfect. While administrative standardisation prevails over most of the territory, the consequences of personal union entail the survival in some areas of pre-union rights and institutional infrastructures which preserve some degree of regional autonomy and serve as agencies of indigenous elite recruitment" (Rokkan and Urwin 1982 p11).

Unexpected rebellion

Due to its assumption that modernisation was eroding national, ethnic or regional attachments, political science was unprepared for the resurgence of ethnic, nationalist and regionalist protests that occurred in Western Europe (and Canada) in the 1960s. Beer (1980) described it as an 'unexpected rebellion'. Before turning to an examination of the explanations proffered of these ethnic nationalist movements I shall briefly outline some features of the resurgence of sub state ethnic nationalism in the United Kingdom.[1]

In Wales the resurgence of cultural cleavages that had seemed to be declining in salience, certainly since 1918, was a significant feature of the 1960s. In 1962, Saunders Lewis, an eminent playwright and Welsh nationalist, gave a radio lecture, *Tynged yr Iaith*, forecasting the death of the Welsh language by the end of the century unless immediate action was taken. *Cymdeithas yr Iaith Gymraeg*, the Welsh Language Society was created in response to this lecture in 1963. Throughout the 1960s, Welsh language activists campaigned for a Welsh language act. Their campaigning action included damage to property and law breaking (but not violence to people) was a hallmark of their activity from the very first. In 1967, they won a partial victory with the passage of the Welsh Language Act, which gave official status to a language that many had thought to be a dying language.

Political nationalism too was resurgent in Wales. Since its creation in 1925, *Plaid Cymru*, the Party of Wales, had enjoyed little electoral success. This changed in 1966 however, when the party president, Gwynfor Evans, won the Carmarthen by-election. *Plaid Cymru* also performed well in the subsequent Caerphilly and Rhondda by-elections almost overturning massive Labour majorities. In the 1970 general election, although it won no seats, *Plaid Cymru* won 10.5 per cent of the vote, its best ever national performance in terms of share of the vote. Thereafter, although its share of the vote declined, *Plaid Cymru* succeeded in gaining seats in Welsh speaking West Wales. In October 1974 it won Caernarfon and Meirionydd in the county of Gwynedd and Carmarthen in Dyfed. In 1992 its tally of seats rose to four, its highest ever, all again in West Wales.

Nationalism in Wales has also had a darker violent side. During the 1960s, the Free Wales Army was active. Two of its members were killed planting a bomb in 1969, during the Investiture of the Prince of Wales. In the 1980s, *Meibion Glyndwr*, the Sons of Glyndwr (a medieval Welsh hero that led a rebellion against

---

[1] For a discussion of ethnic nationalist movements elsewhere see for example Rokkan and Urwin The Politics of Territorial Identity: Studies in European Regionalism London Sage 1982; Colin Williams (ed) National Separatism Cardiff University of Wales Press 1982; M Watson (ed) Contemporary Minority Nationalism London Routledge 1990.

the English), conducted an arson campaign against holiday homes owned by English people in Wales.

This resurgence in ethnic nationalism has not been confined to Wales within the United Kingdom. In Scotland the Scottish National Party, the SNP, has become a significant electoral force. In 1967 it won the Hamilton by-election and in the 1970 general election won the Western Isles seat. In the October 1974 election, with nationalist sentiment running high and the cause of Scottish independence bolstered by the discovery of North Sea oil, the SNP won 30 per cent of the vote and 11 seats. The 1974 Parliament was preoccupied with devolution measures for Scotland and Wales. In 1979 however, the Scottish electorate failed to endorse the devolution measures proposed by the government in a referendum.

Although the devolution debate during the 1970s ended anticlimactically in 1979 this was not the end for political nationalism in Scotland. Although the Conservative Party continued to win parliamentary majorities nationally, their share of the vote and seats in Scotland declined throughout the 1980s. In 1987 the Conservatives won only ten seats in Scotland, barely enough to fill the ministerial posts of the Scottish Office. A 'Doomsday scenario' began to be envisaged where the Conservatives continued to win parliamentary majorities but only a handful of seats in Scotland. This, it was argued by some, would call the legitimacy of Westminster rule over Scotland into question. Nationalist sentiment rose again in Scotland during the 1980s and the main opposition parties (with the exception, paradoxically, of the SNP) sat as a Scottish Convention to agree on a new home rule measure for Scotland. The 1992 election campaign was fought in Scotland with only the Conservative Party committed to constitutional status quo and John Major, the prime minister, made the maintenance of the Union a focal point of the Conservative appeal in Scotland. The result of the election with the Conservatives gaining one seat and the Conservatives increasing their share of the vote seemed to be a (partial) vindication of this strategy. Although the SNP also increased its share of the vote, by 7 per cent, its failure to gain seats resulted in the nationalist campaign again losing momentum.

Nationalist cleavages that had appeared to be dormant also erupted in Northern Ireland in the 1960s. Attempts by the Stormont leader O'Neill to reconcile the Catholic community in Northern Ireland to the union backfired and resulted in a Protestant backlash (led by hitherto marginal figures such as the Reverend Ian Paisley) and more demands by the leaders of the Catholic community. The violence that began in 1969 resulted in the abolition of Stormont, the only successful exercise in devolved rule that has been attempted in the United Kingdom this century. It has also resulted in the Anglo-Irish agreement signed in 1985 and, in December 1993, the Downing Street Declaration. Both documents

8

give the Irish government, the government of a foreign power, an interest in the affairs of a part of the United Kingdom. This is an unique state of affairs in terms of the territorial management of a part of the United Kingdom.

Explanations of minority nationalism

Although the upsurge in minority nationalism was unanticipated, political scientists were not long in seeking to explain it. Explanations can be divided into three types. One group of explanations sees the rise of minority nationalism from the 1960s onwards as a manifestation of other processes that were occurring contemporaneously. The explanations of minority nationalism in Britain offered by Bogdanor (1979) and David Adamson (1991) would fall into this group.

Secondly, there is a group of explanations which, although they may have little else substantively in common with each other, share a common approach in seeking to explain minority nationalism in terms of history. Rokkan and Urwin's analysis in terms of centre and periphery belongs in this category as do Hechter's and Nairn's Marxist inspired accounts of minority nationalism.

Thirdly, there is a group of explanations which although they often share a historic dimension are distinguished by their concern with the actions (and interests) of the state in mediating territorial and ethnic tensions within a polity. Rhodes and Wright (1987) are perhaps the clearest exponents of this view, though versions of it are also presented forcefully by Bulpitt (1983) and Tarrow (1977).

Postmaterialism

It is possible to regard the upsurge in minority nationalism from the 1960s on as another example of postmaterialism. Inglehart believed that greater economic and physical security among western publics was tending towards "a decline in the importance of issues that reflect the stratification system of industrial society; ideology ethnicity, life-style, and so on may assume greater importance. Class politics may decline in favour of status or cultural or 'ideal' politics" (Inglehart 1977 p13). Minority nationalist movements are often concerned (if not exclusively) with issues of culture, identity, community and belonging. Bogdanor saw the demands of minority nationalist movements as being very similar to those of other postmaterialist movements: "Modern ethnic nationalism and movements of regional deconcentration are in essence attempts to humanise the state. Economic and technical developments whose tendency is to make men more and more alike find themselves checked by political pressures – the search for identity and the demand for participation" (Bogdanor 1979 p6).

Also, the reasons for their upsurge are similar; greater economic security enables people to satisfy other 'higher order needs' such as identity and self-expression:

> Only after some degree of affluence has already been achieved, and after the worst problems of deprivation and unemployment have been solved, can men think seriously about the more intangible needs which are essential to their happiness. When this stage has been reached, the old political ideologies cease to have meaning, class conflict declines and there comes to be less intensity of feeling between Left and Right.

> (Bogdanor 1979 p6).

Dealignment

Another explanation for the upsurge of nationalist parties in the United Kingdom can be provided by the class and partisan dealignment thesis. Crewe wrote "In Great Britain, since World War I, class ... has been the primary, almost exclusive, social basis of partisan choice...In the late 1960s the first signs of a weakening in the class-party link appeared. Alternative bases of partisanship emerged (or re-emerged after decades) in some areas: language and culture in rural Wales, national identity in Scotland..." (Crewe 1983 pp192-3). The working class has declined due to the decline in manufacturing employment and support for the Labour party within the working class is no longer as firm as it was previously. Adamson's study of Welsh nationalism reaches similar conclusions about political change in Wales writing of a "gradual erosion and destructuring of the basis of labourism even in the valley heartlands, a process first reflected in the support *Plaid Cymru* gained parts of south Wales in the 1960s and 1970s" (Adamson 1991 p159).

Applying the concepts of postmaterialism and class dealignment to the nationalist movement in Wales is superficially appealing. Developments in Wales during the 1960s and 1970s did share similarities with events elsewhere and some of the aspirations of the nationalist movement bore some resemblance to other non-nationalist protest movements of the period. However, such accounts of minority nationalist movements are unable to explain why forces common to western Europe generally should be expressed in Wales (and elsewhere) precisely in nationalist terms. Arguably, they ignore precisely what is at issue, that is the ethnic background present in Wales and other places where nationalist movements have flourished. Acknowledging the universality of the process of class dealignment which Adamson uses to account for the resurgence of Welsh nationalism in the twentieth century Adamson states that

> The changing occupational structure experienced in south Wales during the post-war period has also been experienced in other regions. However, in

other regions the absence of ethnic differentiation prevented such early opportunity for the new working class to give voice to its increasing alienation from labourism and the Labour Party.

(Adamson 1991 p175).

In order to understand the nature of politics in Wales that makes the rise of a nationalist movement possible it is necessary to examine the social and historical context of politics in places such as Wales. Adamson is aware of the need for grounding an explanation of contemporary nationalism in its social and historical context, writing:

> I have engaged in a historical analysis in the belief that any attempt to understand political and social movements must include a thorough understanding of the precedents and antecedents which shape the particular character of any social practice. Nationalism in contemporary Wales differs, in many ways from its nineteenth-century expression, but cannot be understood without reference to the social forces which existed then and continue to have effect
>
> (Adamson 1991 pp3-4)

Other studies have placed the study of the historical context of places at the heart of their accounts of minority nationalism. These are discussed below.

Territorial politics and history

Centre-periphery

A second group of explanations provide a historically grounded account of ethnic nationalism. Most notable among models that employ history to explain minority nationalism has been Rokkan and Urwin's centre-periphery model. This model posits a division within nation states between privileged locations centres, and peripheries or "those geographical locations at the furthest distance form the centre but still within the territory controlled by the latter" (Rokkan and Urwin 1983 p2). A periphery was distinguished by being

> dependent with little control over its fate and possessing minimal resources for the defence of its distinctiveness against outside pressures. It is often a conquered territory, as it were a kind of colony, administered by officials who are responsive less to the desires of the periphery than to instructions from a geographically remote centre. It will also tend to have a developed economy... one that is dependent upon a single commodity that is sold in

distant markets and this is... easily prey to frequent fluctuations in demand and prices, over which the periphery has little control. Finally, the periphery will tend to have a marginal culture: without unified and distinctive institutions of its own, its culture will be fragmented and parochial

Minority nationalism can thus be explained as a manifestation of the tensions between the centre and periphery, problems arising from the process of nation building and boundary demarcation, or, simply, the 'politicisation of peripheral predicaments' (Rokkan and Urwin 1983 p118). Thus, minority nationalism arises from a historical context where events from several centuries before may still be of significance in contemporary politics. In the case of Wales for example, the military integration of Wales occurred as long ago as 1282, political integration in 1536 and cultural integration (the decline of the Welsh language across large parts of Wales) from 1800 onwards. These dates, have shaped the nature of life in Wales today, are remembered by nationalists and are important to understanding the modern manifestation of Welsh nationalism. In short, history is an essential ingredient of the centre-periphery model. Meny and Wright state that

> in order to study centre-periphery relations one has to resort to history – history as it has been experienced, interpreted and manipulated... any ahistorical approach is doomed to failure: recent centre-periphery relations can be understood only as a combination of past and present. Tensions which emerge within a state are the product of its early formation, its development and adaptation

(Meny and Wright 1985 p3).

The centre-periphery model is opposed to models which seek an explanation for contemporary minority nationalism in contemporary events or delve only as far as the recent past in constructing an explanation for it. Urwin criticised "a bias towards ahistorical treatment, and at the most, a limited comparative view" (Urwin 1985 p155) in many discussions of minority nationalism. He claimed that "Several authors have been content to seek an explanation in contemporary developments" (Urwin 1985 p155) including in a variation of the 'overload' thesis, stressing:

> a continuing internationalisation of territorial economies, accompanied by a persisting erosion of interstate boundaries through a growing diffusion of a more and more undifferentiated blend of messages, ideologies and life-styles...Linked to these trends have been the demands on, and the expectations, the resources and manpower of central machineries in the welfare state era. The pressures to expand social welfare services and to intensify aid to the less productive sectors and regions of the economy have increased the cost of

infrastructural requirements, while at the same time heightened demand has increasingly strained the state's ability to deliver the goods

(Urwin 1985 pp155-156).

However, the centre-periphery model has not escaped criticism. Rokkan and Urwin admit that there are problems concerning the usage of the terms 'centre' and 'periphery' "since neither is a precise technical term" (Rokkan and Urwin 1983 p1). Also, an over-concentration on the historical development of centres and peripheries may ignore contemporary developments of equal territorial significance. Rhodes and Wright maintain that "the term 'centre-periphery' relations is not only magnificently vague but it may also focus exclusively on cleavages which were significant in the evolution of the modern welfare state but which may be of declining relevance for the analysis of advanced industrial societies" (Rhodes and Wright 1987 p4). Like the Marxist accounts of Hechter and Nairn the centre-periphery model tends to ignore the role of the state interceding between the centre and the periphery. Meny and Wright state:

Most observers have focused their attention on the anti-central state activity of those peripheries which are most distinct, most different from the central nation model. Emphasis has been placed on the 'ethnic revival' and often too much importance has been attached to the methods of expressing demands (from dancing displays to bomb outrages) rather than their substance or consequences. Analyses have often, too, been coloured by the sympathies of the observers. The revolution which, it was claimed seemed to be menacing the Western nation states obscured for too many analysts the no less spectacular transfer of the management of policies from the centre to the periphery

(Meny and Wright 1985 p7).

These are discussed further below after an examination of Hechter's internal colonial and Nairn's uneven development accounts of territorial politics.

Internal colonialism

Hechter's account of minority nationalism in the British Isles is, in a sense, an exercise in historical sociology (as was the work of Marx himself). The title of Hechter's book, *Internal Colonialism: the Celtic fringe in British national development, 1536-1966*, is a fair summary of the scale of his project. He uses statistical data from 1851 to 1966 as well as drawing on secondary historical sources to substantiate his claim that Ireland, Wales and Scotland were internal colonies of an English core.

An internal colonial situation arises as:

> The spatially uneven wave of modernisation over state territory creates relatively advanced and less advanced groups. As a consequence of this initial fortuitous advantage, there is crystallisation of the unequal distribution of resources and power between the two groups. The superordinate group, or core, seeks to stabilise and monopolise its advantages through policies aiming at the institutionalisation of the existing stratification system. It attempts to regulate to regulate the allocation of social roles such that those roles commonly defined as having high status are reserved for its members. Conversely, individuals form the less advantaged group are denied access to these roles. This stratification system which may be termed a cultural division of labour, contributes to the development of distinctive ethnic identifications in the two groups. Actors come to categorise themselves and others according to the range of roles each may be expected to play. They are aided in this categorisation by the presence of visible signs, or cultural markers, which are seen to categorise both groups. At this stage, acculturation does not occur because it is not in the interests of institutions within the core

(Hechter 1975 p9).

However, as with Marx's analysis of capitalism, Hechter maintains that the distribution of power maintained by the cultural division of labour contains the seeds of its own destruction as:

> To the extent that social stratification in the periphery is based on observable cultural differences, there exists the probability that the disadvantaged group will in time, reactively assert its own culture as equal or superior to that of the relatively advantaged core. This may help it conceive of itself as a separate 'nation' and seek independence. Hence, in this situation, acculturation and national development may be inhibited by the desires of the peripheral group for independence from a situation perceived to be exploitative

(Hechter 1975 p10).

Hechter's account of ethnic nationalism in the United Kingdom is clearly historical. However, is it historically accurate? Is it accurate to assume a cultural division of labour where elite positions were monopolised by English outsiders? Also, is it correct to portray economic development in Wales for example as complementary and subordinate to the needs of English capital? This is clearly what Hechter maintains but such a view is contradicted by historical evidence. Minchinton (1969) describes the rise of an indigenous bourgeoisie in South

Wales as the industrial revolution progressed. K O Morgan (1980, 1981) describes a vibrant Welsh economy during the latter years of the nineteenth century and the early years of this century. The development of coal and steel and the shipping and transport networks of the coastal plain point to the significant role of Welsh industry in the world economy, not to its subjection to an English core. Indeed, it could be maintained that the core economy was precisely in areas of heavy industry like South Wales (Evans 1983 p2). Although after World War One the fortunes of the industries upon which South Wales had relied for its prosperity declined, leading to economic depression in the region, it is difficult to maintain that the core had forced Wales to concentrate in these industries knowing that they would be depressed industries in the future. Also, as Welshmen were able to play a leading role in business, legal, administrative, political and other high status fields certainly by the end of the nineteenth century, the salience of the cultural division of labour must have declined significantly by that time. This weakens Hechter's analysis of Welsh nationalism in the twentieth century.

Thus, whilst Hechter may be correct in stating that nationalism in Wales and Scotland has been stimulated by "an awareness of persisting regional underdevelopment" (Hechter 1975 p310) and the failure of regional policy, of the Labour Party when in office in the 1960s, and what he generally refers to as 'bureaucratic centralism' (Hechter 1975 p310), to solve the economic problems of Wales and Scotland, he is wrong to imply, as he seemingly does, that inequality has been deliberately perpetuated by the core. It is the ineffectiveness of the core in delivering the fruits of growth equally that may have triggered the most recent 'crystallisation' of Celtic nationalism, not its malign or selfish desire to deny those benefits to the Celtic periphery altogether. Hechter imputes for the state a simple role of serving the interests of dominant, that is, core, economic interests, and thus perpetuating ethnic and spatial economic inequalities. This is not only naively deterministic, it also neglects the important role that the state can serve in mediating territorial conflicts as I discuss below.

Uneven development

For Nairn, "The theory of nationalism represents Marxism's greatest failure" (Nairn 1977 p337). Marx saw, as we noted above, nationalism as a form of irrationality that capitalism would undermine and socialism would erase. However, according to Nairn, Marx had not sufficiently understood the consequences of the uneven nature of capitalist development. Instead of even development, a process of diffusion resulting in a "basically homogeneous enlightened class throughout the periphery" (Nairn 1977 p338), the impact of development in the periphery was experienced as "domination and invasion"

15

(Nairn 1977 p339). Peripheral elites quickly discovered that "tranquil incorporation into the cosmopolitan technocracy was possible for only a few of them at a time" (Nairn 1977 p340) and therefore had to achieve a measure of autonomy from the core elites if they were not to be exploited. Mobilising the peripheral masses was one way of doing this. In order to appeal to the masses however, they had to communicate to them in a language they understood and this was the language of everyday culture, religion or the vernacular language itself. As Nairn puts it, "The new middle-class intelligentsia had to invite the masses into history; and the invitation card had to be written in a language they understood" (Nairn 1977 p71). This accounts, Nairn claims, for the populist nature of nationalism.

Nairn applies the concept of uneven development to the Britain of the 1970s. Here however, neo-nationalism is not a response to exploitation by the centre. Rather, "the key to these neo-nationalist renaissances lies in the slow foundering of the British state" (Nairn 1977 p73). The United Kingdom, undergoing a process of de-industrialisation and decline is described as a "sinking paddle-wheel state" (Nairn 1977 p89) and Scotland and Wales can hardly be blamed for not wanting to go down with the ship.

Also, although neo-nationalism is not itself the social revolution foretold by Marx, "The fact is that neo-nationalism has become the grave-digger of the old state in Britain, and as such the principal factor making for a political revolution of some sort" (Nairn 1977 p71). It should therefore be welcomed as something that might make a future socialist revolution possible.

Nairn's account of minority nationalism in Britain, like Hechter's, suffers from a number of weaknesses. By placing his theory in rather an apocalyptic historical framework, he is left to explain why the British state, apparently in irreversible decline has managed to survive at all. More fundamentally, his suggestion that "those ethnic-linguistic features so prominent in the ideologies of nationalism have always been secondary to the material forces of uneven development" (Nairn 1977 p71) seems too economistic and reductionist. A D Smith criticises the importance attached to economic advantage and disadvantage contained within the model as "such a 'territorial reductionism' fails to do justice to that other crucial variable, history, with all its cultural attributes" (Smith 1981 p35). Other areas that have experienced uneven development to a similar degree (the North of England maybe) have not seen nationalist or separatist movements. A possible explanation for this is precisely because they have no distinctive ethnic or linguistic features around which they can mobilise. Uneven development, an economic concept, cannot itself explain a complex political phenomenon such as minority nationalism. Attempts to explain all manifestations of minority nationalism in terms of one or a very few factors are doomed to failure as "Each situation is distinct, fashioned by myriad variables" (Meny and Wright 1985 p3), and Rokkan and Urwin conclude "the geopolitical, geocultural and geoeconomic map of Western Europe constitutes a veritable mosaic where explanations that seem to be valid in some situations are not so in others" (Rokkan and Urwin 1983 p191). Criticising Hechter's theory in a similar vein, Nairn nevertheless shows why it has been favoured as an explanation by some, "This theory is wrong because it lumps too many different things together. Both in analysing the causes and in considering the effects of new nationalism in Europe, it is too superficial. It may be effective ideology, but it rests on rather poor history" (Nairn 1977 pp201). It is the emotiveness of the internal colonial comparison, not its analytical rigour that has appealed to many nationalists in particular (Rose 1982 p9).

Also, the colonial comparison is invalid because it ignores the role of the state in advanced industrial societies. This point has been made specifically in relation to Wales. Criticising Hechter's application of the internal colonial model to the Welsh case, Lovering maintains that "the attempt to draw an analogy between Wales and an industrially advanced 'third world' country, is misleading because of what it misses out, and this is the ameliorative and modifying role of the unitary British state" (Lovering 1983 p49). It is to a discussion of the role of the state in territorial politics that we now turn.

Bringing the state back in

Tarrow criticises the "diffusion-isolation" and the "dependency-marginality" (1977 p16) accounts of minority nationalism as neither approach "explicitly addresses the question of how the state intercedes between the market and the periphery in advanced societies". Peripheries are not simply prostrate victims of the processes of capitalist development as "public resources find their way to the periphery" and this fact must be acknowledged "in any model of centre-periphery relations that claims policy relevance" (Tarrow 1977 pp16-17).

It is surprising that the state has received comparatively little attention in the study of territorial politics until recently. As Madgwick and Rose (1982 p1) have pointed out "(T)erritory is an essential dimension of government. A modern state can no more exist without territorial limits and divisions than a society could exist without divisions into social classes". Electoral competition (inevitably) inserts a territorial dimension even into functional politics as "Politicians demand equitable treatment for all regions of a country, and institutions of governance must be able to deliver the benefits of public policy to all of its parts. In the competition for electoral advantage, political parties articulate demands for particular areas as well as for the country as a whole. Pressure groups voice what their members want – and where these demands should be met" (Madgwick and

Rose 1982 p1). Lipset and Rokkan (1967 p11) observed that "Historically documented cleavages [are] rarely exclusively territorial or exclusively functional but will feed on strains in both directions." . Madgwick and Rose (1982 p2) concur: "Yet there is a territorial dimension in every functional policy. Political grievances can be articulated in territorial terms, such as complaints about Welsh unemployment or Scottish housing. The substantive problem remains housing or unemployment, but the demand for action is limited territorially" . For Rhodes and Wright (1987 p10), territorial politics is increasingly a question of "who gets what public services, when, where, how and why".

Rhodes and Wright (1987 p2) provide an institutional and public policy focus to their discussion of territorial politics. For them territorial politics, is defined as "the arena of political activity concerned with the relations between central political institutions in the capital city and those sub-central political organisations and governmental bodies within the accepted boundaries of the state". This has several advantages over other accounts of territorial politics. Its subject matter is explicitly political and avoids including, for example purely cultural demonstrations of peripheral identity within the ambit of territorial politics. By focusing on the state and its activities it includes functional issues (the territorial distribution of government resources for example) that increasingly, (though with some significant exceptions) make up the content of territorial politics. By focusing on governmental institutions it is able to consider some of the developments mentioned earlier that have clearly had an impact on life in the peripheries that other, more sociologically oriented, approaches were unable to consider. Such developments would include the creation of the Welsh Office in 1964, the reform of French regional government in 1982 or the granting of regional autonomy to some areas of Spain from 1977 onwards. Lastly, a focus on government enables the investigator to tie in developments in peripheral regions with forces that may have a general impact on the activities (and nature) of government and public policy. This Rhodes and Wright (1987 p13) do by employing the concepts of 'national government environment' and 'central elite ideology'.

The national government environment facing the British government since the 1970s has been one of economic decline, rising unemployment and, consequent upon these trends, the decline of many of Britain's urban areas. Although these are functional problems, the policy response to them is necessarily spatially concentrated (see Madgwick and Rose 1982 p1; Rhodes and Wright 1987 p10). Economic policy and urban policy are therefore suitable policy areas to examine the implementation of government policies in a territorial region. Economic policy and urban policy in Wales are investigated in chapters five and six of the book.

18

Central elite ideology refers to how central elites interpret the problems facing them and what solutions they propose for these problems. Since 1979 central elite ideology has been neo-liberal, monetarist and laisser-faire. The shorthand term for such views in the United Kingdom has been Thatcherism. Conservative governments since 1979 have eschewed keynesian demand management and emphasised instead the control of government expenditure as the primary goal of central government in order to control inflation and create an environment in which the private sector can prosper. Related to a minimal government role in macro-economic policy, central elite ideology has favoured the view that the private sector is more effective and more efficient than public provision of goods and services. Government, both central and local, should therefore play a subordinate, supportive role to the private sector, enabling private initiatives to come to fruition not crowding out the private sector by its expenditure or activities.

Paradoxically, the reduction of the role of government in the economy has required, according to some observers (for example Gamble 1988), a strengthening of central executive authority at the expense of local government and other groups, such as trade unions, that might ideologically oppose the government's economic and social policies. The ideology of British central elites is the subject of chapter four.

The choice of Wales as a case-study for territorial politics arises for several reasons. Firstly, whereas Scotland and Northern Ireland have been studied a study of electoral behaviour in Wales noted that despite renewed signs of political distinctiveness "no general account of Welsh politics in the manner of J G Kellas 'The Scottish Political System' was forthcoming" (Balsom 1983 p27).[2]

Secondly, Wales contains many examples of the problems brought about by the decline of manufacturing industry, rising unemployment and declining urban areas. Wales therefore offers a testing ground for government policies to these problems. The nature of the economic and social situation in Wales is studied in chapter two.

Thirdly, the institutional structure of government in Wales provides the student of territorial politics with an ideal opportunity to study the role of institutions in mediating centre-periphery relations. The range of government institutions unique to Wales has grown during this century, especially since 1964 with the establishment of the Welsh Office. Today, public bodies such as the Welsh

---

[2] On Scotland see for example J G Kellas The Scottish Political System 4th Edition Cambridge University Press 1989; A Midwinter, M Keating and J Mitchell Politics and Public Policy in Scotland London Macmillan 1991; D McCrone Understanding Scotland: The Sociology of a Stateless Nation London Routledge 1992; M Linklater and R Denniston (eds) Anatomy of Scotland: How Scotland Works Edinburgh Chambers 1992; F Gaffikin and Morissey Northern Ireland: the Thatcher Years London Zed Books 1990.

Development Agency, the Land Authority for Wales, the Development Board for Rural Wales and many other organisations spend millions of pounds annually discharging politically important functions in Wales. The Welsh Office and all other public bodies in Wales are part of central government but their territorial rather than functional specification creates ambiguity as to their role. Rhodes maintains that "they are simultaneously in the centre and for a territory" (Rhodes 1988 p144). Such bodies are often assumed to act as instruments of central control and central policy preferences. However, for Bulpitt, they may "be divorced from the local (and national) political process, they may operate in a political vacuum. Alternatively, despite their non-elected character they may be colonised by local political groups. How they operate will be determined in large part by the general structure of territorial politics. The whole subject of non-elected agencies still requires considerable investigation, and nowhere is this more true than the United Kingdom" (Bulpitt 1983 pp24-25). Tarrow discovered that in France and Italy, officials from the centre, "far from behaving like traditional local notables or acting merely as rubber-stamp administrators of programs initiated from above, local officials have become actors in the political adaptation of their communities to social and economic change" (Tarrow 1977 p4). Wales with its profusion of such bodies, would be an ideal place to examine the work of non elected local bodies.

Fourthly, it has been claimed that the government policies in Wales have diverged from those in England. The existence of separate administrative institutions in Wales has been pointed to as one reason for this divergence. Wales has been described as an enclave of 'relative keynesianism' where government intervention is still practised (Barrie Clement 6-6-1991). Gamble observed that:

> establishment of the Welsh Office in 1964 was widely seen as a sop ... But the institution has developed in interesting ways. Having a Cabinet Minister heading the Office has allowed the development of coherent interventionist policies for the whole region. The most striking example of such strategic thinking came paradoxically in the Thatcher years ... Under Walker and Hunt the Welsh Office has practised not the disengagement favoured by Thatcherite ideology but an interventionist industrial policy

> (Gamble 1993 p83)

Peter Walker, a former Secretary of State for Wales also claimed that he was able to implement policy in Wales as he wished and not as the Prime Minister commanded (Walker 1991 p203). The institutions of government in Wales and the possible extent to which they provide some capacity to exercise 'relative autonomy' from the guidelines of Westminster and Whitehall is the subject of chapter three.

The institutional structure of government in Wales is not the only reason offered as to why, allegedly, policies applied in Wales differed from those in England. It is claimed that the political environment, particularly the political culture, in Wales differs from that in England. It has been claimed that a 'regional consensus' exists in Wales which promotes co-operation by business, labour and government to a degree exceptional in the United Kingdom context (Rees and Lambert 1981 p125). Dafydd Elis Thomas, formerly president of *Plaid Cymru*, claimed that "It is not sufficiently recognised by those who look at the Welsh political system from the outside that Wales has developed a distinctive way of operating. It is a kind of 1960s corporatism... The bringing together of trade unions, management, local authorities and the agencies is a feature of the scale of Wales" (Hansard 28 November 1991, Welsh Development Agency Bill Session 1991-1992 col 1131). In chapter two in addition to examining the economic and social problems of Wales I also examine the social, political and cultural environment of government in Wales looking particularly for evidence of a political culture that emphasises consensus and co-operation.[3]

Finally, in chapter seven I conclude by examining what light the book casts on the nature of government, not only in Wales but also in the United Kingdom as a whole. Is it possible to speak of a distinct and separate political system in Wales in the same way as Kellas claimed to find a separate Scottish political system? Or is it more accurate to speak of a Welsh arena of politics integrated within a British political system? This study may be able to shed some light on the question that Aneurin Bevan posed over half a century ago, namely, where is the focus of power in British government? Does it lie in Cabinet, Westminster and Whitehall or is it possible for territorial ministers and political actors away from London to influence outcomes? In an earlier study of territorial politics in the United Kingdom Rose claimed that "To understand the United Kingdom as a whole, we must understand how its diverse territorial parts, England, Scotland, Wales and Northern Ireland are governed" (Rose 1982 pp2-3).

---

[3] The influence of political culture on the outputs of subcentral government has already been observed by political scientists. Agnew notes that "cultural differences can enter into the determination of public policy" (Agnew 1987 p57) and cites as evidence the findings of Newton and Sharpe of a 'Welsh effect' in local government expenditure to support his view.

2 Culture, politics and society in Wales

'At one point a woman, recently moved to Ceredigion, asked: "As an English person, I am trying to understand, but can you tell me exactly what is this Welsh culture you are all so worked up about?"

There was an embarrassed silence while the chairman cast around for someone to say something'

(John Osmond in Wales on Sunday 23-9-1990).

Introduction

Although this book is a study of the government of Wales it also, by implication, studies Wales. Wales is, at least partly, the environment in which the government of Wales operates and it is partly by their success in responding to the problems and demands created by Welsh society that the institutions of Welsh government should be judged. As Greenwood and Wilson state: "Public bodies do not exist in a vacuum but are closely related to the broader environment which they inhabit. They are both influenced by, and themselves influence, that environment'" (Greenwood and Wilson 1989 p4).

Therefore, in this chapter I will outline some of the features of Welsh society and how, and how far, these distinguish the social, cultural and political life of Wales from elsewhere in the United Kingdom. Cultural distinctiveness and a sense of national (or regional) identity are particularly important in any study of territorial politics as these are a necessary condition for the expression of territorial demands. Rokkan and Urwin are explicit on this point:

There are economic peripheries in Europe, but no territorial identity on the continent can be defined solely in terms of a distinctive economy. Similarly, no territorial identity can be distinguished only on the basis of its class character: where identity clashes did have a class basis, as between landlord and rural proletariat in Ireland... they were also grounded in religious, ethnic or linguistic differences. It may well be that class can provide an issue around which identity conflicts can be generated, but it is less probable for it to provide the essence of community feelings

(Rokkan and Urwin 1983 p66).

A recent history of Wales is entitled simply "When was Wales?" (Williams 1985) and it is not the only recent book about Wales to use a question mark in its title ("Wales! Wales?" by Dai Smith). Welshness, *Cymreictod*, the Welsh character, the Welsh 'way of life' are all concepts that seem to have no precise meaning. Perhaps we can say of the Welsh nation what Hugh Seton-Watson said of nations generally – "no 'scientific definition' of the nation can be devised; yet the phenomenon has existed and exists" (Seton Watson 1977 p5).

An equally important question is 'Where is Wales?' Within the peninsula that is Wales there are major differences in language, accent, industry, values and aspirations. The perception of these differences is particularly marked between the North and South of Wales. Jan Morris, perhaps melodramatically, states that:

There is no easily definable hierarchy, no universal kind of patriotism. North Walians think, speak and look differently from southerners, worlds of style and experience divide the anthracite miner's family of Ammanford, the wine-bar flaneurs of the Cardiff suburbs and the severe Calvinist agriculturalists of Y Bala or Tregaron. To observers from more logically arranged countries Wales seems to lack all qualifications or even instincts for cohesion

(Morris 1986 p215).

Generalisations about Welshness that describe parts of Wales may not apply to the culture of other parts of the country. Both may be equally Welsh however.

Today, it is popular to consider nations as "Imagined Communities" (Anderson 1983). Perhaps Wales exists in the imagination. Welshness perhaps is simply a series of myths that the Welsh tell about themselves. Myth making has played an important part in the forging of many nations, not only Wales, as the poet and novelist Emyr Humphreys well knew:

The myths of the Welsh were closely bound up with a living poetic tradition. This meant a degree of discipline in the formal arrangement and a social and political significance attached to correct propagation. Myth-making is a recognised activity amongst defeated peoples. It is not only a source of consolation. Properly understood and used it is a most potent weapon in the struggle for survival

(Emyr Humphreys quoted in Morgan 1986 p18).

Wales is undoubtedly a nation rich in national myths. Wales, after all, is the nation of Arthur, Merlin and the *Mabinogion*. The histories of the early Welsh saints, the Princes of Gwynedd and Owain Glyndwr have also been embellished to add lustre to the history of Wales. Nearer to our own time, the images of radical, rural Nonconformist Wales in the nineteenth century or radical socialist Wales and the legends of Tonypandy or 1926 in the twentieth century may be stories that the Welsh tell about themselves to express their identity.

However, if they tell us little about politics and life in Wales today then we must set ourselves the task of erasing the "prevalent misconceptions" (Cole 1992 p2). To do this we must study and compare the images of Wales we have with the reality of contemporary Wales. We can do this by examining the prevalence of a Welsh identity and exploring some of the possible bases for such an identity.

Welsh identity

Whatever, the ambiguities of Welshness most people in Wales lay claim to a Welsh identity. In the Welsh Election Survey of 1979, 57 per cent of respondents identified themselves as Welsh in preference to English or British. This relatively low figure might have be accounted for by the devolution debacle that had occurred shortly before the 1979 election. In 1968 and in 1981 Welsh identity had stood at 69 per cent.

These figures reveal that most people in Wales think of themselves as Welsh. They do not tell us what it is to be Welsh or how being Welsh differs from being English. Previous studies of Wales and Welsh culture (Butt Philip 1975 Chapter 3; Madgwick et al 1973 chapter 5) have concentrated on such characteristics as the Welsh language, religion and associated values such as temperance and sabbatarianism, a love of learning, and a radical tradition in politics. Other studies, notably Dai Smith's 'Wales! Wales?' defines Wales in terms of the working class communities of 'the Valleys', "of pit-head winding gear... and the defiance of a brass band on the march" (Smith 1984 p3). Perhaps one way to begin examining the culture of Wales is to examine what role these elements play in contemporary Wales.

Table 2:1
Poll Findings of Identity Attitudes in Wales[1]

Percentages

	1968	1979	1981
Welsh	69	57	69
British	15	34	20
English	13	8	10
Other	3	1	1
Totals	100	100	100

Sources: 1968 Opinion Research quoted in Richard Rose, "The United Kingdom as a Multi-National State" in Studies in British Politics (Macmillan 1976); 1979 Welsh Election Study quoted in Denis Balsom et al "The Political Consequences of Welsh Identity" (Centre for the Study of Public Policy, Strathclyde 1982); 1981 Research and Marketing, Wales and the West, published by HTV Wales.

Language

The clearest case for Welsh distinctiveness is the Welsh language. In the 1991 census over half a million Welsh speakers were recorded, some 18.7 per cent of the population of Wales. This figure masked considerable regional variations within Wales; the percentage of Welsh speakers in the counties of Wales varied from 2.4 per cent in Gwent to 61 per cent in Gwynedd. Thus in some parts of Wales, Welsh continues to serve as a living community language whilst in other parts almost all social interaction is inevitably conducted through English. Table 2:2 shows the variation in the proportion of Welsh speakers amongst the counties of Wales.

The Welsh Language has been in decline throughout the twentieth century. The 1901 Census recorded that half the population of Wales were Welsh speaking. By 1991, less than a fifth described themselves as Welsh speaking. However, some comfort for the Welsh language can be drawn from the fact that the rate of decline of the language has declined considerably in recent decades as Table 2:3 shows.

Welsh is the most successful of the Celtic languages in the British Isles. It has been given legal recognition in the Welsh Language acts of 1967 and 1993. The number of pupils educated in Welsh medium schools has been on the increase

---

[1] Table in John Osmond Introduction in The National Question Again: Welsh Political Identity in the 1980s John Osmond (ed) Gomer Press Llandysul 1985.

25

Table 2:2
Welsh Speakers by County 1991

County	Per cent*
Clwyd	18.2
Dyfed	43.7
Gwent	2.4
Gwynedd	61.0
Mid Glamorgan	8.5
Powys	20.2
South Glamorgan	6.5
West Glamorgan	15.0

*Percentage of usually resident population aged 3 and over.
Source: Digest of Welsh Statistics No.39 1993 Govt Statistical Service.

Table 2:3
Welsh Speakers as a Percentage of the Population 1901-91

Census	Per cent*
1901	49.9
1911	43.5
1921	37.1
1931	36.8
1951	28.9
1961	26.0
1971	20.8
1981	18.9
1991	18.7

*Percentage of usually resident population aged 3 and over.
Sources: Carter and Aitchison 1985, p12; Digest of Welsh statistics No.39 1993.

since the 1960s and Welsh is now part of the core curriculum in Welsh schools. The number of adults learning the language has also been increasing in recent years.

The status of the Welsh language has also changed in recent decades. The expansion of administrative jobs that require a knowledge of the Welsh language has enhanced the career opportunities of those who possess it. The advent of *Radio Cymru* and *Sianel Pedwar Cymru*, the Welsh fourth television channel, have also created new opportunities for Welsh speakers. There are therefore some reasons for believing that the future of the Welsh language may be more secure today than it has been for some decades.

Against this however, must be set the fact that the Welsh language continues to decline as a community language in those areas where it has traditionally been strongest. The intrusion of English into the predominantly Welsh speaking communities of North West Wales, thanks chiefly to in-migration, continues to be a challenge to the Welsh language in its heartland.[2] An increasing number of Welsh speakers in the anglicised south east of Wales (where the 1981 and 1991 censuses showed some growth especially amongst the young) may not be sufficient to preserve the Welsh language as a living community language.

The language has also proved to be an important political and social issue in Wales. The activities and demands of *Cymdeithas Yr Iaith Gymraeg*, the Welsh Language Society, have served to emphasise the Welsh language as a political issue to English speakers within and without Wales. Calls for bilingual notices, bilingual government forms, greater provision of Welsh language education can however have a divisive effect. Policies to designate primary schools as officially Welsh medium have caused much controversy in Dyfed for example. If the Welsh language is a necessary part of a Welsh identity then over four fifths of the people of Wales are excluded from that Welsh identity.

Religion

Perhaps the most prevalent misconception is of Wales as a society where the influence of religion, especially Nonconformist religion is considerable. This was the case in the nineteenth century, when issues such as sabbatarianism, temperance and church disestablishment were the central issues of Welsh politics. Then it could be said with some justice, as Gladstone did in 1891, that "the Nonconformists of Wales are the people of Wales" (Quoted in Morgan 1980 p92).

During the course of the twentieth century however, the influence of organised religion, particularly the Nonconformist sects that were such a prominent part of Wales during the nineteenth century, has been in decline. The spread of secularism, affluence and a wider knowledge of other cultures which have led to a decline in religious belief across the Western World partly account for the decline of religious belief in Wales, but the decline of Welsh Nonconformity in particular has also been due to the falling numbers of Welsh speakers (Davies 1990 p214).

The historian Glanmor Williams, writing of religion in contemporary Wales, notes that "the most striking feature of the figures...is the drop of nearly two-thirds among members of those Nonconformist denominations most strongly

---

[2] See for example G Day 'A Million on the move'?: population change and rural Wales' in G Day, G Rees (eds) *Contemporary Wales* vol 3 Cardiff University of Wales Press.

represented in the Welsh speaking Wales of the Nineteenth century" (Williams 1991 p72). Table 2:4 shows the truth of this observation.

Table 2:4
Religious Affiliation in Wales 1905 and 1982

Denomination	1905	1982	Change %
Church in Wales	193,081	137,600	-29
Welsh Independents	175,147	65,200	-63
Presbyterians (Welsh Calvinistic Methodists)	170,617	79,900	-54
Welsh Baptists	143,835	50,200	-65
Welsh Wesleyan Methodists	40,811	25,300	-38
Other Protestants	19,870	35,300	+78
Roman Catholics	64,800	129,600	+100
Total	808,161	523,100	-36

Sources: Report, Evidence and Indexes of the Royal Commission appointed to inquire into the Church and other Religious Bodies in Wales 1910; MARC Europe Survey, 'Prospects for Wales' 1982

Cited in Williams 1991 p72.

More recent surveys reveal that the 1980s were a period of further decline in religious observance in Wales. A survey for S4C in 1990 showed that all the main denominations in Wales had lost adherents during the 1980s. Again the decline was steepest amongst the Welsh Nonconformist churches (Table 2:5)

A survey in 1991 found that 90 per cent of respondents claimed to belong to a Christian denomination (Wales on Sunday 12-5-1991). However, it was also found that 40 per cent never attended services and only 20 per cent were regular attenders. Also, over half the respondents claimed to belong to the Anglican Church and only 26 per cent to the Nonconformist denominations. Thus it is possible to agree with D. P. Davies that religious life in Wales today "may reflect a trend that is identifiable in other areas of life in Wales today, namely that erstwhile differences in attitude, custom and practice between Wales and England are now becoming blurred" (Davies 1990 p216).

The decline in religious practice in Wales has also seen a decline in some of the social characteristics that made Wales distinct. The Welsh Sunday Closing Act passed in 1881 was the first legislative acknowledgement of Welsh

Table 2:5
Percentage Change in Membership of Main Christian Churches
in Wales 1980-90

Denomination	Change in adherents 1980-90 (%)
Church in Wales	-17
Roman Catholics	-11
Baptist Union of Wales	-29
Independents (Presbyterian, Methodists)	-20

Source: *Western Mail* 15-9-1990

distinctiveness in modern times (Morgan 1980 p43). The 1961 Licensing Act provided for local polls to decide on Sunday closing. Carter and Thomas used these polls to measure where the influence of the Nonconformist churches and the Welsh language were strongest and how far (parts of) Wales could be described as a distinct 'culture region' (Carter and Thomas 1969 pp61-71). The results of these polls since 1961 show the decline and contraction of Welshness according to this criterion. In 1961, South East Wales and the anglicised Brecon, Radnor and Flintshire counties voted to go 'wet' (*Western Mail* 8-11-1968). In 1968 these areas were joined by Montgomeryshire, Denbighshire and Pembrokeshire (Liverpool Daily Post 8-11-1968). By 1982 only Ceredigion and Dwyfor districts remained 'dry' and, after the 1989 poll, only Dwyfor district in Gwynedd remains 'dry' (*North Wales Weekly News* 11 November 1982). Temperance and Sabbatarianism, two supposed pillars of 'the Welsh way of life', had disappeared from virtually every corner of Wales.

Education

Education and a love of learning has played a prominent part in the Welsh image of themselves. The self taught artisan, miner or quarry worker represented an ideal figure in the Wales of the nineteenth century. Nor was such a figure wholly mythical. Bob Owen, *Croesor*, a clerk in a north Wales slate quarry, was an eminent scholar, awarded an honorary degree by the University of Wales.

When he died in 1962, he gave his collection of over 47,000 books to the University of Wales (Morris 1986 pp241-242). For Jan Morris, a scholar like Bob Owen Croesor was "unmistakably a child of the Welsh patriotic resurgence" (Morris 1986 p242).

Education was especially important issue to the increasingly self-confident Welsh nationalism of the nineteenth century. It was the Education Report published in 1847, critical of education standards in Wales (and much else besides, including the sexual immorality of the Welsh) which 'stung' a Welsh nationalism, Welsh speaking and Nonconformist in tone, into life (Williams 1985 p208).

It was also through education reforms that a Welsh identity demonstrated its progress through the course of the nineteenth century. The foundation of the University College of Wales in Aberystwyth in 1872, financed by the 'pence of the poor' was a symbol of the centrality of education in the minds of thousands of ordinary Welsh men and women. A history of University College Wales Aberystwyth begins "the struggle for Welsh national identity and the striving for educational opportunity have almost always gone hand in hand" (Ellis 1972 p1).

Legislative and institutional distinctiveness was accorded to Wales in the shape of the Welsh Intermediate Education Act in 1889. This created the first secondary school system with state support in Britain. For K O Morgan the 1889 Act was "educationally, socially and administratively... one of the most impressive memorials of the political awakening of Wales" (Morgan 1980 p102). In 1907 the Welsh Department of the Board of Education was established and its first Inspector of Schools was O M Edwards, a popular hero of Nonconformist Liberal Wales.

This history of national advancement being tied to educational advancement continues to cast its shadow over Wales's image of itself. The Gittins Report on primary education in Wales published in 1967, stated "The Welsh, for example, traditionally regard themselves as having an unusually high respect for education" (Central Advisory Council for Primary Education in Wales 1968 p2). However, recent figures show that such a high self-regard may not be justified. Wales had the lowest percentage of 16 year olds staying on at school or going to further education of any region of the United Kingdom in 1991/92 (HMSO Regional Trends no.28 Table 5.5). When Welsh school children leave school they are likely to do so with poorer qualifications than school children of almost any other region of the United Kingdom. In 1990/91, 8.2 per cent of English school leavers left with no qualifications whatsoever; in Wales the same figure was almost twice this level at 16.0 per cent. Only in Northern Ireland was the same figure even higher at 16.1 per cent. In the same year, 12.5 per cent of English school leavers left with five or more GCSEs (of grades A-C) whereas only 9.3 per cent of Welsh school leavers had equivalent qualifications. Only two regions, Yorkshire and Humberside and Scotland performed worse than Wales (HMSO Regional Trends no 28 1993 Table 5.7). In specific subjects the performance of Welsh school leavers again compared poorly. Welsh school leavers had the lowest proportion of GCSE passes grade A-C of any region of the United Kingdom, only two regions, Scotland and Yorkshire and Humberside had a lower proportion of such passes in Mathematics and Welsh school leavers were bottom of the class in the proportion of French passes at GCSE grades A-C (HMSO Regional Trends no. 28 1993 Table 5.8).

Radicalism

Welsh politics has often been described as radical. It is however, difficult to give a precise meaning to this term. Certainly, since the middle of the nineteenth century Wales has always supported the party of the Left in British politics and has given little support to the Conservative Party (Table 2:6).

Table 2:6
Seats Won in Wales 1906-74

Party	1906	1918	1922	1935	1945	1966	1970	1974 (Oct)
Lib	33	21	11	8	8	1	1	2
Con	–	4	6	6	2	3	7	8
Lab	1	10	18	18	25	32	27	23
Other	1	1	1	4	1	–	1	3*

*Plaid Cymru.
Source: Beti Jones Parliamentary Elections in Wales 1900-1975.

However, 'radicalism' has been used to describe the political culture of Wales, not just its political behaviour. Are there attitudes associated with Welshness that can be described as radical?

Welsh history can provide numerous examples of radicals and support for radical causes. *Iolo Morgannwg*, who by his forgeries 'rediscovered' Wales's 'ancient traditions' of the Druids and the *Gorsedd*, was a fervent jacobin and supporter of American independence. The first freedom *Eisteddfod* in 1789 and the first gorsedd of the Bards in 1792 were influenced by the ideas of liberty, democracy (even atheism) from France and America. Iolo Morgannwg offered "a new Welsh national ideology and some new institutions to serve it" (Williams 1985 p162).

However, a deeper impression on Welsh culture at this time was made by the preachers of nonconformity and dissent. The conversion of Wales to nonconformity which occurred rapidly at the end of the eighteenth and the beginning of the nineteenth centuries was "one of the most remarkable cultural transformations of any people" as "A people which around 1790 was still officially Tory and Anglican, over little more than a generation became a largely Nonconformist people of increasingly radical temper" (Williams 1985 p159).

Nonconformity provided new grievances for the people of Wales. In the 1880s there were anti-Tithe riots in North Wales, Lloyd George won fame (and later electoral favour) over the Llanfrothen burial case and Welsh politics in the end of the nineteenth century and early years of the twentieth century was dominated by the issue of the disestablishment of the Anglican church in Wales. Nonconformist issues were at the heart of Welsh politics as Tom Ellis, Liberal MP for Merioneth and a prominent figure of nineteenth century Welsh politics confirms "... it was the nonconformity of Wales that created the unity of Wales rather than any spontaneous demand for Home Rule" (quoted in Morgan 1980 p164).

Although, nonconformist issues have long disappeared from the political agenda of Wales and the social influence of nonconformity has declined more generally, it can still be argued that nonconformity has shaped the Welsh political culture in a radical direction. Ioan Bowen Rees, for example, ascribes the democratic spirit of Welsh culture to the influence of the chapels when he writes:

> Organised religion carries comparatively little weight in Wales today, but the political ethos of non-conformity still colours social attitudes over much of the country... People who have been used to taking a vote on every question from the selection of visiting preachers to the cost of a new organ – and to discussing abstract questions like 'Are there degrees of sin?' without expert guidance... For better or for worse, democracy is the Welsh way of life

(Rees 1971 pp212-3).

There is some evidence that attitudes to forms of direct political participation are different in Wales from attitudes to direct action in other countries. Analysing data from the Welsh and Scottish Election Studies and comparing it to data on similar issues in other Western democracies, Balsom et al found that there was much greater approval for direct action in Wales than in Scotland, Britain or any of the other nations studied. Part of the reason for this is that Wales has some history of direct action, particularly on Welsh issues.[3] The burning down of the bombing school in Penyberth in 1936, the collection of signatures for the

---

[3] An extract of an interview with Saunders Lewis quoted in Ned Thomas *The Welsh Extremist* second edition Talybont Dyfed Y Lolfa 1991 p69 demonstrates this

"'I personally believe that careful, considered, public violence is often a necessary weapon for national movements, necessary to defend the land, the valleys of Wales from being violated, wholly illegally, by the government and the big corporations in England. I think, for instance, that Tryweryn, Clywedog, Cwm Dulas, are attacks that cannot be justified on moral grounds at all. The fact that they were decided on by the English Parliament confers no moral right. And so I think that any means that hinders this irresponsible violence on the land of Wales by English corporations is wholly just.'

'Do you include the shedding of blood?'

'So long as it is Welsh blood and not English blood.'"

Parliament for Wales campaign in the 1950s and the non-legal but non violent campaigns of the Welsh Language Society show that there is, to some extent, a tradition of direct action, even violent direct action in Wales. Balsom et al conclude : "Welsh attitudes to violence are better defined, they are quite strongly linked to specifically Welsh issues... Politically, Wales is different" (Balsom et al 1982 pp50-51).

It has also been claimed that political culture in Wales stresses social cooperation and collective provision to a greater extent than in the United Kingdom generally. In the nineteenth century Tom Ellis, a Welsh Liberal MP, described Wales as a land characterised by the cooperative traditions of *"cyfraith, cyfar, cyfnawdd, cymorthau, cymanfaoedd"* (custom, co-ploughing, co-protection, co-help, co-assembly) (quoted in Williams 1985 p229).

The claim that Wales is a land characterised by cooperation or partnership has also been heard more recently. During the 1992 election campaign, David Hunt, then Secretary of State for Wales wrote of the Conservative record in Wales: "Our success has been built upon a typically Welsh foundation: our willingness to co-operate with one another, irrespective of party, in the process of developing Wales. This cooperation is in the interests of all the people of Wales" (Conservative Central Office for Wales 1992 p1).

It is difficult to evaluate the veracity of the claim of a Welsh political culture characterised by cooperation or partnership. Elements of a collectivist ethic have existed in the past and the Labour Party's domination of elections in Wales possibly shows that collectivist ideas may have found a receptive audience in the Welsh working class. It is possible to compare Wales with Scotland where, for example McCrone (1992) has put forward the claim that Scottish political culture contains, to a greater degree than England, those elements of collectivism and cooperation necessary to create what Marquand (1988) called a principled society' supporting a 'developmental state' prepared to actively intervene in the economy and society and rejecting a minimal role for the state. One way to test such a thesis is to study the outputs of government in Wales and this I will do in chapters five and six.

Wales today

We have seen above that many of the characteristics that were once said to define Welsh identity and Welshness play a much smaller role in Welsh life today than was the case a century ago. Have there been new developments in the politics and society of Wales that could form the bases of a new Welsh identity? Some areas that might reflect and constitute new bases of Welsh identity are the economic structure, media, politics and government institutions in Wales, contemporary Welsh culture, including verse, drama, prose, film and broadcasting both in English and Welsh, and sport.

Economic structure

Wales is commonly held to be characterised by a distinctive economic structure. The South Wales valleys particularly were said to be characterised by a concentration of coal mining and heavy industry such as steel making. Wales has also been thought of as a country where agriculture makes a major contribution to the economy. Can the Welsh economy be said to be distinctive?

In 1913 employment in coal-mining peaked at 270,000. By 1984-5 employment in coal had fallen to 24,000 and by the end of 1993 was down to a couple of hundred. This was the end of an era in Welsh history. Steel making has also been in decline though less precipitately. The closure of the Dowlais, East Moors and Shotton steel works in the late 1970s and early 1980s however reduced the steel industry in terms of employment and contribution to Welsh GDP to a comparatively minor role. Agriculture too has declined though it continues to play a greater role in the Welsh economy than in the economy of Great Britain. However as the difference in the percentage employed in agriculture in Wales and Great Britain is less than one per cent (2.2 per cent compared with 1.7 per cent in 1991) the significance of this difference should not be exaggerated.

Manufacturing and particularly services have grown as a proportion of Welsh production since the second world war. Wales is not unique in this, indeed it is a trend across the modern developed world. By 1981, about a quarter of Welsh employees were employed in manufacturing and 60 per cent in services. C. J. McKenna notes of the Welsh economy that "The overall impression is that of a mix of activities not wildly out of line with the UK as a whole..." (McKenna 1988 p25). What might differentiate Wales is not the nature of problems in Wales but their extent and the way that they have been addressed by government. How these problems have been addressed in Wales is studied in chapter five.

The level of prosperity in Wales is lower than the UK average. Throughout the 1980s, GDP per head (gross domestic product) in Wales has been some 85 per cent of the UK level. The overall figure for Wales hides some gross regional disparities within Wales. South Glamorgan has a per capita GDP just above the UK average but GDP in Mid Glamorgan is only some 75 per cent of the UK average. Benefits make up a greater proportion of household incomes in Wales than elsewhere in the United Kingdom. For example in 1985, social security payments accounted for 18 per cent of household income in Wales but only 13.6 per cent in the United Kingdom.

Part of the reason for a higher proportion of household incomes in Wales

34

being made up from social security expenditure is the lower level of employment in Wales. Between 1924 and 1990 the unemployment rate in Wales was always higher than the unemployment rate in the United Kingdom as a whole. The activity rate, the proportion of those of working age in employment has also been lower in Wales than elsewhere in the United Kingdom. These statistics clearly set Wales apart but hardly in a positive sense.

Media

A distinctively Welsh media would be expected to reflect the distinctiveness of Wales and, by providing a forum for the discussion of Welsh affairs, play some role in augmenting the distinctiveness of Wales. In Scotland, for example, the existence of a several Scottish newspapers has been cited as one factor that sustains a Scottish political system (Kellas 1989 p7). However, it is true to say that "The Welsh media are much less Welsh than the Scottish media are Scottish" (Tunstall 1983 p228).

The print media in Wales is penetrated to a far greater extent by London based papers than is the case in Scotland. Table 2:7 below shows the readership for the major daily papers in Wales.

Nevertheless the print media does contain some Welsh elements. Over 300,000 newspapers printed in Wales are sold daily in Wales. The *Western Mail* is the

Table 2:7
Daily newspaper readership in Wales January-June 1989

Paper	Readership
Daily Mirror	646,000
The Sun	553,000
Daily Express	217,000
Western Mail	212,000
Daily Mail	155,000
Daily Star	122,000
Daily Telegraph	69,000
Today	66,000
The Guardian	55,000
The Times	34,000
The Financial Times	20,000
The Independent	12,000

Source: Willing's Press Guide 1991 National Readership Survey Half Year Study (Figures not available for the Daily Post).

Table 2:8
Welsh daily newspaper circulation January-June 1989

Paper	Circulation
South Wales Echo (Mon-Fri) (Cardiff)	91,085
Western Mail (Cardiff)	77,830
South Wales Evening Post (Swansea)	68,908
South Wales Argus(Mon-Fri) (Newport)	41,461
Evening Leader (Wrexham)	27,893

Source: UK Press Gazette 25 September 1989
(The *Daily Post*, printed in Liverpool, also offers coverage of the news of
North Wales, but does not attempt to cover the news of Wales as a whole. Its
circulation in 1995 is some 75,000)
(Wales now also boasts its own Sunday paper, *Wales on Sunday*, launched in
1990 with a circulation of some 65,000.)

only daily paper printed in Wales that is sold throughout Wales and tries to cover
events in the whole of Wales. Table 2:8 shows the circulation of the daily papers
printed in Wales.

Numerous local weekly papers are published, though these tend to take a
parochial view of affairs and restrict their news coverage to purely local events.
In North Wales two local weeklies are also published in Welsh, *Herald Mon* and
Herald Gymraeg with circulations of around 2,500. Even more parochial are the
so-called *papurau bro*, literally area papers, which cover the news of very small
areas (a few villages at most). Their function seems to be primarily encouraging
people to read more Welsh rather than covering news and opinion.

Welsh language publications have small circulations, often depend on
government grants for their existence and are marginal in their influence. *Y
Cymro*, a weekly national newspaper has the largest circulation but this is only
some 5,000. Other magazines such as *Y Traethodydd, Golwg, Taliesin* or *Barn*
have small circulations and depend on government support for survival. When
the Welsh Arts Council withdrew its support form *Y Faner* in 1992, it quickly
folded, ending almost a century and a half of publication.

The domination of the London media in Wales constrains the discussion of
Welsh issues in Wales. Osmond claims that "The penetration of English based
newspapers into Wales and their general lack of attention to Welsh issues...is
crucial to an understanding of Welsh political attitudes. It means that the mass of
the Welsh people...are by and large left in ignorance of Welsh political issues and
the arguments that surround them" (Osmond 1983 p164).

This can be clearly seen if the role of the media during the devolution debate of the late 1970s is studied. The most popular papers in Wales, the *Daily Mirror* and the *Sun* gave little coverage to the devolution issue, and, where they did, tended to concentrate on the implications of Scottish devolution and to trivialise the issue. Osmond claims that the failure of the devolution issue to get a fair hearing in Wales resulted primarily "from the lack of an integrated Welsh newspaper network capable of giving the issue comprehensive coverage" (Osmond 1983 p164).

Broadcasting, radio and television, have more Welsh elements. BBC Wales is a separate region and in its television programmes and its radio stations, Radio Wales and Radio Cymru, displays a strong sense of national identity. HTV Wales/Cymru also broadcasts several hours of local news and other local programmes each week. S4C, *Sianel Pedwar Cymru,* the Welsh Fourth Channel, which began broadcasting in 1982 has broadened the choice of viewing in Wales and offers a view of Welsh, British and world events from a Welsh perspective. Generally, however, it is fair to conclude, as Geraint Talfan Davies does, that "broadcasting in Wales is an integral part of British broadcasting" (Davies 1983 p192). Also, the impact of the Welsh broadcast media is further reduced as it is believed that as many as a third of the people of Wales receive transmissions from across the border in England.

Politics

From 1906 to October 1974 Wales consistently elected a majority of MPs from parties of the Left (Table 2:6). Wales has been a comparatively poor prospect for the Conservative party and, from about the end of the first world war a Labour redoubt, as some academics have noted.[4] From 1945 Labour won over half the votes cast in Wales at every general election and in 1966 won 60.6 per cent of the votes cast in Wales and 32 of the 36 seats. The electoral dominance of the Labour Party in Wales seemed every bit as crushing as the Liberal dominance of parliamentary representation had been in the nineteenth century. The fortunes of the Conservatives seemed to have improved hardly at all during the course of the twentieth century.

Nor could the strength of the Labour party in Wales be ascribed solely to the class composition of seats in Wales as a 'British' model of voting would suggest. Balsom et al (1983) found, using data from the 1979 Welsh Election Study, that this divergence was partly attributable to a sense of Welsh identity amongst voters making them more likely to vote Labour and less likely to vote Conservative. This difference was over and above any difference associated with class composition factors that were traditionally used in the British model

---

[4] J Blondel Voters, Parties and Leaders London Penguin 1974.

of electoral behaviour to explain variations in voting behaviour. Members of all classes in Wales were found to be more likely to vote Labour than their counterparts in England and this was ascribed by the authors to a sense of Welsh identity that was related to, and affected, electoral behaviour.

However, electoral behaviour in Wales from 1979 onwards seemed, for a time, to give some confidence to the Conservative Party in Wales that its fortunes might finally be about to improve (Table 2:9).

Table 2:9
Welsh Election Statistics October 1974-83

Party	1974 (Oct)		1979		1983	
	Seats	Vote %	Seats	Vote %	Seats	Vote %
Lab	23	49.5	21	46.9	20	37.5
Con	8	23.9	11	32.2	14	31.0
Lib	2	15.5	1	10.6	2	23.2
PC	3	10.8	2	7.8	2	7.3

Source: The Wales Yearbook 1992

However, from 1974 to 1983 the electoral fortunes of the Labour Party worsened in Wales and those of the Conservative Party improved. Although this reflected a wider UK trend it was taken to mean that the electoral distinctiveness of Wales was being undermined. The rise of Plaid Cymru as an electoral force from the late 1960s onwards was not sufficient to outweigh the impression that Welsh politics was becoming more like British politics. Crewe claimed that class, not religion or language, was the main electoral cleavage even in Welsh speaking rural Wales in the 1979 election (Crewe 1979 p252). J. B. Jones *et al.* talked of a process of 'acculturation' that was eroding the distinctiveness of Welsh politics and submerging it within a wider UK political context. The results of the 1979 (and 1983) general elections in conjunction with the results of the devolution referendum in March 1979 "undermined the persistent belief that Welsh radicalism still remained a potent force" and confirmed the "emergence of a new Welsh political profile" (Jones and Wilford 1983 p225). They ascribed the emergence of this new political profile to a broad process of 'acculturation' that implied "the acquisition of politico-cultural characteristics of the wider, English political and social system" (Jones and Wilford 1983 p226). G. A. Williams concurred in (damning) terms, "By 1983 every political tradition to which the modern Welsh people in their majority had committed themselves was bankrupt" (Williams 1985 p259).

Election results since 1983 have seen some re-emergence of the older pattern of Welsh electoral behaviour though this is partly due to the fact that British

Table 2:10
Welsh Election Results 1987-92

Party	1987		1992	
	Seats	Vote %	Seats	Vote %
Lab	24	45.1	27	49.5
Con	8	29.5	6	28.6
Lib	2	17.9	1	12.4
PC	3	7.3	4	9.0

Source: The Wales Yearbook 1992; BBC Cymru/Wales General Election 92
Results

voting patterns nationally have seen a recovery of Labour support. Support for
the Labour Party had risen to almost 50 per cent by 1992 and the Conservatives
are again decisively a minority party in Wales. Plaid Cymru has established itself
as the party of the Welsh speaking North and West of Wales winning four seats
(its highest ever total) at the 1992 election and performing well in Carmarthen,
another seat where the Welsh language is still strong. What Balsom (1985) called
Y Fro Gymreig (the Welsh heartland) continues to be distinct from Westminster
politics, but it also gives many signs of being distinct from politics in the rest of
Wales generally. Outside north west Wales *Plaid Cymru* continued to perform
abysmally.

At the 1987 election, Balsom found no special Welsh dimension and a profile
of support at the election found few significant Welsh characteristics. He
concluded that "These data are broadly consistent with patterns found for Britain
as a whole and thus cast doubt on the continued distinctiveness of voting
allegiances in Wales" (Balsom 1987 p21). Certainly, the social characteristics
that supported the dominance of the Left in British politics are being eroded by
economic and social change. Social change has eroded the bases of nineteenth
Welsh radicalism to almost vanishing point. *Plaid Cymru* is the beneficiary of
what remains of this political force. Economic change is eroding the one-class
communities of the South Wales valleys that gave Labour hegemony in that
region. David Adamson, for instance, analyses the decline of Labour in Wales in
terms of the decline of the old highly unionised working class living and working
in tightly knit communities (Adamson 1991). The rise of light manufacturing
industries (often employing a high proportion of women) and service industries
has produced a 'new working class' no longer socialised into support for the
Labour Party. As Adamson describes it, "Whilst those already stamped with the
work and community experience of the mining valleys are likely to retain their
political loyalties to the Labour Party, emerging cohorts of voters no longer

experience a reinforcement of familial, political socialisation in their work and community experience. The totality of socialisation in Labour politics has been broken" (Adamson 1991 p165).

The process may well be as David Adamson has described. However, what he has described using a form of Marxist analysis and drawing on the case of Wales is class dealignment, a phenomenon that is hardly unique to Wales. Analysts of British politics, indeed electoral politics in most western countries, would be familiar with what Adamson has described.

Thus, whilst it is clear that some distinctive characteristics of Welsh electoral behaviour remain, the overall picture is indeed one of an erosion of distinctive Welsh characteristics and of an integration into a wider British political context. North West Wales has retained (even consolidated) a distinctive political culture of its own but it is an exception to the rest of Wales, let alone the rest of the United Kingdom. Elsewhere in Wales, Labour retains an electoral predominance but this seems partly at least due to sheer inertia (Miller 1984). The 1992 election was fought mainly on British national issues and issues such as devolution made relatively little impact despite attempts by sections of the Welsh media to raise the profile of Welsh issues. The *Western Mail*, for example, held a 'Great Debate' on devolution before the 1992 general election. However, the fact that any debate at all took place on this issue and that Wales continued to vote for a Labour government when England voted for the return of the Conservative government suggests that G. A. Williams's lament that "Welsh politics had ceased to exist ... Wales had finally disappeared into Britain" is exaggerated (Williams 1985 p297).

Welsh identity and institutions

John Osmond, a journalist and observer of Welsh affairs, has recently claimed that "For Wales in the 1990s there can be no doubt that institutions carry the main weight of the required awareness and solidarity" [for a sense of nationhood] and that "in answer to the national question, Wales consists of a people struggling to become a nation by progressively establishing their own institutions" (Osmond 1992 p12).

However, it is also possible to view the process of administrative devolution that has occurred in Wales as an alternative to or substitute for more far-reaching forms of devolution; forms of devolution that might engage the people of Wales in decision-making.

Many of the administrative institutions that exist in Wales today were the creations of politicians and not the Welsh people. Often they were created as part of a wider reform of the machinery of government and could not have come into existence if the only calls for their creation had come form Wales. Administrative devolution in Wales has often had to wait for general administrative reform in

Whitehall, for example, the creation of Housing for Wales in 1988 was part of a wider reform of government relations with housing associations nationally. Alternatively, several measures of Welsh administrative devolution came about thanks to nationalist calls from Scotland (the creation of the Welsh Development Agency in 1976 for example).

Administrative devolution does not create badges of identity. We must pity the nation that writes folk songs about the activities of its department of transport or eulogises all that its higher education funding council has done to promote a sense of its own identity. Administrative institutions are often remote from people's concerns. The Cardiganshire survey of 1971 for example found that virtually all respondents could correctly identify the current Prime Minister but only just over half could name the Secretary of State for Wales (Madgwick et al 1973 p249).

The public in Wales, as elsewhere, tends only to take an interest in administrative institutions when things are perceived to be going wrong. Public interest might not therefore be an healthy sign. When the Public Accounts Committee of the House of Commons investigated the Welsh Development Agency over allegations of financial impropriety and gross incompetence (including the employment of a convicted con-man without checking his references and the interviewing of models in hotel bedrooms), the public did indeed take notice but this is not, presumably, the sense of identity to which Osmond was referring.

The claim that administrative institutions embody Welsh nationhood is therefore dubious. Perhaps the claim says more about the reduced expectations of Welsh devolutionists than about Welsh identity. It is significant that in the 1970s John Osmond could dismiss the Welsh Office as "not a Welsh institution as such but an outpost of Whitehall in Wales, merely impressing a Welsh imprint on hundreds of circulars that are directed form central government ministries" (Osmond 1978 p76). J. B. Jones's assessment of the role of administrative institutions in Wales may be more accurate. He maintains that "Paradoxically ... the process of building national institutions may be regarded not as a means towards promoting a coherent political identity but as an alternative to it" (Jones 1988 p51).

Arts

Although Wales borders a country that is a major force in the production of popular culture in the areas of publishing and broadcasting, Wales manages to retain a distinct culture. In some respects that culture is more open, more cosmopolitan than it was and is finally winning recognition beyond Wales.

The invented traditions of the *Eisteddfod*, an annual cultural festival, continue

41

to invest Welsh culture with an exalted status. Although, the 'Welsh only' rule on the *Eisteddfod* field might be thought to make the *Eisteddfod* inaccessible and irrelevant to the majority of the people of Wales, this appears not to be the case. Very successful *Eisteddfodau* have been held in largely anglicised areas such as Neath and Newport. Extensive television coverage is given in both English and Welsh languages to the national *Eisteddfod* and it can claim to be a national event for the people of Wales.

The advent of *Sianel Pedwar Cymru*, the Welsh fourth television channel, has been a significant boost to Welsh culture. Television adaptations of the works of Welsh authors such as Kate Roberts have provided a generation of Welsh film makers and writers an opportunity to interpret afresh the classics of Welsh literature. Contemporary writing has been inspired by the expansion of Welsh language broadcasting as the novels of Eigra Lewis Roberts testify. A Welsh film industry has emerged winning some critical acclaim with works like *Un Nos Ola Leuad,* (One Moonlit Night) and *Hedd Wyn* which won an Oscar nomination.

Anglo-Welsh culture has also gained a wider prominence in recent years. R S Thomas is regarded as one of the foremost poets writing in English today and his poetry often deals with Welsh themes. Other Anglo-Welsh poets, such as Dannie Abse and Gillian Clarke, have also won a wide audience for their impressions of Wales. In terms of drama, BBC Wales has felt confident enough of its own Welsh identity to serialise Kingsley Amis's barbed satire on 'professional Welshmen', 'The Old Devils'. It can be said with some justification that there is an air of confidence and vitality about Welsh culture that was lacking even thirty years ago.

Sport

The sporting field is as important for Welsh identity today as the Eisteddfod field. Rhodri Morgan states that, "What is truly remarkable is that much of Wales' self-image as a nation rests on being a separate country from England for sporting purposes. Let's face it, Brittany doesn't play against France in football or rugby; Bavaria doesn't play against Germany. Where would we be today if those international matches had not started to be arranged, originally between Scotland and England, but with Wales and Ireland added on for a bit of a variety in the 1870s?" (Morgan 1994 p17). In addition to competing 'internationally' at rugby, Wales sends a Welsh national team to the football world cup and the Commonwealth games. Some Welsh internationals became household names in Wales during the 1970s.

Conclusion

It is clear that many aspects of Welsh life that were characteristic of a 'Welsh way of life' have been in decline throughout the twentieth century. New developments in Wales this century have failed to create a culture as distinctive or as different from English culture as that which prevailed in the nineteenth century. The Welsh media and even Welsh politics in Wales today share many features with other parts of Britain. Nevertheless, much remains distinctive. The language continues to survive and has made some limited advances in recent years. Politics in Wales continues to display some differences even if these are muted when compared with the differences that prevailed a century ago. Culture and sport continue to provide opportunities for the assertion of a Welsh national identity.

Some other claims about the contemporary foundations of popular Welsh identity seem more dubious. Institutions do not, generally, impinge upon popular consciousness in the same way as sports or the arts. However, it is possible that, although Welsh institutions do not form a basis for a distinct identity, that they may operate in an indirect fashion. It is possible that the institutions of government in Wales have sufficient autonomy to devise and implement different solutions to the problems of Wales, even if those problems are themselves similar to those found elsewhere in the United Kingdom. If the political culture of Wales is more collectivist, imbued with an appreciation of the merits of partnership to a greater extent than is found in England, this could be demonstrated by the actions of the institutions of government in Wales. It is to an examination of the institutions of government in Wales, their evolution, their degree of autonomy and the manner of their operation that we now turn.

3 The institutions of government in Wales

"... The arena of political activity concerned with the relations between central political institutions in the capital city and those sub-central political organisations and governmental bodies within the accepted boundaries of the state"

(Rhodes and Wright 1987 p2)

Introduction

In chapter one I reviewed some of the existing approaches to territorial politics. The approaches by Rhodes and Wright (1987) and Bulpitt (1983) were found to be applicable in the British context. In chapter two I examined the claim that administrative institutions in Wales were important as symbols or representations of Welsh identity. Whilst I concluded that this claim was dubious, in this chapter I study government institutions in Wales in terms of what they do, rather than what, if anything, they might symbolise.

A study of administrative institutions in Wales is important if we are to evaluate the claim that government policies applied in Wales since 1979 have differed from those applied in England. In addition to the claim that Welsh political culture differs from English political culture in being more collectivist and consensual than the latter, this claim to policy divergence rests on the Welsh Office and other institutions of Welsh government enjoying a degree of 'relative autonomy' from the diktat of Cabinet. K. O. Morgan, an eminent historian of

Welsh and British politics, offers the view that "The Secretary of State for Wales has almost a free hand in spending, acting as Prime Minister, Chancellor and Cabinet rolled into one" and claimed that during the 1980s the Welsh Office was "very un-Thatcherite" (Wales on Sunday 25 November 1990). Peter Walker, recalling his years as Welsh Secretary said "I was allowed to do it my way with a range of interventionist policies" (Walker 1991 p203) and implies that these policies were not always the same as policies pursued elsewhere in the United Kingdom by saying "What we achieved in Wales as a result of close government co-operation with industry, councils and trade unions does underscore the weakness of our post-war performance in the rest of the country" (Walker 1991 p212). Rhodes is right to remind us that "Centre-periphery relations cannot be reduced to the study of institutions, but equally such a focus is of far greater relevance than is often allowed" (Rhodes 1987 p35).

Given a focus on administrative institutions, what aspects of these institutions should be studied and how? Here the capacaties of institutions and the relationships and links between institutions, that is intergovernmental theory, will be of special interest. Rose reminds us that

> In order to understand the policy process and, even more, the impact of government upon society, it is important to understand the relationships between organisations. But that can be done only if there continues to be a recognition that the formal structure of each organisation establishes boundaries that separate it from every other organisation. The point is important, for there is a tendency to submerge organisations in a single abstraction, such as the political system...To speak of a system emphasises the interaction and interdependence between organisations. But a system exists only by virtue of the different organisations that form the constituent parts

(Rose 1984 p.165).

For Rhodes and Wright "a focus on territorial politics fuses...the concerns of intergovernmental theory with history" (Rhodes and Wright p2). The historical context has to be explored for three reasons; firstly, in order to locate continuities and discontinuities in the evolution of territorial politics, secondly, because interpretations of the past colour contemporary political debates and such interpretations need to be tested and thirdly, many historical issues can only be explored through historical analysis.

Therefore, in the remainder of this chapter I examines the historical evolution of governmental institutions in Wales before studying the work of the Welsh Office today, its relationships within Whitehall, its relationships with other governmental institutions and levels of government within Wales. Finally, I try to assess the claim that the Welsh Office has acquired the capacity to deal with institutions of government outside the United Kingdom. The conclusion to this final section will provide some indication of the extent of the autonomy of the Welsh Office today.

The development of administrative institutions in Wales

1536-1945

The Acts of Union of 1536 and 1543 were intended to assimilate Wales with England. Williams states that the purpose of the Acts of Union was "with the introduction of uniformity in the legal codes of England and Wales, to have uniformity also in their administration" (Williams 1950 p38). Wales was divided into thirteen shire counties along the English pattern which sent MPs to the Parliament at Westminster. All remaining Welsh laws were abolished and justice in Wales was dispensed by the Courts of the Great Sessions which applied English law to Wales. The Act also established on a legal basis the Council of Wales which oversaw the work of administrators in Wales. These institutions did not (indeed were not intended to) develop a body of Welsh law or administrative practice (as occurred in Scotland) and were in any case abolished before the dawn of modern politics, the Council of Wales in 1688 and the Courts of the Great Sessions in 1830. By 1746 the integration of Wales with England was so complete that the Wales and Berwick Act stated that references to England in legislation referred also to Wales (Bogdanor 1979 p119).

However, towards the end of the nineteenth century demands arose for separate provision to be made for Wales in legislative and administrative arrangements. In 1890, Alfred Thomas, the member for East Glamorgan, proposed the creation of a Welsh Secretary of State (Morgan 1980 p109). Although this measure failed to win much support, Wales began to receive administrative and legislative acknowledgement at this time. The case of separate legislation was conceded in the 1881 Sunday Closing Act and the 1889 Welsh Intermediate Education Act. The demands for different administrative structures were met to some degree in the early years of this century with the creation of the Welsh Board of the Department of Education in 1907, Welsh National Insurance Commission in 1911, and in 1919 the Welsh Board of Health and the Welsh Board of Agriculture.

Randall (1972) found that three factors spurred the creation of these administrative institutions. Firstly, one reason for the separate treatment of Wales was the unique or distinctive circumstances of Wales. Augustine Birrell, President of the Board of Education, in 1907 justified the creation of the Welsh Department of the Board of Education by saying that "... Welsh subjects and

Welsh questions formed a part by themselves and were subject to considerations which did not apply so much to other parts of the country" (quoted in Randall 1972 pp356-7) and Walter Runciman, President of the Board of Agriculture and Fisheries, admitted that the creation of a Welsh Board of Agriculture was necessary "to meet the special requirements and circumstances of Wales" (quoted in Randall 1972 p357).

Randall also found that national sentiment had been an important factor in the process of administrative devolution. Although Lloyd George had initially opposed the creation of a separate Welsh National insurance Commission in 1911 he acquiesced, admitting that it was "one of those questions where you have to defer to sentiment" (quoted in Randall 1972 p357).

The third factor was, however, external to Wales. Randall noted that where Welsh institutions were established "it becomes clear that their creation was closely linked to changes in the central government machine as a whole" (Randall 1972 p358). Administrative devolution to Wales often had to wait for reform within central government and this had consequences for the extent of powers transferred and the degree of autonomy involved. The North Wales Liberal Federation found in 1937 that existing administrative arrangements in Wales were inadequate and incapable of providing "independence of administration" (quoted in Randall 1972 p361). The Welsh Department of Education, for example, had produced "nothing distinctive in policy; in fact it is merely a 'branch' with no independent existence" (quoted in Randall 1972 p361). Administrative devolution before 1945 therefore had failed to produce a substantial degree of autonomy for the institutions of government in Wales.

1945-64

The election of a Labour government in 1945 brought hopes of reform for Wales. For some purposes Wales was considered an administrative unit, for example the area board of British Gas. An attempt was made to give greater coherence to the work of government in Wales by establishing a Conference of the Heads of Government Departments in Wales (Gowan 1970 p53). In 1948 the Labour Government created a Council of Wales and Monmouthshire. However, it was a nominated and advisory body and had little power. Although the Labour party had become the party that most Welsh voters supported by 1945, it was not a party that put Welsh sentiment to the fore.

Further reform came in 1951 when the Conservative government created the post of Minister for Welsh Affairs. Initially, this post was held in conjunction with the Home Secretaryship; after 1957, it was held by the Minister for Housing and Local Government. The creation of this post was explained as a means of "recognising the national aspirations and the special position of Wales" (R. A.

Butler quoted in Osmond 1978 p.107). Again, the reform was largely symbolic and no Welsh dimension was injected into policy-making. Mr Lightman, a civil servant at the Welsh Office states that the role of this minister was to act as a 'liaison officer' (Mr Lightman's lecture 22-10-1987). Bevan's dismissal of a Welsh Secretary as "nothing but a messenger boy" (quoted in Butt Philip 1975 p282) seemed to have some justification.

A notable and notorious example of the Minister for Wales's failure to reflect Welsh interests in policy-making was his approval of the flooding of the Tryweryn Valley despite the fierce opposition of virtually every Welsh interest. The impotence of the Minister for Welsh Affairs was made clear in the case put forward by Liverpool City Corporation in the Tryweryn case before the House of Lords. "There can be no question that emotions in Wales have been aroused" said Geoffrey Lawrence, on behalf of Liverpool City Corporation, "But Liverpool Corporation have to take the constitution as they find it. There is no separate Welsh government. There is no separate demarcation of Wales from England from the point of view of water supplies" (quoted in Osmond 1978 p.113). Administrative reform remained superficial and largely symbolic; "a touch of political lipstick and eyeshadow to heighten the glamour without actually doing much to alter the underlying reality" according to Lightman (lecture 22-10-1987).

Wales had, by the middle of the twentieth century, failed to achieve a significant measure of administrative autonomy. Partly, this reflected the centralist logic of many leading British politicians. These included Welsh figures, notably Aneurin Bevan. In a speech in the first Welsh Day Debate in the House of Commons Nye Bevan denied that Wales had any unique problems and that a solution to Wales's problems could be found within Wales: "My colleagues, all of them members of the Miners' Federation of Great Britain, have no special solution for the Welsh coal industry which is not a solution for the whole of the mining industry of Great Britain. There is no Welsh coal problem." (quoted in Osmond 1978 p23).

However, only twenty years after Nye Bevan denied the uniqueness of Wales's plight and, by implication, the need to address it on a Welsh basis, the distinctiveness of Wales was acknowledged in a new administrative structure for Wales. The Labour Government elected in 1964 created the office of Secretary of State for Wales with a seat at the Cabinet table. How had this reversal come about?

Although Aneurin Bevan spoke for many in the Labour movement in seeing Welsh nationalism as a 'distraction' from the social and economic problems Labour sought to solve his opinion was not the only one expressed within the Labour party. There were others in the party that were a great deal more sympathetic to claims based on Welsh nationhood. Certain Labour MPs, such as

S. O. Edwards and Tudor Watkin had been prominently involved in the Parliament for Wales campaign during the 1950s. Also, as Labour advanced electorally into North Wales in the 1950s, it inherited, to some degree, the mantle of the Liberal Party as the 'party of Wales'. New MPs, representing North Wales seats such as Cledwyn Hughes (Anglesey, elected 1951) represented a new element in the Labour party, an element which was more sympathetic to Welsh sentiment.

Also, certain prominent figures in the Labour party shared these Welsh sentiments. James Griffiths, MP for Llanelli, was deputy leader of the Labour party and chairman of its home affairs policy committee and Butt Philip ascribes some of the pressure within the Labour party for a commitment to the creation of a Welsh Secretary to this 'chance fact' (Butt Philip 1975 p282).

The issue of the administration of Wales was given greater prominence by the Third Memorandum of the Council of Wales and Monmouthshire 'Government Administration in Wales', published in 1957. In this Memorandum the Council called for the creation of a Secretary of State for Wales with a seat in the Cabinet and responsibility for a wide range of government functions in Wales. The Conservative government of the time rejected the main proposals of the report but made some minor concessions including the creation of a Minister of State to assist the Minister for Wales, who devoted his whole time to Welsh affairs. However, the Labour party seemed to have been swayed by the arguments presented by the Memorandum. Possibly, the reform of administrative structures chimed with Labour's new emphasis on reforming the machinery of government to address more effectively social and economic problems. Thomas states "What seems to have finally convinced the Labour Party of the desirability of setting up a Welsh Office ... was the growing perception of the possibility that a Welsh Office could play an important part in the economic development of Wales within an integrated United Kingdom economy" (Thomas 1980 p56). J. B. Smith reveals a similar thesis: "the fact that the crucial economic issue was seen, not as a deterrent to constitutional change, but as a problem whose solution demanded the structural changes to which Labour was now bounden... The coherence which had for so long eluded Labour's thinking on its policy for Wales was now within the movement's comprehension" (Smith 1978 pp112-3).

1964-1979

One function the Welsh Office was intended to fulfil, as previous measures of administrative devolution in Wales had fulfilled, was, as James Griffiths boasted, a "recognition of our nationhood" and to provide "a new status for Wales within the constitution of the United Kingdom" (Welsh Grand Committee First Sitting, Functions of the Secretary of State for Wales and Constitutional Change in Wales

49

16 December 1964 col 10). However, government departments are not intended merely as symbols; they are mechanisms for decision-making. Was the Welsh Office any better equipped to make decisions reflecting the circumstances and needs of Wales than previous measures of administrative devolution had been?

Initial prospects for the Welsh Office were not bright. Edward Rowlands, a former minister at the Welsh Office, wrote "Whitehall had made little or no preparation for the coming of the Welsh Office" (Rowlands 1972 p333). Opposed by the civil service and some ministers (interviews with Cledwyn Hughes and John Morris)[1] "moves were afoot to confine his role his [the Welsh Secretary's] to that of a watchdog" (Rowlands 1972 p334). Thus, one of the first tasks of the Welsh Office was to extract some real and effective powers "from a reluctant Whitehall" (Rowlands 1972 p334).

Initially, too, the Welsh Office had few resources to undertake any functions. In 1965, 225 civil servants worked in the Welsh Office and there was some difficulty in finding civil servants of a high calibre to work in the department. Cledwyn Hughes, Welsh Secretary from 1966 to 1968 had to draft in Sir Algernon Rumbold, a former Deputy Secretary at the Commonwealth Office, where Cledwyn Hughes had been a minister, to prepare "Wales: The Way Ahead". This document, claimed to be a great achievement for the Welsh Office at the time, required the services of a retired civil servant with no connection to Wales to be completed (Osmond 1974 p.107).

Nevertheless, despite the opposition of the civil service and other ministers, the Welsh Office grew, acquiring functions from other government departments. The acquisition of functions by the Welsh Office after 1964 was aided by appeals to Welsh sentiment or conditions in Wales (education and agriculture for example) and also by the fact that the machinery of government was being overhauled nationally. It is claimed that it was easier for the Welsh Office to gain responsibility for health functions because the health service was already undergoing the upheaval of being amalgamated into the Department of Health and Social Security nationally (Rowlands 1972 pp334-5). The pressures of national sentiment, special conditions in Wales and wider reform of the machinery of government were the forces cited by Randall (1972) as driving the creation of Welsh governmental institutions before 1964.

The pressures of national sentiment, in the form of calls for devolution in Wales (and Scotland) were particularly important for the growth of the Welsh Office during the 1970s. A Labour minority government was dependent on the support of nationalist MPs (11 Scottish Nationalist and 3 Plaid Cymru MPs were

---

[1] Crossman's reaction to the creation of the Welsh Office as recorded in his diaries may serve as an illustration "Another...idiotic creation ..., a completely artificial new office for Jim Griffiths and his two Parliamentary Secretaries, all the result of a silly election pledge" (Crossman 1976 p63).

elected in October 1974) in order to remain in office. It conceded the devolution of certain powers to elected assemblies in Scotland and Wales. The Welsh Office was in danger of losing most of its responsibilities to a Welsh assembly. John Morris admitted that the increase in the number of functions performed by the Welsh Office during the 1974-9 Labour Government was intended to preserve some substantial role for the Secretary of State for Wales after devolution (Interview with John Morris).

Table 3:1
Growth of the Welsh Office 1964-79

Year	Function	Former Ministry
1964-5	Roads	Transport
	Housing, Local Government, Town and Country Planning, New Towns Water and sewerage, forestry, Tourism, National Parks, Ancient Monuments & Historic Buildings, Welsh Language, Regional Economic planning (Shared with DEA)	Housing & Local Government
1969	Health Service	Health (in England
	Local Authority Health and Welfare	to DHSS)
1970	Primary & Secondary Education	Education & Science
1971	Child Care	Home Office (in England to DHSS)
(1974)	(Staff of Welsh Hospital Board Absorbed)	
1975	Industry Functions	Trade and Industry
1978	Higher & Further Education (excluding Universities)	Education & Science
	Agriculture	MAFF
	Manpower Policy	Employment

(Source: Thomas 1987 p.146)

Much of the growth of the Welsh Office has been the result of re-allocating branches of existing departments to the Welsh Office. The growth of the Welsh office is paved with Transfer of Function orders. Rose states "The Welsh Office is a paradigm case of the process of re-allocating programmes, for it was created by subtracting Cardiff regional offices from existing offices and adding them to the remit of the Secretary of State for Wales" (Rose 1987 p46).

Growth in this way, however, brings its own problems. Civil servants transferred to the Welsh Office in this way may be more familiar with implementing policies devised elsewhere rather than implementing policies to suit Welsh conditions. A subordinate cast of mind among Welsh Office officials would clearly hamper the autonomy of the Welsh Office. However, such a limited approach would be expected to diminish over time as civil servants became used to the greater scope for autonomy or older civil servants retired. Even so, John Morris found in 1974 (a full decade after the establishment of the Welsh Office) that some officials still wanted to refer every decision to a functional ministry (interview with John Morris).

In order to discharge the increased number of functions the Welsh Office had to grow in size. In 1964 225 civil servants worked in the Welsh Office. In 1979 this figure stood at 2,300. Growth was most rapid during the 1960s (from 225 to 750 during the years 1964-70) and from 1974-9 when a number of functions were transferred to the Welsh Office from the regional offices of other ministries. The recruitment difficulties that had existed in the early years of the Welsh Office's history (see Evidence to Royal Commission on the Constitution Welsh Office Evidence p108) appeared to have been overcome. This was partly due to the expansion of the Welsh Office; a career in the Welsh office offered greater opportunities for advancement as a result. Partly, the attractiveness of Cardiff as a place to live and standard civil service procedure that requires civil servants to serve in a number of ministries also aided recruitment of talented officials to the Welsh Office.

Another measure which enhanced the status of the Welsh Office came in 1974, when the senior civil servant in the Welsh Office was given the title of Permanent Secretary, enhancing his status to the level enjoyed by the senior civil servant in all other departments of state. As John Morris, the then Welsh Secretary, said "my top man was equal to other people's top men" (John Morris quoted in The Welsh Office: 25 Years, BBC2 23 November 1989).

The power of the Welsh Office was further augmented by the accretion of associated non-departmental public bodies. These covered a wide range of functions. Some, such as the Welsh Development Agency, the Development Board for Rural Wales or the Land Authority for Wales, had large budgets and responsibilities for politically sensitive matters such as economic growth. Thus, by 1979, the Secretary of State for Wales stood at the pinnacle of a large and complex array of governmental organisations.

By 1979 the Welsh Office had almost gained parity with the Scottish Office in terms of functions. The functions proposed for a Welsh Office by the Third Memorandum of the Council of Wales and Monmouthshire in 1957 had finally been transferred to that body. Much of that growth had been piecemeal, motivated by considerations of electoral appeal or partisan advantage, responses to Welsh sentiment, especially at the time of the devolution debate, or the result of Whitehall empire-building.

The Conservative Party has not historically been regarded as sympathetic to Welsh sentiment. It was the only party opposed to the devolution proposals for Wales in the 1970s and the result of the devolution referendum in 1979 seemed to be a vindication of the Conservative opposition to devolution. In the following general election, in May 1979, which brought the Conservatives back into office nationally, the Conservatives gained 11 seats and 32 per cent of the vote in Wales, the highest number of seats they had won in Wales up to that time this century.

One of the first measures by the Conservative government was to repeal the Wales [Devolution] Act. However, the existence of a Welsh dimension in Government was acknowledged to some extent as the Conservatives also created a Commons Select Committee to oversee the work of the Welsh Office. The new government was also pledged to reduce public expenditure and lessen the role of the state in people's lives. Wales felt some of the force of this drive, for example with the abolition of the Welsh Council, an advisory body, in 1979.

However, the Conservative government elected in 1979 was, in some respects, more sympathetic to Welsh concerns than first impressions might have indicated. The new Secretary of State for Wales, Nicholas Edwards, sat for a Welsh constituency, Pembroke. Thus, the first Thatcher government chose a member for a Welsh constituency with Welsh connections as Welsh Secretary, although this meant that the Welsh Secretary was chosen from the ranks of the small number of Welsh Conservative MPs. In 1970, by contrast, Heath had chosen Peter Thomas as Welsh Secretary. Although he had strong Welsh connections, and was formerly MP for Conway, by 1970 he was the member for Hendon South.

The Conservatives also carried through an important extension of the Welsh Office's powers in relation to bargaining with other Whitehall departments. In 1980 the Welsh Office was given a block grant for the expenditure on most Welsh Office programmes. The two main components of Welsh Office expenditure outside this block were expenditure on agricultural support and aid to industry. The Welsh Office Block was determined according to a population-related formula related to changes in expenditure for comparable programmes in England. Within programmes covered by the Block (roads and transport; housing; environmental services; education; health and personal social services; and Welsh Office administration costs) the Secretary of State has the "freedom to decide the distribution of resources between the programmes which comprise the Welsh Block in the light of his own priorities reflecting the particular needs of Wales" (Memorandum by the Welsh Office HC 259 Session 1992-93 p75). Thus, the Secretary of State has, theoretically, greater discretion to vary expenditure on programmes in Wales than was the case before 1980. However, the need to achieve minimum uniform standards nationally mean that this power is not as great as it may seem. Nevertheless, Peter Walker claimed that he could re-allocate expenditure between programmes so that it would achieve a greater impact in the Valleys programme for example (Walker 1991 pp209-10).

The 1980 Local Government Planning and Land Act transferred responsibility for setting local government expenditure in Wales to the Welsh Office. The Welsh Office has become the centre as far as local authorities in Wales are concerned. Within Wales a Consultative Council on Local Government exists and its subgroups dealing with specific areas of policy (housing for example) have created new channels of communication between the Welsh Office and local authorities. Welsh local authorities have historically had a low rate base and the formula for calculating grants to local authorities in Wales differs from that applying in England. This may partly account for the comparatively good relations that have prevailed between local and central government in Wales.

The early 1990s have seen a renewed burst of function acquisition by the Welsh Office. In April 1992, responsibility for training was transferred from the Department of Employment to the Welsh Office. Simultaneously, the funding of higher and further education institutions in Wales was transferred to new Welsh funding councils. David Hunt, then Welsh Secretary, used this opportunity to create a new department within the Welsh Office, responsible for training, education and enterprise. This co-ordinates the work of the training and enterprise councils, the local enterprise agencies and the local careers services within Wales.

Thus, since 1979, the Welsh Office has continued to acquire functions, although at a slower pace than in the 1970s when the pressure of devolution created a momentum for change. In addition to the growth of the Welsh Office, the number and expenditure of non-departmental public bodies in Wales has grown (see below). The Welsh Office has become a more powerful administrative machine than it was in its early years and now affects many aspects of daily life. As an administrative body the Welsh Office has come of age.

However, other developments since 1979 cast some doubt on the Welsh Office as a recognition of Welsh nationhood. In 1987 Peter Walker's appointment to the Welsh Office marked a constitutional development in the history of the Welsh Office. Peter Walker, MP for Worcester, was the first Welsh Secretary to have no connection with Wales. The Conservatives' tally of eight Welsh MPs meant that the pool from which Welsh Office ministers could be drawn was not deep. In May 1990, David Hunt was appointed Welsh Secretary. His Welsh connections were again tenuous (though he was at least born in Wales). John Redwood, MP for Wokingham, appointed Welsh Secretary in 1993, appeared to have no previous connection with Wales whatsoever. William Hague, MP for Richmond in Yorkshire, appointed Secretary of State for Wales in June 1995, is a Yorkshireman and not a Welshman. As far as Conservative governments are concerned, the office of Welsh Secretary is now a Cabinet post like any other, sitting for a Welsh constituency or having strong Welsh connections is no longer a necessary qualification.

The appointment of non-Welshmen to the Welsh Office carries with it overtones of colonialism to some in Wales. It seems to indicate that Welsh national sentiment can be more easily disregarded than Scottish national sentiment. The Conservatives have continued to fill all offices in the Scottish Office from a dwindling number of Scots Tories (10 MPs in 1987; 11 in 1992) even though there are a number of 'expatriate' Scots amongst English Conservatives MPs such as Teddy Taylor, member for Southend East. The strength and sensitivity of Scottish national sentiment is shown by the fact that what has already happened in Wales is there labelled the 'Doomsday scenario'. Wales, it must be concluded, is a more integrated and less politically nationalist part of the United Kingdom than is Scotland.

Nevertheless, in conclusion, we can say that the history of the Welsh Office has been one of growth and that it has now acquired the functions, powers, personnel and coherence of a department of state. History has equipped the Welsh Office with a wide range of functions and a measure of resources, in terms of personnel, institutions, finances and control over those finances that are unprecedented in the history of Wales. Whether this in fact makes the Welsh Office a 'miniature Whitehall' (Peter Thomas quoted on The Welsh Office : 25 Years, BBC2 23 November 1989) or merely a small and peripheral part of a large and complex system (Kellas and Madgwick 1982 p29) is examined below.

The power of the Welsh Office

The Welsh Office and Whitehall

The Welsh Office is clearly a part of Whitehall, albeit at 150 miles remove. Its existence affords access to officials and ministers representing Welsh interests that would otherwise not exist or exist only fortuitously. Access to Whitehall and the 'corridors of power' was one of the major justifications for the creation of the Welsh Office. James Griffiths considered it of the utmost importance for Wales to have "its own representative in the seat of power" (quoted in Randall 1972 p365). David Hunt, in evidence before the Welsh Affairs Select Committee stated that the Welsh Office contributed to many areas of policy-making by the fact "that it has a Secretary of State in the Cabinet" and that the Welsh Secretary has "an immediate input into policy formation... even when Welsh interests are not involved (Q512 HC 259 Session 1992-3). Also, Welsh Office "officials are involved whenever Welsh interests are part of the overall picture" (Q512 HC 259 Session 1992-93). This degree of access can be important. Welsh Office civil servants played a prominent role in drawing up the Severn Bridges bill for example. Also, in his autobiography Peter Walker recounts how, as Welsh Secretary, he was able to bring forward plans to build the second Severn crossing, thus amending the priorities of the Department of Transport (Walker 1991 p210).

Nevertheless, the Welsh Office and the Secretary of State for Wales are comparatively minor figures in Whitehall. Rose (1987) using several measures of departmental status found the Welsh Office to be the bottom ranking of the Cabinet departments. However, on some of the measures that he used, the Welsh Office has arguably gained in status since the late 1980s. The Welsh Office is no longer the dead end it was once considered to be. David Hunt was promoted to Employment Secretary in 1993, a position with a large budget and a high political profile. John Redwood managed to be a more publicly prominent figure than previous Welsh Secretaries. His comments on single mothers in the St Mellons estate (July 1993) sparked a national debate, something few previous Welsh Secretaries had been able to do about any topic. In the summer of 1995, John Redwood launched a leadership challenge against John Major, the Prime Minister. Though unsuccessful in his challenge, John Redwood was able to raise the public profile of the office of Welsh Secretary. More importantly, the Welsh Secretary has been revealed to play a more significant role in Cabinet committees than had been thought in the past.

A previous study of government in Wales found that "The secrecy surrounding the constitution and functions of the various Cabinet committees prevents a judgement being made as to the position occupied by the Secretary of State" (Randall 1972 p365). However, in May 1992, a full list of Cabinet Committees and their memberships was published and it is now possible to measure what role the Welsh Secretary plays in Cabinet Committees. This information reveals the Welsh Secretary to sit on the main domestic policy committees, including the important Ministerial Committee on Economic and Domestic Policy. Altogether, the Welsh Secretary was a member of the Ministerial Committee on Economic and Domestic Policy (EDP), the Ministerial Committee on Industrial, Commercial and Consumer Affairs (EDI), Ministerial Committee on Home and Social Affairs (EUR), Ministerial Committee on Local Government (EDL), Ministerial Committee on Legislation (LG), Ministerial Sub-committee on Health Strategy (EDH(H)) and the Ministerial Sub-committee on European Questions (OPD(E)). Welsh Office ministers were also members of the Ministerial Sub-committees on Drug Misuse (EDH(D)), Co-ordination of Urban

Policy (EDH(U)), Alcohol Misuse (EDH(A)) and Women's issues (EDH(W)) (Independent 20 May 1992 p9).

Before the Welsh Affairs Select Committee, David Hunt also claimed that he had access to Cabinet committees of which he was not a regular member when he requested the right to attend their meetings. He said "... on those occasions when I have asked to be present at meetings of OD [Overseas and Defence Cabinet Committee] I have been invited. I have never knowingly been excluded. Indeed, I believe that the Prime Minister goes out of his way to ensure that whenever any interests that would involve Wales are concerned then I am present" (Q539 HC 259 Session 1992-93).

Around the Cabinet table the role of personality cannot be discounted. It is possible that David Hunt's participation in a number of Cabinet committees reflected good relations with the Prime Minister or his clubbability rather than the clout of the Welsh Office. Peter Walker too claims that, as Welsh Secretary, he played a major role in the government. In his autobiography he says, "I was conscious that the high ranking the Prime Minister gave me in the Cabinet pecking order, above the Secretaries of State for the Environment, Trade and Industry and Defence, meant that the officials from major departments had to come to my small department to discuss proposals" (Walker 1991 p215). However, he goes on to imply that it was his personal qualities, rather than the status of the office he held which ensured this high profile for the Welsh Office in Whitehall: "I suspect the officials who worked for me in a series of small departments positively enjoyed the reversal of the normal roles and senior civil servants having to come to them" (Walker 1991 p215).

The power of the office of Welsh Secretary in relation to other departments in Whitehall remains unclear. For example, although the Welsh Secretary is not responsible for law and order functions in Wales (they are the responsibility of the Home Office) David Hunt met the four chief constables of Wales in order to look for ways to "better co-ordinate the whole area of crime prevention and dealing with the effects and after-effects of crime" (Q525 HC 259 Session 1992-93). He continued "Strictly,... that is not an area of my responsibility but the Home Secretary had no objection to my meeting the four chief constables of Wales because of my special responsibility for Wales (Q525 HC 259 Session 1992-93). The 'oversight' power over the work of government in Wales that was given to the Welsh Secretary from its earliest days can aid him in his dealings with other departments with regard to Wales. However, there are limitations to the oversight powers, especially if matters are not brought to the attention of the Welsh Secretary in time or if they are even hidden from him. Edward Rowlands, writing about the early years of the Welsh Office found "It has been and still is possible for major decisions on a pit closure... to be formulated in advance of any consultation with the Welsh Office. Consultation has sometimes meant merely being informed" (Rowlands 1972 p338). The Welsh Secretary's apparent ignorance of British Coal's decision to shut the Point of Ayr colliery in Clwyd in October 1992 might indicate that little has changed. David Hunt does not agree, however, that the case of the pit closures is evidence that the powers of the Welsh Office are deficient. In evidence to the Welsh Affairs Committee he said

> I was kept fully informed by the President of the Board of Trade regarding discussions with British Coal over the pit closures issue ... However, the detailed content of the closure list was considered by the Government to be a matter for British Coal ... I understand that the decision on the Point of Ayr was not passed to the President of the Board of Trade until the day before his announcement... I do not regard the fact that I was told the following morning, that is, on the day, that the Point of Ayr was to be included as one of the list of 31 pits as a matter of great difference between myself and the President of the Board of Trade

(Q516 HC 259 session 1992-93).

The Memorandum by the Welsh Office to the Welsh Affairs Committee states that the work of the Welsh Office involves "in particular circumstances the development of specific policies; the adaptation of policies to the situation in Wales; and the delivery of policies through distinctively Welsh mechanisms" (Memorandum by the Welsh Office HC 259 Session 1992-93 Evidence p75). Although there are examples of distinctive policies pursued by the Welsh Office, for example the Mental Handicap Strategy or Welsh Language policy (including the passage of a Welsh Language Act in 1993), much of the work of the Welsh Office involves adapting policies to Welsh needs or delivering policies through distinctively Welsh mechanisms. Nevertheless, the Welsh Office may enjoy a significant degree of autonomy as a result.

There are numerous examples of policies that have been adapted by the Welsh Office to meet circumstances in Wales; David Hunt has claimed that "... there are differences to be found in every area of policy where we have adapted to the Welsh dimension" (Q514 HC 259 Session 1992-3). He claimed that he had "... very much a free hand with my colleagues within the Welsh Office in determining in consultation with other interested groups in Wales and the other representative bodies what is the right approach for Wales" (Q513 HC 259 Session 1992-93). An example of where the institutional structure gives Wales the power to vary policy and adapt it to Welsh needs, he suggests, is the Curriculum Council for Wales. The teaching of history differs in Wales from that in England and, reflecting (perceived) Welsh characteristics, "... in the curriculum on music and literature we have taken performance as a much higher priority than theory because in Wales we have a great tradition in singing and performing the arts and music" (Q513 HC 259 Session 1992-93).

However, 'the free hand' the Welsh Secretary enjoys to vary policy is bound to some degree, as the Welsh Secretary admitted, by the fact that "We work of course within a common government framework ..." though he insisted "differences of detail can always be seen and highlighted" (Q514 HC 259 Session 1992-93). Also, in some policy areas such as the development of town and country planning "it is necessary for the Welsh Office, the Scottish Office, the Northern Ireland Office and the Department of the Environment to sit round a table and work through the way in which policy is to be developed. There may be occasions on which a different path is followed in the territories from what is followed in England, and it will be as a result of that co-operation and co-ordination" (Q515 HC 259 Session 1992-93). This answer indicates that the 'free hand', even where policy differs, is constrained by a need to consult and negotiate with other departments.

One advantage that is claimed for the Welsh Office in terms of making and implementing policy is that it is a multi-functional department. David Hunt, compared his experience as a local government minister in England with being Welsh Secretary thus: "When I was minister for local government, minister for inner cities, energy minister, often I should be wanting to achieve objectives that would involve a number of other government departments. With those same objectives within the Welsh Office I can ask my private secretary... to set up a meeting for me... I have the housing department, I have the local government department, I have the education department, I have the health department, I have all these different departments then sitting round the same table..." (Q477 HC 259 Session 1992-93). Such co-ordination is possible in England, but is more difficult and does involve at the local level, special teams of officials from different departments, the City Action Teams, to co-operate in devising policies (Q479 HC 259 Session 1992-93).

"The other side of the coin, however," as the Report of the Welsh Affairs Committee points out, "is that in most areas the policy framework is set by English government departments and copied by the Welsh Office with greater or lesser variations to suit Welsh circumstances" (HC 259 Session 1992-93 Report p1). It is difficult to see how this could be otherwise, as the Welsh Office contains relatively few civil servants and lacks the resources to devise distinctive policies in a large number of areas. Thomas compares the numbers of Welsh Office civil servants engaged in a specific policy area with the number of civil servants working in the same area in an English 'functional' department. Unsurprisingly, the Welsh Office can devote relatively few civil servants to a specific policy area compared with Whitehall functional departments (Thomas 1987).

In addition to its role in Whitehall the Welsh Office is also the focus for numerous public bodies and local authorities within Wales. For these bodies the Welsh Office, not a department in Whitehall, is effectively their 'centre'. Does the Welsh Office's relationships with these bodies enhance the authority and autonomy of the Welsh Office or diminish it?

The Secretary of State for Wales can draw on non-departmental public bodies for help, advice and expertise on specific issues. On tourism, for example, an important issue for the Welsh economy and thus for the Welsh Secretary, the Wales Tourist Board is a reservoir of expertise whereas "the Civil Servants who work on tourism matters in the Welsh Office, generally speaking, have a non-tourism background" (Wales Tourist Board Memorandum HC 259 Evidence p45) and thus it is the Wales Tourist Board that is formally designated the adviser to the Secretary of State (HC 259 Q293 Session 1992-93). Most of the work of the Welsh Office itself "is of a policy nature; local authorities, health authorities and non-departmental public bodies (NDPBs) undertake many of the executive responsibilities" (Cm 1916 p87). Thus, the 2,400 or so civil servants at the Welsh Office are relatively free to concentrate on making or adapting policy to meet Welsh needs.

Also, as Mr Lightman, a civil servant at the Welsh Office found, Wales "contains relatively few people and relatively few organs of local government and other elements of organised society" (Mr Lightman's Lecture 22 October 1987). For example, "There are eight counties against 39 in England, 37 districts against 296; 9 District Health Authorities against 192; and no health regions (unless you count the Welsh Office itself) against fourteen" (lecture 22-10-1987). As one Welsh Office official told me, whilst knowledge of factual details is inevitably less (though not by much) "personal knowledge and expertise is greater" (Interview with Welsh Office civil servant).

The small size of Wales and the small number of people and organisations the Welsh Office has to deal with creates a situation where, claims Mr Lightman, "we in Cardiff are infinitely more closely in touch with – and I think influenced by – the local authorities, the health, housing and education authorities, individual companies in industry and indeed individual consumers than our London colleagues" (Mr. Lightman's lecture 22-10-1987). This creates another resource for the Welsh Office, and one study of the government in Wales described it as 'government by consultation' (Madgwick and James 1979).

Sir Geoffrey Inkin, chairman of the Cardiff Bay Development Corporation, claimed that the chairmen of English urban development corporations "envy the direct access my Board has politically and at senior Civil Service level, and more particularly the access to people taking decisions and people involved in the decision-making process" (Q229 HC 259 Session 1992-93).

Michael Boyce, chief executive of Cardiff Bay Development Corporation and formerly chief executive of South Glamorgan County Council, described relations with the Welsh Office as 'regular', explaining:

> the opportunity to have a regularity of contact arises because there is a Welsh Office and particularly because the Welsh Office, as far as I am concerned, is only half a mile up the road" and, "through regularity you build up understanding, confidence and trust and it is those issues that secure this relationship rather than frameworks, rules and regulations. They become the canvass against which you know you have to operate. They may not always be happy or jovial ... but they are done on the basis of understanding

(Q229 HC 259 Session 1992-93).

The growth of governmental institutions at the Wales level can be expected to augment the autonomy of the Welsh Office from Whitehall functional departments by creating new channels or Welsh forums of communication. One example of this might be housing policy in Wales. In 1988, the Welsh functions of the London based Housing Corporation were placed in a new non departmental public body, Housing for Wales (Tai Cymru) sponsored by the Welsh Office. Simultaneously, housing associations in Wales, which had previously been represented in an England and Wales wide body, founded a Welsh Federation of Housing Associations. Discussions between the Welsh Office and local authorities about housing were already conducted through a subcommittee of the Welsh Consultative Council on Local Government. The possibility of a distinct Welsh housing policy network, and thus of a distinct Welsh policy on housing, had come into being. Also, such a network can take greater account of the particular needs of Wales and given Wales's size develop a deeper knowledge of the housing situation in every part of Wales. John Allen, chairman of Housing for Wales said in evidence to the Welsh Affairs Committee "Undoubtedly very strong benefits have emerged from the ability in Wales to have its own organisation, both in terms of the board being representative of the various parts of Wales, the board being able to direct its attention specifically to the particular problems of Wales which in many ways are quite different from some of the problems of industrial England ... and it also provides a much firmer and more direct interface with the housing association movement in Wales and with the local authorities and all other interested parties in Wales" (Q403 HC 259 Session 1992-93). (Whether this distinct Welsh structure of organisations concerned with housing policy in fact produces distinctive Welsh housing policies is discussed in chapter 5 below).

The nature of the Welsh Office's relationships with the local authorities and non-departmental public bodies has become a matter of some controversy. Traditionally, it has been thought that the Welsh Office retained a 'slightly old fashioned democratic flavour about it' (Kellas and Madgwick 1982 p13). Giving evidence to the Royal Commission on the Constitution the Permanent Under Secretary at the Welsh Office remarked that "a public servant...ought always have at the back of his mind the thought that he may be called to account for his actions to a body which consists of freely elected representatives of the people he is serving" (Royal Commission on the Constitution Welsh Office interviews p10). Mr Lightman claimed that the Welsh Office is a 'Westminster' department rather than a 'Whitehall' one, meaning that there is an emphasis on "political responsibility through political institutions rather than administrative ones" (Mr. Lightman's lecture 22-10-1987).

It is true that the existence of the Welsh Office makes some of the trappings of government more accessible to people in Wales. The Welsh Office as a building provides a focus for protest and a stage for demonstrations. Welsh language rights marches have ended there and a dead cow was dumped on its steps by farmers protesting at the imposition of milk quotas. However, it is unclear whether the existence of the Welsh Office makes the conduct of government in Wales any more accountable to the people of Wales.

Since 1979, Wales has been governed by a Conservative government although it has never won a majority of seats in Wales. Conservative strength reached a peak of 14 seats in 1983, by 1992 the number of seats in Wales held by the Conservatives was down to six. As in Scotland, nationalists have claimed that Conservative rule in Wales lacks legitimacy. The imposition of non-Welsh politicians as Welsh Secretary can only have added to an impression of colonial rule for some. In particular, concern has been expressed about the growth of the non-elected component of government in Wales, the non-departmental public bodies (Osmond 1992). It has been alleged that through appointments to these bodies and through the instructions he gives these bodies, the Welsh Secretary can govern almost like a viceroy.

The 'imperial domain' of non-departmental public bodies in Wales is extensive. The 1993 edition of 'Public bodies' lists 23 executive, 28 advisory and 4 tribunal non-departmental public bodies sponsored by the Welsh Office. In addition, there are 14 National Health Service Trusts in Wales as well as nine district health authorities, eight Family Health Service Authorities, the Health Promotion Authority for Wales and the Wales Health Common Services Authority. Altogether, there are almost a hundred non-departmental public bodies in Wales sponsored by the Welsh Office. Their combined expenditure in 1992-3 was some £2.4 billion pounds (the total expenditure by local authorities in Wales was forecast to be £3.3 billion in 1991-92, Cm 1916) or some 40 per cent of the expenditure plans for the Welsh Office as a whole in 1992-93 (Cm 1916 p5). Non-Departmental public bodies (NDPBs), or quangos as they are also known, have a wide variety of functions in Wales and vary greatly in size and expenditure. The Higher Education Funding Council for Wales had an expenditure of some £500,000 in 1992-93 but Housing for Wales spent over £187 million and the Welsh Development Agency £165 million in the same year (Public Bodies 1993). The Secretary of state for Wales appoints most of the board members, chairmen and chief executives of the NDPBs in Wales. The 1993 edition of Public Bodies lists the total number of appointments made to non-departmental public bodies sponsored by the Welsh Office as 1277 (Public Bodies 1993 viii).

Thus, the Secretary of State for Wales enjoys great powers of patronage. It has been alleged that these powers have been used by successive Conservative Welsh Secretaries to appoint Conservatives to positions of responsibility in Wales, positions few Conservatives in Wales could expect to hold through election. Whilst this is difficult to confirm empirically (members of the boards are not required to list their partisan affiliations when appointed) some appointments would seem to indicate that there is possibly some truth to this charge. Geoffrey Inkin, chairman of Cardiff Bay Development Corporation and the Land Authority for Wales is a former Conservative parliamentary candidate. Two Conservative MPs defeated after the 1992 election quickly found appointments to two quangos in Wales. One of the new Conservative MPs in Wales, elected in 1992, Jonathan Evans, had previously been a board member of Housing for Wales. Beata Brookes, the former Conservative MEP for North Wales became chair of the Welsh Consumers Council after her election defeat in 1989. The current chairman of the Welsh Development Agency was formerly organiser of Conservatives Abroad in Monaco.

It has also been claimed that the accountability of the non-departmental public bodies in Wales is inadequate. The Public Accounts Committee severely criticised the Welsh Development Agency for profligacy and mismanagement (Public Accounts Committee HC 353 Session 1992-93). A marketing director was appointed without his (bogus) references being checked, £1.4 million was lost through inappropriate redundancy payments, the chairman of the Agency failed to notify the Agency of the change of use of a building he had received a Rural Conversion grant for, and it was revealed that his references had not been checked by the Welsh Secretary (then Peter Walker) when he was appointed chairman. An investigation into the feasibility of privatising the functions of the Welsh Development Agency (Operation Wizard) was not revealed and an attempt was made to conceal Operation Wizard from the attention of Parliament. The Public Accounts Committee concluded with regard to Operation Wizard " ... we are concerned that there might have been a deliberate attempt by the Agency to conceal Operation WIZARD within their Accounts by spreading the costs under several headings. We do not believe this to have been compatible with Parliamentary accountability, especially as some of the options identified by the consultants involve major restructuring of the Agency, with changes to its objectives and the possible reduction of its specific commitment to Wales. We are concerned that not only was Parliament denied information, but that this Committee would have remained unaware of the project's existence had it not been for unofficial revelations from within the Agency" (HC 353 Session 1992-93 Forty-seventh Report of Public Accounts Committee para 41).

Whether the claims of partisan appointment and unaccountable public bodies deserve the sobriquet 'Quangoland' (Osmond 1992 p16) is a matter of political controversy. However, if 'Quangoland' does exist, presided over by the Welsh Office and the Welsh Secretary, then it can be claimed that the Secretary of State for Wales does enjoy considerable influence and maybe a degree of autonomy. In this sense, it might actually serve as another resource for the Welsh Secretary to make and implement policies as he thinks fit.

The Welsh Office abroad

The conventional picture of the Welsh Office is that of a small department engaged in "the humdrum business of implementing policies decided elsewhere" (Kellas and Madgwick 1982 p29). However, it has also been claimed that the Welsh Office is able to engage in the high politics of dealing with foreign companies and even foreign governments, at least in matters of commerce. Peter Walker, as Welsh Secretary, used his status as a Cabinet minister to impress potential foreign investors to Wales. In his memoirs he recounts how he would telephone executives of companies that were considering inward investment into Europe saying "I am the Secretary of State for Wales. Wales is part of the United Kingdom ..." (Walker 1991 p211).

Wales is now linked to the so-called four motor regions of Europe. These are Baden Wurttemberg, Lombardy, Rhone Alpes and Catalonia, major regional economies in each of their states. Together, since 1987 they have been developing inter-regional co-operation in terms of technology transfer, science and technology policy, and research and development. In 1990 Wales entered the European High Technology Confederation upon signing a partnership agreement with Baden Wurttemberg and became, potentially a 'fifth motor' (Morgan and Cooke 1991 pp28-30). Wales was very fortunate in securing this link (interview with Kevin Morgan) as Baden Wurttemberg had initially looked to a prosperous UK region such as the South East as a possible partner. However, it could 'find no-one to talk to' in the South East. Cooke and Morgan conclude that in terms of fostering inter-regional co-operation "The Welsh Office, with a cabinet-ranking

Secretary of State, and the Welsh Development Agency are significant ports of entry ..." (Morgan and Cooke 1991 p49). Wales, thanks to its governmental structure, possesses the elements needed to foster inter-regional co-operation and in this respect is better placed than any English region.

Another development, that shows the governmental structure of Wales can speak for Wales overseas is the establishment in 1992 of the Wales European Centre in Brussels. This is supported and funded by a number of Welsh bodies including the Welsh Development Agency, Welsh county and district councils, the Development Board for Rural Wales, the University of Wales and the Training and Enterprise Councils in Wales. The Wales European Centre acts as a clearing house of information for foreign companies that might want to know more about Wales and a source of information about the current developments, programmes and future plans of the European Union.

However, Wales's 'foreign policy' remains comparatively narrow, focused almost exclusively on commercial and economic objectives (though it is difficult to see what other objectives it might wish to pursue internationally). More importantly, as with domestic policy, the Welsh Office can only conduct its activities in accordance with the framework of policy laid down by Whitehall. Wales cannot have a separate policy in applying for available European Union funds for example.

Conclusion

Thus, in conclusion, it is clear that during the course of the twentieth century governmental institutions in Wales have acquired greater resources than at any time in the nation's history. With this has come some measure of autonomy from Whitehall. This is mainly confined to relatively mundane matters but this is not to minimise the importance of education, housing, health or the clearance of derelict land. Organisations and institutions in several policy areas increasingly operate at a Welsh level and this opens up the possibility of distinctive policies being applied in Wales. It is possible that the Welsh Office, Housing for Wales, the Welsh housing associations and the Welsh local authorities could form a distinctive 'policy network'. Wales, with a high degree of institutional distinctiveness and a sense of national consciousness may be fertile ground for the creation of networks based on co-operation and consultation between different governmental institutions. Rhodes has spoken of 'territorial communities' which like policy communities are " integrated stable networks with continuity of membership and a high degree of vertical interdependence" (Rhodes 1988 p284) .

In order to study whether the opportunity afforded by the distinct structure of government in Wales to develop and implement distinctive policies has been exploited, chapters five and six study the making of economic policy in Wales and urban regeneration policies in Wales during the 1980s and early 1990s. These are areas where government in Wales has invested much of its resources, and by making grand claims as to its success, its prestige. These areas are therefore important in terms of expenditure and in terms of the actors involved. They are also areas where the allegedly more collectivist political culture of Wales, if it has any influence on policy-making, may be expected to reveal a contrast with the policies applied in England, informed as they were by a new right ideology of reliance on market forces. If distinctive policies are found then the claim of exceptionalism will have been substantiated. However, I must firstly distinguish what these policies might diverge from. It is to an examination of Thatcherism that I now turn.

4 The territorial dimension of Thatcherism

Thatcherism sometimes seems to have acquired almost as many meanings as there are people who mention it"

(Jessop et al. 1988 p5)

"a regime of markets, monetarism and authoritative government"

(Kavanagh 1987 pp1-2)

"Thatcherism is then seen as a sharp break from the post-war consensus, being identified with the downfall of Keynesianism for monetarism in economic policy, the contraction of the state, including the privatisation of nationalised industries, the erosion of the nanny state by reform of social security, health care, and education provision and the selling of council houses, and the promotion of an enterprise culture most notably by freeing up the usage of land, de-regulating capital and de-rigidifying the labour market primarily by combating strike activity. Thatcherism emerged out of the apparent inability of governments to meet the needs of the country during the 1970s..."

(Bradbury 1993 p11)

The terms 'Thatcherite' and 'Thatcherism' have been frequently applied to British politics during the 1980s. Frequent use has also resulted in several different meanings being attached to the terms. In this chapter I will concentrate on those aspects of Thatcherism that had a particular impact on territorial politics.

Briefly, these aspects are the public policy dimensions of Thatcherism, the electoral dimension of Thatcherism and the 'British' patriotic resonance of Thatcherism. In order to understand the term more fully however (or at any rate my uses of it) I shall begin by outlining some of the key features of Thatcherism identified by others.

Understanding Thatcherism

Philosophically, Thatcherism may be termed an individualist reaction to the drift to collectivism that was implied in the post-war consensus in British politics. Consensus politics involved acceptance by both the Conservative and Labour parties of a mixed economy with a large public sector, a welfare state, a commitment to full employment achieved by keynesian demand management policies and the inclusion of representative bodies, primarily trade unions and business organisations, in consultation with the government over economic policy. Opposition to collectivism (or Butskellism or consensus politics) did not originate with Mrs Thatcher. Free market, laisser-faire liberalism was the operating code of British politics for much of the nineteenth century. The opposition of individual freedom to collectivism is central to the political theory of Hayek; the Institute of Economic Affairs propagated such ideas in Britain after 1957. From the late 1960s new right ideas, advocating a limited role for government and emphasising the role of markets and individual action gained ground across much of the western world. Although some authors (Kavanagh 1987 p251) have also identified Mrs Thatcher's own background as contributing to these beliefs, Thatcherism in a philosophical sense is older than Mrs Thatcher herself and may be regarded as the reassertion of old (Victorian) values, a return to old certainties.

Pragmatically, Thatcherism represents a response to the failure of collectivism to deliver growth, satisfy societal demands and ensure the authority of government. These failures were becoming apparent by the 1970s. For Dahrendorf "The story of Thatcherism starts in the 1970s – the decade as it now seems, of the gathering crisis" (Dahrendorf 1988 p191). By the 1970s, unemployment was rising and by the mid 1970s over a million people were unemployed in the United Kingdom. Simultaneously, inflation was rising rapidly. The 1970s were the era of stagflation. Governments were unable to prevent rising unemployment, and, arguably, by the mid 1970s, government economic policy was directed at the control of inflation not the achievement of full employment. One cause of inflation was thought to be the power of trade unions. Trade unions were able to undermine successive Conservative and Labour governments. Incomes policies, a staple of economic policies during the

1960s and 1970s, were trampled by industrial action in 1973/4 and 1978/9. The notion of 'ungovernability', was coined to describe the inability of governments to authoritatively implement their preferred policies when faced by opposition from powerful social interests, in short to govern. Brittan (1975) claimed that as governments were forced to make unaffordable promises to vested interests in order to win votes then the future of democracy itself was imperilled.

Economic decline was also partly ascribed to a growing public sector. Bacon and Eltis (1976) argued at the time that the public sector was 'crowding out' the private sector, driving down investment, output and growth whilst encouraging inflation and union power. The public sector was assumed, by definition, to be more bureaucratic, wasteful and inefficient than the private sector and a growing public sector was thus a brake on economic growth.

Thatcherism offered not only a diagnosis of Britain's economic ills, it was also a policy prescription. Collectivism was eschewed in favour of individual effort, initiative and enterprise. Government should offer incentives, chiefly in the shape of tax cuts, to encourage a spirit of enterprise amongst individuals and eventually an enterprise culture. The role of the state was to be limited in order to give the private sector room to flourish. Government intervention had failed and undermined the credibility and authority of government. Government should restrict itself to setting out a framework for economic actors to follow. In monetarism, Thatcherism discovered such a role. Controlling the money supply was (seemingly) within the government's capacity and did not require the government to deal with business or unions as 'social partners' in order to be implemented.

Obstacles to free enterprise had to be removed. Trade union power was regarded as driving up the level of wages excessively and protecting restrictive practices that made British industry uncompetitive and therefore had to be curbed. The public sector was overlarge and inefficient, a drain on public expenditure, a burden on private industry and a haven for trade union militancy. The reduction of the size of the public sector, through privatisation, was therefore crucial to Thatcherite economic strategy. The free market was to be preferred wherever possible, and a great deal of Thatcherite policy since 1979 has aimed to increase the role of the market mechanism in allocating resources even to areas not thought possible in 1979 such as the provision of local authority services, public utilities such as water or electricity, and the National Health Service. Thus, in addition to monetarism there was a reliance on markets.

The third element of Thatcherite policy was not directly economic but was a necessary support for Thatcherite economic policies. Radical economic change would have to be implemented in the face of opposition from those that had benefited from the expansive social democratic state (such as the providers of government services in local government and other public sector bureaucracies) and those that stood to lose out from a greater reliance on the free market (trade unionists in inefficient industries for example). The reduction of the public sector's role in the economy and the inculcation of an enterprise culture would, of necessity, take time, and a strong state was necessary to defend progress towards this goal from possible counterattacks by opponents of this strategy in the interim. Hence it is possible to describe Thatcherism as a policy prescription as combining the free economy and the strong state (Gamble 1988 p32).

The 'free economy and the strong state' doctrine of the Conservatives under Mrs Thatcher also served to consolidate support for the Conservative Party according to several left-wing observers. For them, Thatcherism combined (contradictory) appeals to popular prejudices on issues such as 'law and order', immigration, anti-permissiveness, opposition to trade union excesses, and support for 'lame duck' nationalised industries into 'a kind of reactionary common sense'. Thatcherism is not simply concerned with economic reform or rolling back the state, it seeks to establish itself as the dominant paradigm within which economic, social and political debate takes place within Britain. For Marxist analysts of the phenomenon, the authoritarian-populist tone of Thatcherism is an essential ingredient of Thatcherism as a hegemonic project. Peregrine Worsthorne detected a similar current in Thatcherism describing it as "bitter-tasting market economics sweetened and rendered palatable by great creamy dollops of nationalistic custard" (Worsthorne quoted in Crewe 1988 p32).

A more prosaic account of Thatcherism focuses on Mrs Thatcher herself and her 'style' of leadership. 'Thatcherism' after all refers to Mrs. Thatcher and for many voters, it is the personality they think of, not the policies or hegemonic project, when they hear the term. Crewe notes that "Thatcherism's statecraft, to use Bulpitt's happy term, is at least as distinctive as its economic and cultural prejudices and is the neglected element of its electoral success. Mrs Thatcher's warrior style – setting objectives, leading from the front, confronting problems, holding her position did make a major electoral impact in both 1983 and 1987" (Crewe 1988 p45). Mrs Thatcher's personality and leadership qualities were as important in many voters' minds in those elections in influencing how they cast their votes as conventional issues like the health service or defence.

Studying Mrs Thatcher's personality and upbringing may tell us something about Thatcherism. Some such as Riddell seem to feel that a good deal of the phenomenon can be explained in terms of the Iron Lady herself. He writes "Thatcherism is essentially an instinct, a sense of moral values and an approach to leadership rather than an ideology. It is an expression of Mrs Thatcher's upbringing in Grantham, her background of hard work and family responsibility, ambition and postponed satisfaction, duty and patriotism" (Riddell 1983 quoted in Riddell 1991 pp2-3). However, studying the Iron Lady cannot tell us why her qualities were suddenly those of a leader of the Conservative party in 1975 whereas she had not been a prominent Cabinet minister before this time. Also, even a strong willed Prime Minister as was Mrs Thatcher cannot simply impose her will on events and shape the country exactly as she would wish. A fixation on Mrs Thatcher's personality in short ignores the context in which this powerful personality had to operate, and without this dimension, the evolution of Thatcherism cannot be understood.

A concentration on what Mrs Thatcher said Thatcherism was or wanted it to be might also exaggerate the degree of coherence of the doctrine that bears her name and the degree of consistency with which it was translated into policy. Riddell (1991) in particular, does not feel that Thatcherism was a coherent philosophy or applied consistently as policy. Rather, it is for him "a personal, highly distinctive approach to politics rather than a coherent set of ideas" (Riddell 1991 p2). In implementation too, Riddell claims that "there was no master plan" (Riddell 1991 p5) and that many of Mrs Thatcher's radical policies were based on the successes and failures of earlier policies. Studies of public policy under Mrs Thatcher's government's have found far less consistency and coherence (and success) than Thatcherites and critics of Thatcherism have been willing to admit (Rhodes and Marsh 1992; Savage and Robins 1990). Also, importantly, the policies pursued by Mrs Thatcher were "in line with the policies practised by the Labour Government [of 1974-1979] " (Riddell 1991 pp8-9). It was Chancellor Healey who first initiated monetarism and the control of public expenditure as central features of government macro-economic policy. In some respects Thatcherism developed trends that were already established in British politics and emerged shortly afterwards in the United States and some other European states.

Thatcherism and territorial politics

Bulpitt (1983,1986,1989) offers an account of Thatcherism that suggests it is less of a break with the past than some accounts have suggested, and ties in a discussion of territorial politics to that of Thatcherism more generally. For him, Thatcherism represents Conservative party *statecraft*. Statecraft for the Conservative party is concerned with winning and holding power at the centre, and, once there, insulating the centre, as far as possible, from low politics (local government, education, drains etc.), leaving the centre to engage in what it prefers, high politics (foreign policy, diplomacy, defence etc.). Low politics, is hived off to (hopefully) compliant local elites giving the centre the autonomy it needs to pursue its own interests. Central elites and local elites each go about their business, and minding their own business, in their sphere of politics. Bulpitt terms this a Dual Polity. This situation, argues Bulpitt, prevailed from about the end of the first world war to the 1960s when, due to a weakening economy and the loss of an external support system (the empire), the Dual Polity broke down.

Mrs Thatcher was elected leader of the Conservative Party under fairly desperate circumstances in 1975. Not only had the Conservatives lost four of the previous five general elections, the whole tenor of political and economic debate seemed to have tilted against them. Central autonomy had given way to enforced co-operation with business, local authorities and, especially trade unions in order to govern. This was very much against the instincts of the Conservatives, according to Bulpitt. What they sought was an automatic policy that could be implemented without entangling government with other groups. Such a policy appeared to be monetarism. Control of the money-supply would be sufficient to ensure the fulfilment of a government's inflation (and other macro-economic) targets. And a key to controlling the money supply was controlling and curbing government expenditure.

Monetarism, as a theory, appealed because it seemed to remove the need for government to deal with other interests in order to govern. Central autonomy could be restored and local authorities could be allowed to do their dreary duties undisturbed. However, as the Conservatives discovered after 1979, in practice, monetarism did not seem to work and curbing central government expenditure was far harder than imagined in opposition. Bulpitt colourfully describes how central government turned on local government in response to its own failures: "Local government spending was a more convenient scapegoat for this failure than the centre's own weaknesses on this account. Moreover the Government's gradual realisation that 'monetarism was not enough' shifted attention to the supply side of the economy. Once again this put local government in the firing line as a prime obstacle to a more efficient economy" (Bulpitt 1989 p69). Control of local expenditure was a necessity, and after it became clear that local electorates could not impose sufficient financial discipline on local authorities, ministers intervened with block grants, rate capping, the poll tax and local government reorganisation. In addition, central government increasingly did not regard local government as a fit agent to boost the supply side of the economy by promoting enterprise, attracting business to run-down areas and educating and training the workforce. These functions were removed from local government and vested either in the centre (Training Agency for example) or, if returned to the local level, were given compliant like-minded local elites in Urban Development Corporations or Training and Enterprise Councils for example. Bradbury asserts that "The battles with local government which did involve and still do involve considerable increases in central control were an attempt to make them reliable handlers of low politics concerns again. The failure to do so has resulted in the later Thatcher governments continuing in to the Major administrations in the creation of new unelected local government, or what John Stewart calls the new magistracy, which is reliable. This is the reconstruction of the dual polity on a different unelected basis" (Bradbury 1993 p15).

However, it should not be concluded that Thatcherism necessarily disavows government intervention at the local level. Whilst there has been an attempt to "re-peripheralise responsibilities for low politics via the removal of governing responsibilities to the private sector and to the individual" (Bradbury 1993 p15) through compulsory competitive tendering, opted out schools and local management of schools for example, government activity is not restricted to mundane matters of providing public utility services. Nicholas Ridley, as Secretary of State for the Environment stressed that local authorities had a role to play, albeit an *enabling* role, assisting other bodies, chiefly in the private sector, to provide public services or assisting in creating the conditions in which the private sector could prosper (benefiting in theory at least the wider community). Section 33 of the 1989 Local Government and Housing Act makes consideration of promoting local economic development a function of local authorities. More generally, urban development corporations, local economic agencies, training and enterprise councils and other bodies with a spatial component, are all involved in delivering economic policies. Jessop et al, note that:

> new forms of intervention through the Manpower Services Commission, the Urban Development Corporations, new technology programmes or state support for the allegedly self-starting small business sector – belie the government's claim to be rolling back the frontiers of the state. In fact, of course, Thatcherism is merely rolling back the frontiers of the social democratic state; disengagement here is accompanied by deeper involvement in other areas of post-Fordist promotion

> (Jessop et al 1988 pp140-1).

Thatcherism then, according to this view does not disengage government from the economy, rather what distinguishes Thatcherism from previous government strategies is a concentration on inserting market mechanisms into the provision of public services and using public bodies more generally to support, encourage and foster enterprise and the private sector. A government, can be interventionist but still be Thatcherite if its interventions are designed to support the private sector, foster an enterprise culture and uses market mechanisms where possible in its activities. Duncan and Goodwin (1988) make this point – rather polemically, stating that the Conservative Government's solution to urban problems has been to "dilute and shrink the boundaries of local government powers while inserting business influence more strongly into the local state" (Duncan and Goodwin 1988 p141) but in order to do this "centrally promoted local state institutions have had to be used" (Duncan and Goodwin 1988 p135) which "act as state development agencies, employing large sums of money and owning (i.e., nationalising) large areas of land so that they can make sure the free market works" (Duncan and Goodwin 1988 p134). This point will be important when evaluating government policy in Wales in subsequent chapters.

Two other dimensions of Thatcherism that have had a marked territorial dimension are worth noting in passing. These are the pattern of support for the Conservative Party in Britain during the 1980s and the use of British or English patriotic imagery in Thatcherite rhetoric.

Firstly, it has been generally observed that the 1980s witnessed a marked polarisation of electoral behaviour geographically. It is now common to speak electorally of two nations, the South, a conservative stronghold and a North where Labour is the dominant electoral force. Crewe described Labour as no longer party of the working class as a whole but only the party "of a segment of the working class – the 'traditional' working class of Scotland and the North, the public sector and the council estates" (Crewe 1985 p195). The polarisation of the electorate during the 1980s has also been explained by differing levels of prosperity in the regions of Britain. Johnston et al.'s study "A Nation Dividing" found that vote varied with levels of economic satisfaction and that this was influenced by regional economic conditions. Thus, an electorate divided geographically reflected economic differences in the regions. The economic policies of the 1980s, accentuated these differences. Regions with heavy concentrations of employment in nationalised industries or manufacturing industry generally fared badly during the recession of the early 1980s.

The electoral appeal of Thatcherism might not have extended to the North or Scotland or Wales, partly for cultural reasons. Chancellor Lawson ascribed the lack of success for the Conservative Party in Scotland to the fact that "Scots exhibit the culture of dependence rather than the culture of enterprise" (quoted in Keating et al. 1991 p8). Mitchell has claimed that "the post war settlement and Keynesian welfare state, central to many discussions of Thatcherism, were important in making Britain attractive to Scots" (Mitchell and Bennie 1994 p6). A policy agenda that might appeal to the affluent working class of the South East of England (the archetypal Essex man) might not appeal in Scotland or elsewhere.

Finally, the Englishness of Mrs Thatcher and her use of British patriotic rhetoric might have offended voters in Scotland or Wales. Riddell observes that "she is very much an English phenomenon" (Riddell 1991 p3) and earlier noted that "her political antennae tend to be of the crude Daily Telegraph kind – sensitive to murmurings in Finchley but not in Falkirk" (Riddell 1985 p10). Not only is Mrs Thatcher deeply English, so is the creed which bears her name. Gamble notes that "despite its pretensions to making Britain great again, Thatcherism can do little more than aspire to be the latest religion of little England" (Gamble 1988 p172). Electoral considerations for the Conservative party no longer require them to win large numbers of seats in Scotland or Wales. The electoral arithmetic of 'statecraft' means that the Conservatives need not worry overmuch about their lack of support in Scotland or Wales. Under Mrs Thatcher the Conservative nation has become the 'south'; a nation of private housing estates, skilled workers working in service or high tech industries with the resources and confidence to turn increasingly to the market for the provision of health, education or insurance. No longer is the Conservative Party the party of Union and Empire, an appeal that could extend to 'One Nation'.

Conclusion

Discussions of Thatcherism have identified a number of themes. Thatcherism has been described as Mrs Thatcher's style and personality, a repudiation of the post-war settlement, a theory that holds that individualism is superior to collectivism and a term that has been overused and ascribes more coherence and consistency to the actions of the Thatcher governments than they in fact deserved.

However, for my purposes the most useful definition relates to policy-making at the local level. Here, Thatcherism refers to the exclusion or demotion of local authorities from important areas of public provision, the promotion of market mechanisms in public provision and the re-orienteering of the role of public agencies (local authorities and non-departmental public bodies) to an enabling role supportive of and subordinate to the needs of the business community. In the next two chapters I examine how far this definition describes economic and urban regeneration policy-making in Wales during the 1980s.

5   The Welsh Office and the Welsh economy

Introduction

Underlying the claims to exceptionalism in the administration of Wales is the claim that government policy in Wales has transformed the Welsh economy. During the 1980s, it has been claimed, there was an 'economic miracle' in Wales with strong rates of growth being recorded in productivity, manufacturing output and employment. The Welsh economy was also transformed in the sense that it diversified away from the declining industries of coal and steel towards expanding sectors such as consumer electronics, car components and financial services. This transformation, it has been claimed, was achieved (partly at least) through policies that were more interventionist and corporatist than those pursued in England. Thus, I will begin this chapter by examining the claims made for the Welsh 'economic miracle', then examine how the record of the Welsh economy compares with the claims made for it, and then study to what extent the policies pursued in Wales were distinctive from policies applied in England and how, if at all, they might have contributed to the Welsh 'economic miracle'.

The claims that the performance of the Welsh economy was remarkable during the 1980s have received a wide currency. Nicholas Faith, for example, wrote in the Independent on Sunday 4 October 1992:

> ... over the past decade, despite the closure of the Ebbw Vale steelworks and the virtual disappearance of coal mining, it looks as though the fortunes of the employment war have turned in favour of the principality.

This is due largely, if not entirely, to the fact that government policies there have been totally at odds with the pure Thatcherite doctrine being purveyed in the rest of Britain. A series of Secretaries of State for Wales, notably that arch-Heathite Peter Walker, have forged ahead with a highly interventionist policy, crusading for new investment at home and abroad, and supervising a dense network of government funded bodies – the sort of positive policy scorned by the rest of the administration

We shall examine the truth of how far government intervention contributed to a Welsh economic miracle below. Firstly we must examine the nature of this 'miracle', and, fundamentally, whether talk of a Welsh economic miracle is justified.

Welsh economic miracle

The Welsh 'economic miracle' contains a number of distinct elements. The 'miracle' refers to the diversification of the Welsh economy away from its traditional reliance on coal and steel towards new 'sun-rise' industries. The 'miracle' encompasses the attraction of investment into Wales from elsewhere in the United Kingdom and from overseas. The 'miracle' describes the creation of new employment in Wales at a time when old industries were shedding jobs. The miracle describes a transformation of the Welsh workforce as they acquire the spirit of enterprise and start up new businesses of their own or acquire new skills through enhanced training programmes.

Much evidence has been cited to support this favourable view of the performance of the Welsh economy during the (late) 1980s. Employment in Banking, Insurance and Financial Services grew in Wales from 50,000 in 1981 to 75,000 by 1991 (Digest of Welsh Statistics no.39 1993). Wales, with only five per cent of the population of the United Kingdom, in 1988 attracted over a fifth of the inward investment coming into the United Kingdom (Economist Intelligence Unit 1991 p42). Unemployment fell from 181,496 in 1985 to 87,161 by 1989, a fall of over 50 per cent (Digest of Welsh Statistics no. 39 1993 table 4.06). The unemployment rate fell from 12.2 per cent in 1987 to 6.1 per cent in 1990. In April 1992 the unemployment rate for Wales fell below the unemployment rate for the United Kingdom as a whole, the first time this had happened since 1924. Manufacturing output in Wales increased at twice the rate of manufacturing output for the UK between 1985 and 1989. The number of businesses registered for VAT in Wales grew from 72,987 in 1981 to 86,741 by 1991, an increase of 18 per cent over the decade (Digest of Welsh Statistics no.39 1993).

These figures apparently support the claim that the performance of the Welsh economy improved substantially during the course of the 1980s. The 1990 issue of Regional Economic Prospects, produced by Cambridge Econometrics described Wales as having migrated from economic periphery to core and stated "Wales now performs more like a midlands region than a northern region" and that "the boundary of the north-south divide now clearly lies at the northern edge of the midlands" with Wales now being regarded "as an integral part of the southern half of Great Britain" (cited in Thomas 1991 p39).

Causes of the Welsh economic miracle

The claim that this transformation is due largely to the distinctive government policies pursued in Wales during the period is also supported by some observers and commentators. Peter Walker, obviously, ascribes much of the success to himself and his policies "I was allowed to do it [being Welsh Secretary] my way with a range of interventionist policies..." (Walker 1991 p.203) and "What we achieved in Wales as a result of close government co-operation with industry, councils and trade unions does underscore the weakness of our post-war performance in the rest of the country" (Walker 1991 p.212). More objective sources have also remarked on the distinctive tone of policies pursued in Wales during the 1980s. Gamble observed that "Under Walker and Hunt the Welsh Office has practised not the disengagement favoured by Thatcherite ideology but an interventionist industrial policy..." (Gamble 1993 p83).

Before examining how distinctive the policies pursued in Wales were it is necessary to study the performance of the Welsh economy during the 1980s in greater detail. This reveals that to talk of a 'miracle' is to take a very partial view of the Welsh economy.

Welsh economic miracle – assessment

The statistics quoted above indicated an economy that was forging ahead, creating new jobs, diversifying into new industries and improving its performance. However, other statistics indicate that Wales' major economic problems remain and indeed in some respects economic life in Wales did not improve during the 1980s. Wales' gross domestic product, relative to the UK level has barely risen during the 1980s. In 1982 Wales' GDP per head was 85.6 per cent of that of the United Kingdom; by 1991 that figure was 86.5 per cent (Regional Trends no.28 1993). Social security benefits made up a greater proportion of household income in Wales in 1990/1991, 16.1 per cent, than for any other standard region on mainland Britain. The same was true ten years before when social security benefits made up 16.6 per cent of household income in Wales. This can only partly be explained by Wales having a higher proportion of elderly in its population than the national average.

Earnings in Wales in 1992 were significantly lower in Wales than elsewhere in the United Kingdom. In 1992 all full time male employees in Wales earned on average £304, only slightly above the Northern Ireland figure and the lowest figure for any standard region on mainland Britain. Full time manual male employees earned £258.1 weekly, the lowest figure in Britain. Full time non-manual male employees fared relatively worse still, their pay at £357.4 weekly was the lowest throughout the United Kingdom and almost fifty pounds or a quarter less than the average for Great Britain of £406.7 weekly. Although the pay of female employees is lower than that for men absolutely, the position of Welsh women workers relative to other female employees within the United Kingdom is somewhat better. The average weekly pay for all full time female employees in Wales in 1992 was £223.2 which was slightly better than the pay of women employees in Yorkshire and Humberside, the East Midlands and the West Midlands, although well below the Great Britain average of £246.0 (Figures are for July 1992, source *Employment Gazette* November 1993 p.591). Weekly earnings in Wales have fallen in relative terms during the course of the 1980s. In 1980 weekly earnings of all male workers were 95.5 per cent of the English average and was fifth of the ten standard regions in mainland Britain. By 1991 Welsh weekly earnings for men were only 86.8 per cent of the English average and Wales ranked bottom of the British standard regions. The table below gives an indication of how pay in Wales has fallen relative to pay in England during the 1980s.

Prosperity continues to be unequally distributed within Wales. GDP in Mid Glamorgan was only 75.7 per cent of the UK average in 1981. This made Mid Glamorgan the poorest county in Britain. All the Welsh counties save South Glamorgan had GDPs per head below the UK average. By 1989 Mid Glamorgan's per capita GDP remained the lowest in Britain, having worsened relatively to stand at only 72.2 per cent of the UK average. Again, save for South Glamorgan, GDP in Welsh counties remained significantly below the UK average (Source: Regional Trends no.28 1993 Table 14.3)

Thus, in terms of GDP, few parts of Wales can be said to have experienced a miracle. Only in the eastern counties of Gwent, Clwyd and South Glamorgan was there a marked improvement in the relative level of GDP. The West of Wales, West Glamorgan, Dyfed and Gwynedd saw either little improvement or a deterioration in their relative GDPs. A report for HTV Wales identified an East-West divide within Wales in terms of prosperity (Morris and Wilkinson 1989). As we shall see below, some government policies such as the attraction of inward investment, may actually have worsened this regional divide as inward investment locates predominantly in the east of Wales with easier access to

Table 5:1

Weekly Earnings of all Male Workers

Year	Wales	England	Wales as %age of England	Position*
1980	119.1	124.7	95.5	5
1981	132.7	141.0	94.1	8
1982	146.9	154.8	94.9	4
1983	156.3	168.1	93.0	7
1984	165.8	179.4	92.4	9
1985	179.1	193.3	92.7	8
1986	190.5	209.0	91.1	10
1987	204.3	226.0	90.4	9
1988	217.8	248.4	87.7	10
1989	238.6	272.9	87.4	10
1990	258.6	299.5	86.3	10
1991	280.1	322.8	86.8	10

*Position refers to ranking among the 10 Treasury Standard regions of Great Britain

Source: New Earnings Surveys 1980-1991

England and often better infrastructure. Certainly, when studying the economy of Wales it would be mistaken to regard developments in eastern Clwyd or Gwent or South Glamorgan as indicative of the Welsh economy as a whole. Thomas and Day (Thomas and Day 1992) reminds us that "Optimistic accounts of the Welsh economy in the 1990s, narrowly focused on Wales' eastern corners, have largely ignored the considerable variation in regional circumstances within Wales, particularly those of the regional heartland, ...a large part of Wales, left to its own devices will remain a poor relation in a British context."

Unemployment

A much cited indicator of the transformation of the Welsh economy is unemployment. During the late 1980s Wales experienced one of the most rapid falls in unemployment of any British region and by April 1992 the rate of unemployment in Wales was lower than the rate for the United Kingdom as a whole. This happy state of affairs had not occurred since %1924. However, some qualifications to this apparent improvement must be made. Firstly, the economic activity rate in Wales continues to be the lowest in the United Kingdom and this suggests that many Welsh people may simply have dropped out of the labour market altogether. At least some unemployment in Wales may be hidden.

Table 5:2
Economic Activity Rate by Region 1984-92

Region	1984	1989	1992
North	59.7	61.0	60.0
N. West	61.0	62.8	61.1
Yorkshire & Humberside	61.1	61.9	62.1
East Midlands	63.2	65.6	64.3
West Midlands	61.8	64.3	63.0
South West	59.8	63.3	62.3
East Anglia	61.9	65.0	63.9
South East	64.5	66.0	64.8
England	62.4	64.3	63.2
Scotland	61.4	62.4	63.1
Wales	57.4	59.4	57.9
Northern Ireland	58.8	59.7	60.1
United Kingdom	62.0	63.8	62.8

(Economic Activity rate is defined as economically active persons as a percentage of all persons over the age of 16.)
Source: Labour Force Surveys 1984-92
Employment Gazette March 1993

Secondly, unemployment started to rise in Wales in 1990 and the achievement of a rate of unemployment lower than the UK average in 1992 was thus achieved when unemployment was in fact rising in absolute terms. This suggests that the achievement of a Welsh rate of unemployment below the UK average has much to do with unemployment rising more rapidly elsewhere in the United Kingdom, especially in populous regions such as the South East of England during that time. The table below shows that unemployment more than doubled in the populous and previously prosperous regions of the South East and East Anglia between 1990 and 1992, raising the UK rate of unemployment more rapidly than the rate of increase in Wales.

As the level of unemployment began to level off at the end of 1993 the rate of unemployment in Wales again pushed above the level for the United Kingdom (September 1993 figures UK 10.3 per cent; Wales 10.4 per cent). This too suggests that the relative improvement in the performance of the Welsh economy with regard to unemployment owed a great deal to formerly prosperous regions of the United Kingdom performing very poorly.

Lastly, the decline in the value of the ratio of the rate of unemployment in Wales and the rate of unemployment in the United Kingdom is not a recent

Table 5:3
Unemployment as a Percentage of the Workforce (seasonally adjusted)

%age

Region	1990	1991	1992	1993 (July)
South East	4.0	7.0	9.3	10.2
East Anglia	3.7	5.9	7.8	8.5
South West	4.4	7.1	9.4	9.8
West Midlands	5.8	8.5	10.6	11.0
East Midlands	5.1	7.3	9.1	9.6
Yorkshire & Humberside	6.7	8.7	10.0	10.3
North West	7.7	9.4	10.8	10.8
North	8.7	10.3	11.3	12.2
Wales	6.7	8.9	10.0	10.4
Scotland	8.1	8.6	9.4	9.7
Northern Ireland	13.3	13.4	14.2	14.0
United Kingdom	5.8	8.1	9.8	10.4

(National and regional unemployment levels are calculated by expressing the number of unemployed claimants as a percentage of the estimated total workforce at mid 1992 for 1992 and 1993 figures and at the corresponding mid year estimates for earlier years).
Source: Employment Gazette December 1993

phenomenon. In 1966 this ratio was 1.93; by 1978 it had fallen to 1.36 and by 1986 it stood at 1.22. The relative improvement in recent years has been relatively modest and may have had as much to do with a more rapid deterioration of the UK labour market as a whole than an improvement in the Welsh labour market.

Although the comparison between levels of unemployment in Wales and elsewhere in the United Kingdom may not be as unfavourable as it used to be, there continue to be areas within Wales that suffer very high levels of unemployment. Unemployment rates within travel to work areas within Wales reveal blackspots of severe unemployment such as Aberdare with an unemployment level of 16.3 per cent of the workforce, Holyhead with 14.2 per cent of its workforce unemployed and South Pembrokeshire with an unemployment rate amongst its workforce of 14.2 per cent.

The Welsh economic miracle in perspective

A longer perspective casts doubt on whether the performance of the Welsh economy during the 1980s was 'miraculous'. Firstly, although the Welsh economy grew more rapidly than the UK economy during the latter half of the 1980s, the Welsh economy contracted much more sharply than the UK economy during the early 1980s. Between 1979 and 1982 Welsh industrial output fell by 15 per cent and was not restored to its 1979 value until 1988. By contrast, the UK figure fell by just 8 per cent between 1979-82 and was restored to its 1979 level by 1985. A report by the Economist Intelligence Unit prepared by two Welsh economists concluded that "the relatively rapid growth in the late 1980s represented in large part, a delayed recovery from earlier recession" (Economist Intelligence Unit 1990 p17).

Secondly, the late 1980s is not the first period in recent history where Wales has outperformed the UK economically. Between 1960 and 1972 GDP in Wales grew at an average annual rate of 3.57 per cent compared to 2.94 per cent for the UK. By comparison, the period after 1972 was rather depressing, with GDP growth in Wales averaging only 0.7 per cent a year between 1972 and 1984, well below 1.6 per cent in the UK as a whole. The period 1978-84 saw a particularly dismal performance; GDP growth in Wales averaged only 0.48 per cent compared to 1.20 per cent for the UK (figures from McKenna 1988 p22). Thus the recent improved relative performance might, viewed on a longer perspective, indicate a continuation of 'trendless fluctuation' rather than an economic transformation.

A longer perspective also injects some scepticism into the debate as it reminds observers that the claims of economic transformation in Wales have a familiar ring. Long before the Welsh Development Agency, the Valleys Initiative and even the Welsh Office commentators claimed to detect the economic transformation of Wales. Mainwaring and George's study of the Welsh economy (George and Mainwaring 1988) begins by reproducing some observations made of the Welsh economy in the early 1960s:

"Of all the old depressed areas Wales has been by far the most successful since the war in attracting new industries and in creating for itself a new economic base capable of sustained growth in the future... the long term outlook is more hopeful than it has been for half a century".

The *Guardian* on 2 March 1962:

"The redevelopment of South Wales has been one of the great success stories of the past 30 years. Even if the recovery in other parts of Wales has not been stimulated to a like degree by government action, the achievements in the South must repay study because of any light they may throw on the way to tackle similar problems in other parts of the country on a regional basis".

The Times 2 March 1963:

Even the reasons given for this optimism, government policy and the utilisation of new technology is familiar:

"The keynote of the resurgence since 1945 is a combination of government-sponsored investment and diversification; there has been a striking technical revolution in steel production and the expansion in manufacturing has been nearly twice the rate in Great Britain as a whole. Wales shared with other regions the benefits of the Distribution of Industry Act, and the strength of her present economy is shown by her negligible loss through migration in contrast with Scotland and Northern Ireland".

(Preface to Thomas, 1962).

Thus, on a number of socio-economic indicators Wales enters the 1990s with problems that despite the 'miracle' of the late 1980s remain severe. Parts of Wales in particular continue to suffer deprivation in terms of low incomes and low levels of employment. Dennis Thomas, an economist, concludes, "... large parts of Wales will continue to remain the poor relations in Britain and the much lauded 'economic miracle' associated with Wales may prove to be limited and transient, if not entirely illusory" (Dennis Thomas August/September 1993 p18). Perhaps, it is possible to agree with Davies and Thomas (1976 p149) who describe studies of the Welsh economy as "always being eager to welcome a series of false dawns". Recent optimism may be simply the most recent of a long line of such false dawns.

Inward investment into Wales

Great emphasis has been placed in recent years on the fact that a large number of inward investment projects have been attracted to Wales. Peter Walker, records with pride that "In the three years I was there, Wales, with five per cent of the population, got twenty-two per cent of all the inward investment in Britain" (Walker 1991 p.204).

The attraction of inward investment into Wales has been held to be important for two reasons. Firstly, the new industries and new jobs brought to Wales have diversified the Welsh economy and compensated for the jobs lost in the old declining industries that once characterised the Welsh economy. Secondly the nature of the effort to attract that investment into Wales has, it is claimed, displayed a remarkable degree of co-operation between trade unions, local authorities, the Welsh Office and the Welsh Development Agency acting as a 'team' for Wales. Before assessing these two important topics it is as well to have some idea of the extent of the attraction of inward investment into Wales.

Table 5:4 which shows the number of new and expanded inward investment projects attracted into Wales since 1979, the numbers of jobs associated with these projects and these figures as a proportion of the UK totals. This shows that, by the late 1980s, Wales was attracting more inward investment, and, at least as importantly, was attracting a greater share of UK inward investment.

Table 5:4
Announced Overseas Investment Projects and Anticipated Associated Jobs in Wales 1979-89

Year	No of Projects (new & expansions)	% UK	new jobs	% UK
1979	18	9.8	854	6.0
1980	16	10.3	3332	17.9
1981	20	15.0	1986	12.1
1982	17	12.8	901	8.6
1983	31	13.1	2116	13.6
1984	42	12.8	3958	14.6
1985	45	12.0	2416	9.4
1986	49	14.5	2364	14.6
1987	58	17.8	4054	18.7
1988	56	15.9	6006	21.7
1989	40	12.2	3664	11.9

Source: Invest in Britain Bureau

This performance by Wales during the 1980s compared very favourably with the record achieved by other UK regions as the table below shows.

Another way in which the relative success of Wales in attracting inward investment can be measured is the number of inward projects attracted per 100,000 population (Table 5:6). In terms of capital investment too, the figures for inward investment are impressive. Between April 1983 and September 1990 Wales secured 155 new projects from overseas, with a total capital investment of £1,560 million. In addition there were 171 expansions of existing projects from overseas, with a capital investment of £910 million. In total, there were 372 new projects, expansions, acquisitions and joint ventures with a total capital value exceeding £2.5 billion (Economist Intelligence Unit report 1991 p43).

Table 5:5
Proportions of New Overseas Projects and Jobs for
Selected Regions 1981-89

Region	% of UK Projects			% of New Jobs			% UK Employment
	81-83	84-86	87-89	81-83	84-86	87-89	
Scotland	20.9	16.1	12.1	28.1	16.3	12.7	9.0
Wales	13.6	13.1	15.3	11.3	14.9	17.1	4.4
North East	10.1	8.2	10.0	6.1	11.5	12.7	5.2
North West	9.6	9.9	11.0	8.0	7.2	7.0	11.1
West Midlands	3.8	14.3	21.5	3.7	17.6	15.3	9.5
South East	18.4	20.5	12.1	12.6	12.5	9.4	32.9

Source: Invest in Britain Bureau

Table 5:6
Number of Inward Projects Secured per 100,000 Population

Wales	13
Northern Ireland	9
West Midlands	8
North East	7
Scotland	6
North West	4
East Midlands	2
Yorkshire & Humberside	2
South East	2
United Kingdom (average)	2

Source: Invest in Britain Bureau 1991

Origin of inward investment into Wales

Historically, America has been the major source of inward investment into Wales and the American presence in Wales remains large. Over 40 per cent of employment in overseas owned manufacturing plants in Wales in 1992 was in American owned plants. However, during the 1970s and 1980s there was an expansion of inward investment from Europe, especially Germany and also from Japan. In 1992 there were 33 Japanese plants operating in Wales, making Wales one of the most concentrated areas of Japanese owned production in Europe. In addition, there were other inward investors from a number of countries including, for example, Australia, Canada, and Switzerland. Table 5:7 shows the extent of overseas ownership of plants in Wales and employment in Wales by country of ownership.

Table 5:7
Ownership of Plant and Employment in Wales by Country of Ownership

Country	Number of plants	Employment (thousands)	Employment %age overseas total
USA	112	27.8	42.1
Japan	33	12.2	18.5
Germany	41	5.1	7.7
France	22	4.5	6.8
Eire	14	0.9	1.4
Other EC	33	4.0	6.0
Canada	16	4.3	6.5
Switzerland	14	1.3	2.0
Others	59	6.0	9.1
Total	344	66.1	100.0

Source: Welsh Economic Trends 1992

Inward investment and employment

The primary aim of attracting inward investment into Wales is to "improve the general prosperity of Wales and in particular increase employment opportunities" (HC 86 Session 1988-89 Vol. 2 p1 Evidence Welsh Office memorandum para.1). At a time when many of the industries traditionally associated with Wales such as coal, steel and agriculture are in decline, the jobs that inward investment brings are vital to maintain and improve the level of employment in Wales. Also, inward investment often brings new occupations and new career opportunities giving job opportunities for different groups in the jobs market (such as women). The diversification that inward investment can bring also provides a broader foundation for the level of employment in Wales than a concentration on a few (declining) industries can provide.

In 1992 it was estimated that employment associated with foreign owned manufacturing plants in Wales was 66,100 or about 30 per cent of the manufacturing workforce in Wales (Source: Welsh Economic Trends 1993 No 14). Clearly, inward investment now makes a substantial contribution to employment in Wales. However, it should not be imagined that inward investment can itself provide a solution to the unemployment problem in Wales. The number of jobs in overseas owned plants fluctuates with the overall level of economic activity, as do jobs at all plants. Between 1979 and 1983 for example the number of workers employed in foreign owned manufacturing plants in Wales fell from 53,200 to 40,300. The increase since 1983 again therefore represents something of a 'catching up exercise'. A broader lesson might be that employment in foreign owned plants is subject to the consequences of recessions as is employment in domestically owned firms.

Also, inward investment must not be regarded as sufficient to solve the problem of unemployment. Dr. Bridge of the Northern Development Company stated "... in any one year in the North of England and in Wales, 85 per cent of new jobs are going to come from domestic job creation, whether it be through expansion of existing companies or through the creation of new companies. That is where the bulk of employment is going to come from" (Q927 HC 86 Session 1988-89 Vol. 2). Although somewhat dated by now George and Mainwaring's observation that "Despite the publicity given to every major opening by a foreign firm, the attraction of overseas investment has not made a significant impact on Welsh unemployment levels. Openings by overseas firms since 1976 accounted for only 4,500 surviving jobs in 1984 (approximately equivalent to 5 per cent of job losses in the same period)" (George and Mainwaring 1988 pp8-9).

Only limited comfort can be drawn from the fact that employment in foreign owned plants represents a growing proportion of the total manufacturing workforce. In 1979 53,200 workers in foreign owned plants represented 16.9 per cent of the total manufacturing workforce. In 1989 51,300 workers employed at foreign plants represented 22 per cent of the manufacturing workforce. This indicates that the manufacturing workforce as a whole has declined, not that inward investment transformed the situation of manufacturing employment in Wales.

Criticism has been made of the type of jobs created as a result of inward investment (HC 86 Vol. 2 Session 1988-89 Memorandum by Institute of Welsh Affairs). It is alleged that many of the new jobs created by inward investment have been low skilled, low paid, often part time, and have been predominantly filled by women. In evidence to the Welsh Affairs Committee the Wales TUC claimed "The jobs we have lost tended to be those of men in manufacturing and quite well paid in the steel industry and the coal industry and so on. The jobs that are coming to replace them are generally geared more for women, for young people and relatively much lower paid" (Q428 HC 86 Vol.2 Session 1988-89).

Some support for these criticisms comes from the studies of the Institute of

Welsh Affairs (HC 86 Vol.2 Session 1988-89 Evidence p316). Its evidence to the Welsh Affairs Committee noted that "... many of the jobs that have become available in manufacturing have been for women and have involved unskilled, light assembly work" (HC 86 vol.2 Session 1988-89 Evidence p316 para 9). The IoWA memorandum stated that "more than two thirds of the workforce in Japanese companies is female. Despite the favourable rewards these companies pay, it is still the case that women's wages are considerably lower than for male workers and that job losses experienced in Wales have been predominantly amongst men. This shows that unemployment and poverty can still increase despite the growth of new jobs" (HC 86 vol.2 Session 1988-89 Evidence p.317). Also, in terms of research and development and "the application of new product and process technology ... the record for Wales ... is especially poor. In terms of employment, the Welsh share of research activities is the lowest among all the standard regions" (HC 86 Vol.2 Session 1988-89 Evidence p316 para 9).

Criticisms of the low quality of the types of jobs created do not appear to concern some government members too much. Nicholas Bennett, then MP for Pembroke, rejected criticisms of inward investment jobs being low tech by saying "I certainly do not turn up my nose at assembling and other low tech work because that provides employment both full time and part time" (Q136 HC 86 vol.2 Session 1988-89).

Also, in evidence to the Welsh Affairs Committee the Welsh Counties claimed to have detected an improvement in the quality of inward investment (HC 86 vol.2 Session 1988-89 Evidence p47 para 10). The need to foster more research and development operations in Wales is an issue that the Welsh Development Agency are aware of (Q203 HC 86 Session 1988-89 Vol. 2 Evidence p86). The WDA were hopeful that the "quality of jobs will tend to increase as the company has been here longer, ...there is a time process" (Q280 HC 86 Vol. 2 Evidence Session 1988-89 p97).

Some support for this view comes from Rees and Thomas (Rees and Thomas 1994). They report that, during the 1980s, employment of technicians in Welsh engineering plants grew by over 20 per cent (compared with a fall of equivalent size for Britain as a whole) and the employment of professional engineers and scientists increased by 324 per cent! These figures indicate that during the 1980s "the Welsh engineering industries have moved some distance from the 'screw-driver economy stereotype'" (Rees and Thomas 1994 p50). However, they also go on to say that "it is important not to overstate these occupational shifts. There remains a relative preponderance of less skilled jobs in Wales," and, whilst "there is certainly general evidence of important changes taking place in the engineering sector in Wales... these fall far short of a fundamental transformation: even in these key industries, Wales remains a low skill economy when compared with Britain as a whole" (Rees and Thomas 1994 p50). Importantly, they stress that inward investment may not be sufficient to create a more skilled and well trained workforce (see below).

Although the main purpose of the attraction of inward investment is the creation and safeguarding of jobs, doubts have been raised about how effectively this goal is pursued (and measured) in Wales. A National Audit Office report (NAO October 1991) reviewed the 347 schemes granted Regional Selective Assistance grants, the main grant offered to inward investors, during 1984-5 and 1985-6. It was found that only 16,745 of the 25,715 forecast jobs had been created by February 1991. Also, although most of the schemes were due to be substantially completed within three years, 182 projects (52 per cent of the total) were incomplete. At least 65 of these projects were considered unlikely to ever get off the ground and others were unlikely to ever fulfil the forecast job totals. Information collected by the Welsh Office on firms accepting Regional Selective Assistance between April 1987 and March 1991 showed that of the 48,799 jobs originally forecast as being created or safeguarded, 28,100 had so far been achieved, some 56 per cent of the forecast total (Cm 2515 1994 para.3.04). As the Welsh Affairs Committee report concluded in 1988 "The jobs linked to projects are hypothetical and relate to some unspecified date in the future" (HC 86 Vol. 1 Session 1988-89 Report p.x). For example the Trustee Savings Bank relocation of its insurance business in Newport was supposed to yield 2,000 jobs when it was announced in December 1987 but instead yielded only some 400 jobs by 1991 (Thomas 1994 p187).

Inward investment and diversification

Inward investment has helped in the process of diversification within the Welsh economy. Inward investment has brought thousands of jobs in industries such as automotive components and electrical and electronic engineering to replace jobs lost in declining industries such as steel and heavy mechanical engineering. Inward investment has covered a wide range of industries and products including plastics, electrical products and car components as table 5:8 shows. (The table does not include figures for those employed in service companies that have located in Wales from overseas, although there are a number of these such as Banque National de Paris, and Chemical Bank.)

There has been some criticism, however, that inward investment into Wales is failing to achieve its full potential in transforming the Welsh economy because inward investment plants often source their components from outside Wales. The Welsh Affairs Committee concluded in its report (HC 86 1988 Vol. 1 Report Session 1988-89 p.xx) that "...if inward investment attraction is to remain an important economic objective for Wales, attention must be given to improving the quality of the investment and improving the benefits it brings. To achieve

Table 5:8

Employment in foreign owned plants in Wales by sector 1992

Sector	No. of Plants	Employment (000s)	Employment as %age of FOC
Electrical	52	16.0	24.2
Auto Components	24	9.5	14.4
Chemicals	50	8.3	12.6
Metal Manufacturing	18	3.5	5.3
Paper Products	25	4.4	6.6
Rubber & plastic	33	3.9	5.9
Food, Drink & Tobacco	15	2.3	3.5
Mechanical Engineering	27	2.5	3.8

Source: Welsh Economic Trends 1993

this the multinational and UK owned sectors must be more strongly integrated and rooted within the Welsh economy".

Inward investment and regional inequalities

Although the figures indicate that Wales has enjoyed a 'boom' in inward investment during the 1980s, the majority of that inward investment has been concentrated to the South East and North East corners of Wales. Over 70 per cent of the employment in overseas owned manufacturing plants in 1992 were in industrial South Wales, the counties of Mid, South and West Glamorgan and Gwent. A further 18.8 per cent was to be found in Clwyd. The rural counties of Gwynedd, Powys and Dyfed have been comparatively neglected in terms of the attraction of inward investment.

The distribution shown in Table 5:9 indicates that inward investment has not reduced the inequalities that exist within Wales. The distribution of inward investment within Wales is broadly similar to what it was a decade ago, though it is significant that Clwyd has seen its share of employment in overseas owned plants rise form 8.4 per cent of the Welsh total in 1981 to 18.1 per cent in 1992. Most other counties have seen small increases in their share, mainly at the expense of Mid Glamorgan.

The distribution of inward investment has therefore helped in perpetuating and deepening the economic divide within Wales. Nor has the situation improved since the creation of the Welsh Development Agency which has as its objective to improve economic conditions in Wales (the whole of Wales and not just the most advantaged areas). Also, the present distribution of foreign owned plants in

Table 5:9
Employment in overseas owned manufacturing plants by county 1992

County	number of plants	employment (000s)	%age employment
Clwyd	76	12.4	18.8
Dyfed	25	4.4	6.7
Gwent	73	12.9	19.5
Gwynedd\Powys	14	1.4	2.1
Mid Glamorgan	91	17.9	27.1
South Glamorgan	29	8.4	12.7
West Glamorgan	36	8.6	13.0
Wales	344	66.1	100.0

Source: Welsh Economic Trends No 14 1993

Wales does not differ a great deal from the distribution found in 1974. In 1974 nearly one half of the total number of overseas owned plants were in Mid Glamorgan and Gwent and about 70 per cent were in the four counties of Gwent, Mid South and West Glamorgan (Davies and Thomas 1976 p.48). This was before the WDA was created and indicates that it has had little effect in influencing the location of inward investment. This may be because industrialists do not wish to move into rural western Wales. The Chief Executive of Gwynedd County Council saw some truth in the agencies' claim "Who would come a hundred miles further west when Deeside, say, can offer all the facilities and is close to the market and has a big labour market as well as these good communications" (Q127 HC 86 Volume " Evidence Session 1988-89) but this did not stop him saying "... the rural counties have been criticising Winvest and WDA for years" (Q127 HC 86 Volume 2 Evidence Session 1988-89). This criticism appeared to attack the WDA for too readily accepting the existence and deepening of an east-west divide in Wales. However, in its 1991-92 annual report it did claim that it was aware of this problem and was implementing strategies to tackle it. For example the report states "We continue our drive to encourage investment towards the west. I am pleased that in the year [1991-92] a record 23 projects were secured for Gwynedd, a number which exceeds the total of the previous five years" (WDA 1991-92 p7).

The causes of inward investment into Wales

Given the impressive figures for the level and share of inward investment coming into Wales it is hardly surprising that academics have joined politicians in remarking on a 'boom'. Stephen Hill and Max Munday conclude "There is evidence of a substantial and sustained boom in overseas inward investment in Wales in the latter 1980s" (Hill and Munday 1992 p290). What is less clear however, are the causes for this 'boom' in inward investment. As Hill and Munday state elsewhere "... there is no lack of political commitment to the importance of attracting inward investment, both nationally and regionally, it is unfortunate that such commitment has yet to find expression in the collection of appropriate data to evaluate public policy" and "In the absence of such information it is difficult to envisage how to evaluate the performance of agencies responsible for the attraction of inward investment" (Hill and Munday 1991 p1768). Requests for the information necessary to evaluate the performance of persons or agencies involved in attracting investment into Wales can receive a brusque reply, witness Peter Walker's evidence before the Welsh Affairs Committee when it discussed this issue: "Can I say that I am very much more anxious to get on with getting more inward investment than with satisfying the demands of academics of various universities to give more information for learned treatises which are four years out of date when they are published" (Q5 HC 86 Volume 2 Session 1988-89).

Part of the reason for this reluctance to ascertain the reasons for the attraction of inward investment into Wales may be that so many individuals and organisations are keen to take the credit for themselves. Peter Walker in his autobiography naturally emphasises his own role, recounting how he would phone the chief executive of a company that was contemplating coming to Europe and say "'I am the Secretary of State for Wales. Wales is part of the United Kingdom...'" (Walker 1991 p211). In terms of inward investment Wales, it seems, benefited merely from having a Secretary of State sitting in the Cabinet. This was the view of rivals such as the NDC who felt that the ability to 'wheel out' ministers was a great advantage for Wales (Q789 HC 86 Volume 2 Session 1988-89).

Walker also commends the role of co-operation and partnership in attracting inward investment saying "we established a terrific relationship between the trade unions and local authorities" (Walker 1991 p204). The Welsh Development Agency, whilst keen to stress its own contribution to the attraction of inward investment also emphasises the role of co-operation in this field. In its annual report for 1992-93 the Welsh Development Agency describes its Team Wales Initiative. It describes Team Wales as "Another successful initiative, the Team Wales approach to winning inward investment, is working well and giving the

Principality a competitive edge over the UK regions and most in Europe. Team Wales encourages all those involved in the process of inward investment – local authorities, other public bodies, the Welsh Office and supporting professional organisations such as management consultants and solicitors – actually to become part of the overall strategy of marketing and selling Wales. Conferences are held twice a year where contacts can be made, key issues discussed and new tactics devised. Team Wales acts as a framework for the whole inward investment activity with the Secretary of State for Wales continuing to play a prominent role at its head" (WDA 1993 p22).

One member of this team, whose contribution has been much lauded, has been the Wales TUC. Trade unions in Wales, unlike trade unions in some parts of the United Kingdom, were prepared to co-operate with inward investors from the first and "recognised that for any major inward investment good industrial relations should be a critical issue affecting location" (Jenkins 1993 p32). Stressing its contribution to the attraction of inward investment, David Jenkins of the Wales TUC claimed "The Wales TUC confidently believes that the role it has undertaken, together with government and government agencies in the area of winning new inward investments, has been a significant factor in Wales' success in securing so much new inward investment in the last decade or so" (Jenkins 1993 p32).

Such a co-operative stance, one that even in the mid 1970s regarded the attraction of inward investment as a more realistic way of securing a high level of employment than the import controls then suggested by the left (HC 86 Vol. 2 Evidence Session 1988-89 p.139 para 1.4) did not go unobserved. The Wales CBI described how in Wales "there is a very close working relationship, almost like a community spirit, really, between employers and trade union leaders" (Q379 HC 86 Vol. 2 Evidence Session 1988-89).

However, whatever the contribution towards the attraction made by the Wales TUC in the past the ability of the trade unions to negotiate single union deals with new employers as a collective entity or 'social partner' has been weakened by the government's latest piece of employment legislation. The Employment Rights Act 1993 removed the right of the TUC to regulate inter-union disputes and, according to David Jenkins, this will "undermine our role in regulating membership competition between unions, and risk seriously disrupting established bargaining arrangements, especially those based on single union agreements" (Jenkins 1993 p33). As he goes on to say, "This is a particularly important issue in Wales" as "for many years unions in Wales have worked under an agreed arrangement regarding the establishment of single union arrangements on greenfield sites. This has assisted in no small part, the attraction of new jobs into Wales, impressing new and existing companies in Wales with the quality of industrial relations which trade union recognition brings" (Jenkins

1993 p32). Perhaps a shade apocalyptically, the Wales TUC concludes "It is to be deeply regretted that the government's inherent hostility towards trade unions now looks set to destabilise industrial relations throughout the UK. It is to be doubly regretted that a side product of their legislative action will be to remove an important ingredient from the menu which we in Wales have so successfully offered our prospective inward investors" (Jenkins 1993 p33). Whatever the truth of this analysis, it does serve to show that policy in Wales is largely governed by the British context of policy-making and an attempt to insulate policy from the British context will be very difficult.

In any case the exceptionalism of the close links between trade unions, employers and regional development agencies seen in Wales during the late 1980s should not be exaggerated. Mr Jeuda of INWARD, the body charged with the attraction of inward investment into the North West of England, described how the chairman of the regional council of the TUC sat on the board of INWARD and two members of the general council of INWARD were nominated by the regional council of the TUC (Q833 HC 86 Vol. 2 Evidence Session 1988-89). Trade Unions in the North East also gave every impression of bending over backwards to attract inward investment into their region. Dr Bridge of the Northern Development Company, the body charged with the attraction of inward investment into the North of England said in evidence to the Welsh Affairs Committee, "For instance, one point on which Nissan commented after the event was that they were very impressed with the fact that when they came in to talk about industrial relations we were able to put four unions and the regional secretary of the TUC in one room and they created a statement of intent which they gave to Nissan and said 'Whatever you would like to do in the region, we will support'" (Q885 HC 86 Volume 2 Evidence Session 1988-89). This is echoed when Dr Bridge reveals that the board of NDC has four directors nominated by the regional TUC (Q910 HC 86 Volume 2 Evidence Session 1988-89) and the NDC receives "considerable moral support from the trade union movement within the region and enormous help in inward visits (Q910 HC 86 Volume 2 Evidence Session 1988-89).

Team Wales: local authorities

As part of the Team Wales concept, the WDA emphasise the contribution that good relations with local authorities make to the attraction of inward investment. Many have referred to instances when co-operation between the Welsh Development Agency and the local authorities have been excellent and fruitful (Toyota claimed that "the experience of the Welsh Development Agency and Clwyd County Council in dealing with Japanese inward investment helped significantly, and at Deeside we received tremendous support form both of the above and also from Alyn and Deeside District Council" (Toyota 1993 p24).

However, others, such as Wrexham Borough Council, were critical of the relationship with the Welsh Development Agency in the late 1980s. The Welsh Affairs Committee on inward investment report criticised links between WDA and the local authorities severely, comparing them negatively with relations between Locate In Scotland and local authorities in Scotland. The Welsh Affairs Committee reported that "We were disturbed by what we heard about the relationships between WDA, WINvest and local authorities, the various public sector bodies involved in inward investment promotion activities within the Principality" (HC 86 Volume 1 Report p.xliv session 1988-89). An unfavourable comparison was drawn with the situation in Scotland where Locate in Scotland stated it had a far more formal and regular form of consultation with regional authorities (and other interested parties) than was the case in Wales (HC 86 volume 2 Evidence session 1988-89 p156 para 10; Q473). Evidence to support this view comes from Livingston Development Corporation who said "We are willingly partners with the Scottish front... in overseas advertising and marketing efforts... I have statistics... which quite clearly show the benefits derived on the ground from that type of partnership. I can give as an example the fact that 61 per cent of my meaningful inquiries which resulted in settlements in the last five years have been introduced by Locate in Scotland (HC 86 Vol. 2 Evidence Q532 Session 1988-89).

Livingston's favourable impression of its relationship with Locate in Scotland contrasts sharply with Wrexham Maelor Borough Council's description of its relationship with the Welsh Development Agency. In its evidence to the Welsh Affairs Committee it claimed that "they [WINvest] receive many enquiries that are not notified to the Council or passed on by the WDA. This has caused friction as many of the enquiries involve using Council sites unknown to the Council's Officers" (HC 86 Volume 2 Evidence p186-7 Session 1988-89) and that until shortly before the memorandum was written "The Japanese division of WINvest... consistently ignored contacting Wrexham directly with Japanese enquiries. This has caused a considerable amount of bad feeling especially as Wrexham has managed to attract five Japanese companies with seven factories" (HC 86 Volume 2 evidence p187 session 1988-89). Wrexham claims that the Sharp corporation was attracted directly by the Borough Council, Brother Corporation was located directly by the Borough Council, Hoya Lens were contacted in the first instance by the Borough Council and Tsuda Plastic Industry Company Limited made direct contact with the Borough Council (HC 86 Vol. 2 Evidence p187 Session 1988-89).

Relationships with other bodies involved in the attraction of inward investment also came in for criticism. Wrexham described the relationship between counties and districts as not good, and although finding the Welsh Office helpful in encouraging the Borough Council's industrial activity made the adverse comment that cuts in the allocation of capital spending mean "a much smaller capital amount being allocated for industrial purposes" (HC 86 Vol. 2 Evidence p188 Session 1988-89).

Inward investment and the Welsh Development Agency

The Welsh Development Agency is also keen to publicise its own contribution to the attraction of inward investment into Wales. They have a number of representatives in the markets from which inward investment is likely to come such as North America, Japan or Europe. In order to raise Wales' profile abroad the WDA has sponsored tours of the Welsh National Opera abroad as a cultural ambassador for Wales. WDA officials are always at the ready with accounts of their marketing role and the lengths they will go to win investment projects. The Welsh Development Agency does have the resources to give inward investors a complete package, land, premises, planning permission, negotiations with training organisations, local authorities, public utilities etc. and this is a valuable though difficult to quantify contribution to the attraction of inward investment. For example, planning permission for the Bosch alternator plant at Miskin was obtained in only four weeks.

Although the contribution of any agency or organisation to a process as complex as inward investment is difficult to measure accurately it is at least possible to measure the inputs into development agencies and the number of projects attracted to the areas these development agencies cover. In a memorandum to the Public Accounts Committee the Welsh Development Agency did this and produced the figures shown in Tables 5:10 and 5:11.

The Welsh Affairs Committee felt obliged, however, to report "We are bound to say we observed a sharp contrast in the Memoranda we received from WINvest and LIS, and in their relative presentations and performances as witnesses. As well as being more open, SDA/LIS seemed much more professional, more customer oriented in their activities and more sharply focused in their objectives and operations" (HC 86 Vol. 1 Report p.xli session 1988-89).

For example, Cllr Williams of Wrexham Borough Council said in evidence to the Welsh Affairs Committee "Part of the unfortunate role that we had to fulfil in Japan was in persuading Japanese companies actually to meet the Secretary of State. Because they had had such bad experiences with some of the agencies run by the Welsh Office, presidents of companies had actually decided not to meet the Secretary of State on his visit" (Q634 HC 86 Volume 2 Evidence Session 1988-89).

Table 5:10
Projects Attracted 1988-90

Region	1988	1989	1990
North West (INWARD)	30	52	53
North East (NDC)	22	46	44
Yorkshire & Humberside	23	11	26
Scotland	58	34	41
Wales	56	40	70

Table 5:11
Costs per Project (agency running costs/number of projects)

Regional Agency	1988/89 (£000)	1989/90 (£000)	1990/91 (£000)
INWARD	25	16	24
NDC	–	–	66
YHDA	–	109	58
LIS	60	85	73
WDI	45	78	50

(Committee of Public Accounts Fifth Report Session 1992-93 Creating and Safeguarding Jobs in Wales Appendix 3)

Structural reasons

Quite apart from the efforts of ministers, agencies and local authorities and others in Wales to attract investment to Wales there may be general or structural reasons why Wales saw an increase in the volume of investment during the 1980s. These need not have been peculiar to Wales. The boom in the late 1980s in the UK economy led to rapid increases in rents, labour turnover and congestion in the South East of England and this appears to have prompted some companies to consider relocation (FT May 27 1994). The Wales CBI cites "the favourable location of Wales in relation to the South East and the Midlands of England" (HC 86 Vol. 2 Evidence p215 session 1988-89) as one cause of Wales' success in attracting relocating firms. No Secretary of State for Wales can claim the location of Wales as an achievement of government policy.

Secondly, the late 1980s saw rapid progress towards the creation of a single European market and fears by some foreign companies that a fortress Europe mentality might emerge. Inward investment into Europe could therefore be interpreted as a rational desire to be within the fortress before the drawbridge was raised (FT May 27 1994). Thirdly, for Japanese companies Wales enjoyed the advantage that it is an English speaking country, and English is the foreign language taught in Japanese schools (Toyota for example) (Munday 1987).

Wales may have enjoyed some success in some markets during the 1980s due to its previous success record in these markets. This is not to understate the efforts made by the WDA and others during the 1980s but does qualify the contribution those efforts made to more recent successes. Munday for example found that one factor that may have influenced Japanese companies to come to Wales during the 1980s was the success the first Japanese investors to Wales had had in the early 1970s, attracted by the Development Corporation for Wales, the forerunner of the Welsh Development Agency (Munday 1990 p41, p39).

Regional grants

As is mentioned below, inward investment into Wales has been attracted partly by regional financial assistance available from the government. In a report prepared for the Welsh CBI Stephen Hill stated "It has been shown that the attraction of new firms from overseas has been heavily reliant on the financial assistance that is associated with assisted area status. Any reduction in assisted area status in Wales, with consequent reductions in regional aid, would exacerbate existing inequalities and constrain the one engine of economic growth in the region, inward investment" (quoted in *Western Mail* 9-10-1992). However, despite the centrality of regional financial assistance to economic regeneration in Wales it would appear to be an aspect of policy over which the Welsh Office had relatively little control. Payments to firms through the government's regional development policies did not become part of the Welsh Office Block, over which the Secretary of State for Wales has some discretion to vary expenditure between different programmes according to his interpretation of the needs of Wales, until 1994-95. Until then expenditure on regional assistance in Wales had always been described as being "influenced to a considerable extent by United Kingdom ... policies" (Cm 1916 1992 para 1.06). The National Audit Office found most of the employment creation measures available in Wales, including regional selective assistance, operating "under similar guidelines elsewhere in Great Britain" (NAO HC 664 1991 para. 1.1).

In this respect the Welsh Office cannot compare with the degree of autonomy displayed by an independent sovereign state. In evidence to the Welsh Affairs Committee a representative of Locate in Scotland compared Scotland to Ireland saying, "It is the Republic's tax package which is most difficult for Scotland to match [because] as a national fiscal measure, it escapes EEC control" (HC 86 Vol. 2 Evidence Q506 Session 1988-89).

Also, expenditure on regional assistance has been declining both within Wales and the United Kingdom since 1979. A further step in this process took place in July 1993 when the map of areas eligible for regional assistance in Britain was redrawn. The proportion of the Welsh population living in development areas was reduced from 86 per cent to 70 per cent (before 1984 all of Wales had qualified for regional assistance) and key areas of employment growth in Wales during the 1980s (such as Cardiff and Newport) lost their assisted status. Cities such as Cardiff or Newport on the South Wales coast, provide a great deal of work for people living in the South Wales Valleys (*Western Mail* 24 July 1993) and so cutting aid to these areas may actually blight the growth areas of the South Wales region. The redrawing of the assisted areas was based mainly on headline unemployment rates (*Western Mail* 24 July 1993) and failed to take into account the low activity rates and low rates of pay that characterise the Welsh economy. The economist Stephen Hill stated "By all the objective criteria, Wales is the poorest region in mainland UK and needs all the help it can get" (quoted in *Daily Post* 24 July 1993).

Low pay

More negatively, there may be some causes of Wales' success in attracting inward investors of which Wales can hardly be proud. Some have pointed to the relatively low labour costs in Wales as a major reason for investors preferring a Welsh location. S Hill and M Munday (1991) for example found that The Wales/UK Earnings ratio, the rate of output growth in Wales, the level of regional incentives and infrastructure spending could account for most of the inward investment attracted to Wales between 1983 and 1990. Of these variables, the Wales/UK earnings ratio was the most important explanator, followed by regional preferential assistance. Wales is a low cost region, and, coupled with generous (though declining) regional financial assistance, this makes Wales very attractive to inward investors. An earlier survey of inward investment into Wales quoted an economic paper on 'Industrial Location and Economic Potential' which stressed regional wage differentials as one factor on the distribution of industry. The paper said in part "If we could re-establish really striking differences in money wages today, to bring them even further above the national average in London and Birmingham, and even further below it in Scotland and Wales, we could perhaps do a great deal more to re-locate industry" (quoted in Davies and Thomas 1976 p148). Arguably, this is what has occurred in Wales during the 1980s.

Welsh Development Agency

A study of economic and industrial policy in Wales would not be complete without an examination of the Welsh Development Agency. Created in 1976, it has sometimes been regarded as an element of the exceptionalism of government policy in Wales during the 1980s. Barrie Clement wrote of it thus: "The Welsh Development Agency, a non-Thatcherite institution if ever there was one, was given the power and the resources to attract new industry to the area" (*Independent* 6-6-1991).

However, in terms of resources the Welsh Development Agency bears a closer resemblance to a Thatcherite institution, relying to a greater extent on private sector sources of finance than Clement seems to imagine. Whilst gross expenditure by the WDA rose from £63.5 million in 1985-1986 to £165.9 million in 1992-93, an increasing proportion of this came from the WDA's own capital and current receipts and not from government sources. As Welsh Office reports make clear, this is a deliberate part of government strategy. The Government's Expenditure Plans Cm 1916 states that "Some 55 per cent of this expenditure will be financed by receipts, principally from factory sales and rents. In keeping with the aim of developing a self-sustaining market economy, the Agency is expected to finance an increasing proportion of expenditure from receipts" (Cm 1916 1992 para 3.14). In the following report on Government's Expenditure Plans in Wales (Cm 2215) the emphasis on non-government funding is perhaps stronger; "In accordance with the aim of developing a self-sustaining market economy, the Agency is expected, wherever appropriate, to maximise receipts to finance its expenditure programmes. Plans for 1992-93 are based upon receipts of 55 per cent of gross expenditure and for 1993-94 it is proposed that this will rise to 64 per cent. The increase reflects the policy of planned disposal from the Agency property portfolio of holdings which can be transferred to the private sector" (Cm 2215 1993 para 3.16).

Maximising receipts from rents and the disposal of assets can however have adverse consequences for many businesses helped by the Welsh economy. Allan Rogers, Labour MP for the Rhondda, spoke of firms facing rent increases of up to 400 per cent as a result of Inland Revenue valuers applying 'market' rents (*Western Mail* 9-3-1992). A WDA spokesman responded to this situation by saying "The WDA has always charged market rents. That does not mean to say they are economic rents, due to the fact that supply and demand dictates the market rent" (*Western Mail* 9-3-1992). In a Parliamentary answer to Ted Rowlands MP, the Welsh Secretary revealed that in 1990-91 some £11 million worth of premises and property were sold but in 1991-1992 this figure was thought to have risen to £26.3 million (*Western Mail* 2-1-1992). A WDA spokesman said that "It is a policy we intend to continue because we want to encourage private sector investment and encourage people to own their own premises" (*Western Mail* 2-1-1992). In response to the charge that the middle of the recession was the wrong time to divest itself of factory land and premises, Duncan Poole of the WDA admitted "If we did not have cash flow demands I am sure as a totally independent company we would not be selling property today" and on the issue of raising rents to market levels he said "... we are trying to stimulate the market. If we allow property values to stay too low we will have a big problem getting the private sector to do the work the WDA have in the past" (*Western Mail* 23 -11-1992). This attitude appears to ignore the fact that one role of organisations such as the WDA is to intervene in cases of market failure, where the forces of supply and demand fail to provide adequate levels of economic activity. This original aim is however, seemingly subordinated to a new aim more in keeping with the Government's free market ideology, namely the privatisation of publicly owned assets wherever possible. The WDA's Annual Report and Accounts for 1992-1993 states: "Fulfilling its increasingly significant role as the Agency's main generator of income, the Division sold £49.6 million of completed assets – almost doubling last year's sales. The progressive disposal of Agency owned premises to both tenants and investors is in line with Government policy to broaden the ownership of public sector industrial assets in Wales by transferring them to the private sector" (WDA 1993 p33).

The encouragement of the private sector to become involved in functions that were formerly done (solely) by the public sector is also an aim of the Welsh Property Venture. This programme commenced in 1989 and has its aim the levering in of private funds into the building of new industrial property and premises in Wales. The 1992-1993 WDA Accounts, for example, note that the WDA contributed "£13.8 million to this scheme which in turn attracted £56.6 million of private investment – a private to public leverage ratio of more than 4:1" (WDA 1993 p32). The WDA describe the Welsh Property Venture as "our initiative to attract private sector investment in providing business space, has substantially reduced reliance on public funds and is set to operate on a far wider remit" (WDA 1993 p11). This is in keeping with the WDA Property Division's emphasis on its "enabling role, encouraging market efficiency ..." (WDA 1993 p.11).

It is clear from the above discussion that aspects of the work of the Welsh Development Agency operate with a far greater reliance on the private sector than hitherto. Thus, far from being a 'non-Thatcherite institution if ever there was one' the Welsh Development Agency increasingly applies the free market logic of Thatcherism.

This logic was being applied in the late 1980s, during the incumbency of the interventionist 'wet' Peter Walker as Welsh Secretary. It was in the Spring of 1988 that the WDA and the Secretary of State for Wales agreed that the operations of the Welsh Development Agency should be examined by private consultants in what was termed Operation WIZARD. Part of the terms of reference to Barclays de Zoette Wedd, one of the consultants hired, was (as reproduced in Committee of Public Accounts HC 353 Session 1992-93 Appendix 6) "As the Agency has mentioned, an increasing percentage of its activities are funded from self generated funds. Its assets now approach £200 million. The management style of the Agency is, and needs to be, very much concerned with the use of private sector techniques and disciplines in order to be as effective and efficient as possible" and "... you have requested us to consider a preliminary examination of the Agency's business and activities as a public sector body but from a private sector viewpoint". Whilst the full privatisation of the WDA was rejected (one of the options considered by the consultants), other options drawing in the private sector into the work of the Agency and involving the WDA itself operating in a more commercial manner were implemented. As Philip Head, then Chief Executive of the WDA, revealed before the Committee of Public Accounts "We looked at various aspects of the Agency's activity from the point of view of privatisation and also from the point of view of getting some of our departments to operate on a more businesslike commercial basis. In fact quite a lot of that work has been taken into account in the way that the Agency fulfils its functions now" (CPA HC 353 Session 1992-93 Q226).

The privatisation of the Welsh Development Agency would have belied the image of an interventionist Welsh Office. However, the appearance of a Welsh Office and Welsh Development Agency committed to government intervention in the economy of Wales was sustained by concealing Operation WIZARD. As the CPA conclude in their report "... we are concerned that there might have been a deliberate attempt by the Agency to conceal Operation WIZARD within their accounts by spreading the costs under several headings. We do not believe this to have been compatible with Parliamentary accountability, especially as some of the options identified by the consultants involved major restructuring of the Agency, with changes to its objectives and the possible reduction of its specific commitment to Wales. We are concerned that not only was Parliament denied information, but that this Committee would have remained unaware of the project's existence had it not been for unofficial revelations from within the Agency" (CPA HC 353 Report para. 41).

Training

A skilled workforce has been acknowledged as vital if Wales is to benefit as much as possible from inward investment and economic growth more generally. The recognition of this need is not new as Brinley Thomas (1962) made clear in the preface to "The Welsh Economy: Studies in Expansion": "There should be ample opportunities in future for foreign as well as British investment in the expanding industries, but it will be necessary to ensure that technical education and the supply of skilled labour will develop at the right pace" (Thomas 1962 Preface). Yet it has been claimed that the quality of the workforce in Wales in particular, and the United Kingdom more generally, compares poorly with those of other countries. In investigating the impact of government policy on the Welsh economy it is therefore important to examine training policies in Wales.

The skills base in Wales

Although Wales has a reputation as a country where education is valued (see chapter 2) a report of the academic and vocational performance of its people would read, in some respects 'unsatisfactory' or 'could do better'. In particular, Wales had the highest proportion of its school leavers leaving school with no qualifications of any region in Britain, had one of the lowest participation rates in education amongst 16 year olds, amongst the lowest proportion of its workforce with an apprenticeship qualification and amongst the lowest proportion of its workforce receiving some form of job related training in Britain.

Table 5:12
School Leavers Without Qualifications by Region 1991/92

Region	Percentages	
	Males	Females
North	7.7	5.9
Yorkshire & Humberside	7.9	7.5
East Midlands	4.6	4.3
East Anglia	5.0	5.9
South East	5.3	5.0
South West	3.4	2.3
West Midlands	6.5	4.7
North West	7.0	7.0
England	5.8	5.3
Wales	14.2	10.4
Scotland	11.2	8.7

Source: Regional Trends 1994 No 29 Table 4.7

Table 5:13
16 Year Olds Staying on at School or Going Into Further Education
1992/93

Region	Participation (percentage)
North	69.1
Yorkshire & Humberside	71.1
E Midlands	73.8
East Anglia	74.7
South East	80.6
South West	81.3
W Midlands	74.5
North West	72.6
England	76.3
Wales	75.0
Scotland	76.8

Source: Regional Trends 1994 No. 29 Table 4.5

Table 5:14
Economically Active of Working Age: by Highest Qualification
Spring 1993

Region	Degree or Equivalent	Higher below degree	A Level or Equivalent	Apprenticeship	O Level or Equivalent	Other & CSE	None
North	8.6	9.0	12.4	15.7	18.0	13.1	23.3
Yorkshire & Humberside	10.0	7.3	13.1	15.3	17.1	12.8	24.5
East Midlands	9.6	8.0	13.3	12.5	16.3	12.4	28.0
East Anglia	11.1	6.5	13.1	13.5	17.8	13.5	24.4
South East	17.2	7.9	14.3	10.4	17.8	12.6	19.9
South West	12.1	9.4	15.0	12.7	16.9	12.2	21.7
West Midlands	10.2	7.9	13.6	10.6	16.2	13.1	28.3
North West	11.1	9.0	13.2	14.3	18.1	11.1	23.2
Wales	9.3	8.8	13.5	12.0	18.0	12.9	25.5
Scotland	11.8	10.7	19.4	15.3	13.3	7.5	22.2

Source: Regional Trends 1994 No. 29 Table 5.11

Table 5:15
Employees of Working Age Receiving Job-related Training

Region	1986		1991		Training leading to qualification
	on the job	off the job	on the job	off the job	
North	4.9	8.3	7.5	10.0	6.2
Yorkshire & Humberside	4.2	7.4	6.7	9.9	6.5
East Midlands	4.4	8.4	5.5	9.7	5.2
East Anglia	5.2	8.8	6.8	11.4	7.0
South East	5.5	8.1	7.0	11.6	6.7
West Midlands	5.0	7.0	6.4	9.6	6.5
North West	3.9	7.2	6.5	11.0	7.0
Wales	5.1	6.6	6.5	9.3	5.2
Scotland	3.6	5.0	6.0	8.6	5.3

Source: Regional Trends 1994 No 29 Table 4.19

Training initiatives in Wales

It would seem therefore that promoting the creation of a skilled workforce is a particularly pressing need in Wales. A targeted, adequately resourced, co-ordinated approach to training within Wales would seem to be called for. A step towards this would appear to have been taken in 1992 when responsibility for training policy in Wales was transferred from the Department of Employment to the Welsh Office. A new department was created within the Welsh Office, the Training Enterprise and Education Department. This allowed, according to David Hunt, then Welsh Secretary, the development of "a corporate or co-ordinated approach to training education and enterprise" (HC 259 Evidence p79 Session 1992-93). David Hunt claimed this as a personal achievement and the result of his own lobbying in Whitehall (Q522 HC 259 Session 1992-93). Earlier, in the same vein, he had claimed that the acquisition of training functions would give the Welsh "even greater opportunity to co-ordinate the strategy in our distinctly Welsh tradition" (*Western Mail* 9-1-1992) and "The transfer will give me the opportunity to develop comprehensive policies in the areas of training, enterprise and education, which will help us to make the most of our most valuable resource – the Welsh workforce" (*Western Mail* 26-11-1991).

What policy innovations have there been therefore? How has the Welsh Office demonstrated the value it attaches to training and how are these in keeping with Welsh traditions?

As in England, training programmes in Wales are now delivered through Training and Enterprise Councils (TECs). These were described at their launch as organisations "born of the enterprise culture, with a bold vision that extends beyond existing programmes, institutions, and traditional methods of delivery" (Training Agency quoted in Peck and Emmerich May 1993 p7). Their structure too reflects a business bias, as they are established as private companies whose boards must contain by law at least two thirds business people. There is no obligation that trade unionists, voluntary organisation representatives or representatives of the local authorities should sit on these bodies. Peck and Emmerich state that "The TEC initiative... had been designed in such a way as to marginalise these other voices... While TECs talked of a community partnership, this could only be an unequal one, in which the interests of business were afforded a dominant role" (Peck and Emmerich 1993 p4).

Also, whilst TECs have been described as part of a 'skills revolution' concern has been expressed as to whether the rhetoric matches reality. In particular, Peck and Emmerich (CLES 1992) found that many TECs continued to concentrate on providing (the heavily criticised) Youth Training and Employment Training, with few new, more relevant training programmes. Also, at a time when unemployment was increasing Peck and Emmerich found that funding for the TECs was in fact being cut by the government. The attraction of private sector investment into training, another aim of the TECs, was slowed by the recession. Training, like the economy, was now cyclical, Britain now had a Stop Go training policy.

There is some evidence that these tendencies towards a business bias and the exclusion of trade union representatives, the continuation of existing policies with little innovation, a continued reliance on 'voluntarism' and reductions in government expenditure on training as unemployment increased (Peck and Emmerich 1992 pp24-26) have also been displayed within Wales despite the rhetoric of 'distinctly Welsh traditions' in this field.

Firstly, the composition of TEC boards in Wales displays the same preponderance of business interests as do TEC boards in England. An examination of the memberships of the boards of the seven TECs in Wales shows that councillors are absent from the boards of Welsh TECs (Welsh Yearbook 1994). Local government representation on these boards came from district and county officials such as chief executives or directors of education. Anachronistically, a degree of spatial representation was inserted by the inclusion of the Lord Lieutenants of Gwent and Gwynedd onto the boards of two TECs in Wales. The education sector was represented in some cases by including the principals of further education colleges on three TEC boards. The voluntary sector was sparsely represented and one voluntary sector representative was Sir Donald Walters, Chairman of the Wales Council for Voluntary Action, and also a former businessman and WDA official. A Wales TUC report in 1992 found that there were only six employee representatives out of a total TEC board membership in Wales of over one hundred (Wales TUC 1992 p46). By 1994, the number of trade union representatives had actually decreased to only four representatives amongst the seven Welsh TECs. The application of the continental European concept of social partnership was missing in the structure of TEC boards in Wales as in England. This was so despite the fact that Peck and Emmerich have claimed that the inclusion of more social partners in the process of decision-making is necessary to emphasise the social functions of training (Peck and Emmerich (CLES) 1992 p102).

Secondly, training in Wales has suffered cutbacks in government spending at the very time that unemployment was rising. In a written Commons answer, Wyn Roberts, Minister of State at the Welsh Office admitted that in 1991-92 TECs in Wales spent £27.7 million but that in 1992-93 government support for training measures in Wales was to fall to £24.9 million (Hansard Written Answers 10-11-1992, *Western Mail* 11-11-92).

The recession during the early 1990s also acted as a deterrent to investment in skills by the private sector in Wales. A scheme to provide electronics courses for trainees in the Cynon Valley was initially supported by local industrialists but the same industrialists failed to take up the training places created as the recession deepened (*Western Mail* 12-9-1991).

Thus it is arguable that the structure and funding of the TECs in Wales have, as in England, led to a situation where employer dominated boards are liable to replicate the inadequate skills of the existing workforce rather than enrich the stock of skills within the local workforce (Wales TUC 1992 pp47-48; Peck 1993 pp289-305). It has been argued that certain marginal groups within the workforce, the disabled or ex offenders, are likely to be excluded form schemes run by TECs who are seeking to maximise their results (Wales TUC 1992 p47).

As was discussed above, inward investment is seen as a catalyst for change within the Welsh economy. Inward investment has been welcomed for the new jobs and new types of jobs that it can bring to Wales. However, skill shortages may act as a constraint to inward investment. An Employment Department report for example found that 70 per cent of personnel managers at Japanese owned factories in South Wales said candidates for jobs had serious skill problems (Western Mail 29-1-1992). In a survey of 300 companies undertaken on behalf of the Audit Commission it was found that 58 per cent of surveyed companies felt that the limited availability of skilled labour was a constraint to their development. This group included most expanding and large companies. Some

43 per cent of the surveyed companies – mainly expanding companies – reported that they had experienced difficulties with the availability of suitable training programmes (National Audit Office HC 664 October 1991 p22).

Also, although inward investment projects such as Bosch, Sony and the British Airways Maintenance facility at Cardiff create a number of highly skilled jobs it is still the case that these types of jobs are untypical of Welsh manufacturing as a whole. Large firms such as these have a good record of developing, often in close co-operation with local further education colleges, tailor made training schemes. Smaller indigenous establishments are however, unlikely to be involved in developing training programmes for their employees either on their own or in conjunction with further education colleges. Rees and Thomas conclude that "it is entirely unrealistic to envisage the regional economy developing wholly on the basis of ... major inward investment projects... despite the region's relative success in attracting such important developments, their overall employment contribution remains limited" and "in an economy characterised by 'low skills' production employees are restricted to semi- or unskilled jobs, irrespective of the level of training they have received. What is required therefore in order to raise the skills level of the regional economy, is the formulation and implementation of regional strategies which integrate skills enhancement programmes with appropriate economic development policies" (Rees and Thomas 1994 p58). A reliance on training by the private sector is likely to simply reproduce the strengths and weaknesses of the existing private sector. A policy designed to improve the relative competitiveness of Wales as a whole requires a powerful actor with a regional training strategy. Wales does not have such an actor currently.

Enterprise

One of the much trumpeted aims and claimed achievements of the Thatcher governments was the creation of an enterprise culture. The creation of small businesses was seen as the solution to economic problems (Action for Cities 1988 for example). This emphasis on enterprise as an engine of economic growth has also been heard in Wales. Peter Walker, then Welsh Secretary, declared in 1988 "The speed with which the enterprise culture is developing in Wales is impressive to witness. Large numbers of new businesses, the activities of the enterprise agencies, the creation of a whole range of small firms".

If the presence of individual entrepreneurs and small businesses are the solution to economic problems then Wales might be expected to fare relatively well. In 1991 the self employed numbered 163,600 in Wales and made up 13 per cent of the economically active population of Wales. This was a higher proportion of the economically active population that in Great Britain in 1991 which was 11.5 per cent. The corresponding figures for Wales in 1981 were 126,100 and 10.4 per cent. This would indicate that the 1980s had been a decade of enterprise for Wales.

However, some qualifications are in order. Firstly the percentage of self-employed persons amongst the economically active population of Wales has long exceeded the percentage on the population of Great Britain, mainly due to the relatively large proportion of farmers in the Welsh economy. Therefore, the 1991 figures do not represent a relative improvement in the enterprising spirits of the Welsh. The 30 per cent increase in the percentage of self-employed as a percentage of the economically active population of Wales during the 1980s was still lower than the 34 per cent increase experienced in Great Britain (Source: Welsh Economic Trends no.14. 1993)

Table 5:16 shows the rate of growth of new businesses in Wales and other regions of the UK between 1980 and 1989. The stock of businesses in Wales grew by 21 per cent over this period (Employment Gazette November 1990). This placed Wales eighth amongst the eleven standard regions of the UK, above Northern Ireland, the North and the North West but below the UK average of 29 per cent. Thus, although Wales briefly performed outstandingly well during the late 1980s, its performance during the 1980s overall places it amongst the regions with low rates of entrepreneurial activity.

Table 5:16
Percentage Change in Stock of Business in The UK, by Region 1980-89

Region	Ranking 1980-1989	Percentage Increase 1980-1989
South East	1	40.0
East Anglia	2	31.1
South West	3	30.1
East Midlands	4	28.7
West Midlands	5	26.1
Scotland	6	21.3
Yorkshire & Humberside	7	21.2
Wales	8	21.2
Northern Ireland	9	20.7
NORTH	10	19.2
North West	11	16.3
United Kingdom		29.0

Source: Employment Gazette November 1993

The relatively poor performance of the Welsh economy in generating new businesses has been attributed by some to a lack of entrepreneurial spirit amongst its people. The Times once described Wales as "a small country ... with an indifferent soil and inhabited by an unenterprising people" (*Times* 14 September 1866 quoted in Morgan 1980 p1). However, it is also possible that the reasons for Wales' poor record of entrepreneurship may be structural. Wales' history of a small number of heavy industries employing large numbers of people may be inimical to the development of the spirit of enterprise amongst its workforce.

Government policies to foster enterprise in Wales during the 1980s have been similar to those operating elsewhere in the United Kingdom. In Cm 2515 it is stated that "the [Welsh Office] Industry Department .... promotes in Wales a number of Department of Trade and Industry advisory and support schemes. These include the Small Firms Merit Awards for Research and Technology (SMART) competition and the Support for Products Under Research (SPUR) programmes" (Cm 2515 Welsh Office para 3.13 1994). Also administered by the Welsh Office are Regional Enterprise Grants to firms in assisted areas. These programmes, although significant for businesses in Wales, give little room for the Welsh Office to display much capacity for autonomy.

Greater autonomy has been displayed by the Welsh Office however, in its promotion of Welsh businesses, both overseas and within the United Kingdom. The autonomy created by the existence of the Welsh Office enabled Wales to participate in the Four Motors programme with Baden Wurttemberg, Catalonia, Rhone Alpes and Lombardy. The first agreement was signed with Baden Wurttemberg in March 1990 and since then closer links with these regions have been forged including the trade, education and cultural agreements with Catalonia (October 1991) and the establishment of a permanent Welsh desk at the Milan Stock Exchange. This programme fosters trading and research and development links between firms in Wales and in the four motor regions. Also, the Welsh Office in co-operation with the Welsh Development Agency and others in 1992 established the Wales Euro Centre. This functions primarily as a source of information for Welsh businesses about developments and opportunities within the European Union. An ambassadorial role for Welsh business has further been played by Welsh Office ministers by their participation in trade missions and a scheme which provides Welsh firms with representation at selected trade fairs. In 1993/94 89 Welsh companies participated in trade fairs, 6 trade missions were undertaken by the Welsh Office and as a result of these, 42 companies started export activity or exporting (Source Table 3.06 Cm 2515 Welsh Office 1994). At home, the promotion of Welsh companies has been undertaken through the Source Wales Initiative which seeks to raise the profile of Welsh companies amongst other businesses and thereby increase the opportunities for companies in Wales to win contracts from other businesses. A similar scheme is operated in Scotland by Scottish Enterprise.

Regional variations in entrepreneurship in Wales

Measured by county, there were wide variations in the growth in businesses within Wales during the 1980s. Whilst within Wales as a whole, the total number of businesses registered for VAT increased by about 19 per cent, this figure concealed considerable regional variations. Once again it was only part of Wales that enjoyed the fruits of the 'economic miracle'.

Table 5:17
Total Number of Businesses Registered for VAT, 1981 and 1991

County	Year		Percentage
	1981	1991	increase
Clwyd	10196	12700	25
Dyfed	15733	17658	12
Gwent	8297	10903	31
Gwynedd	8736	9525	9
Mid Glamorgan	8036	10470	30
Powys	7258	8211	13
South Glamorgan	8269	9663	17
West Glamorgan	6461	7611	18
WALES	72987	86741	19

Source: Welsh Economic Trends 1993 No.14

A comparison of the creation of businesses by each county on mainland Britain found that the disparity between the performances of Welsh counties was so great that Wales contained amongst the most successful and unsuccessful counties. Gwent ranked tenth overall in terms of the net increase of business registrations between 1979 and 1989 (possibly the beneficiary of 'Severnside spillover'; Tony Moyes quoted in the Western Mail 28-9-1991). However, the county of Gwynedd which saw a net ten per cent increase in its stock of businesses during the 1980s ranked 63rd nationally. With Dumfries and Galloway in Scotland this as the worst performance of any county in Britain (Daly 1990 pp553-563).

If the emphasis on enterprise has been similar in Wales to elsewhere in the United Kingdom even if the performance has not been, have the mechanisms and policies to foster enterprise been similar in Wales? In recent years the Welsh

Development Agency has moved away from the support of business start ups (WDA 1992). Local Authorities too, which have traditionally offered advice, consultancy, assistance in the purchase factory or workshop units and financial assistance in some cases (Economist Intelligence Unit 1991 pp39-40) have reduced their role as sole providers of these services in recent years. As in England the provision of information and assistance to small businesses is a role increasingly played by the Training and Enterprise Councils (TECs) and Local Economic Agencies (LEAs). Training and Enterprise Councils are chiefly responsible for advising, counselling, and providing consultancy and business skills information to new or small businesses. The Local Initiative Fund (LIF) run by the Welsh Office for TECs is used as 'seed money' to "draw in support in cash and kind form the local community" (Welsh Office Cm 2515 1994 para 4.33).

Also, as in England Local Enterprise Agencies (LEAs) are becoming increasingly important in the provision of assistance to enterprise. These bodies are coalitions of local business, though often with some public funding, who provide advice, premises, small loans and a voice for business at the local level. Hudson and Sadler describe them as "the classic characteristic of Conservative self-help philosophy" (quoted in Moore 1988 p21) and Chris Moore described their insertion into economic policy at the local level as 'quasi-privatisation' (Moore 1988 pp21-29). However, he also stated that whilst "they are based on market assumptions and objectives ... they represent intervention in the market and rely extensively on public support" (Moore 1988 p27). Such intervention however, represents support for business and business values and whilst it is possible to speak of partnership, it is a partnership where other interests are subordinated to business interests. Moreover, it is a form of partnership between the public and private sectors that is hardly unique to Wales despite the rhetoric of some Welsh Office ministers. There are currently over 300 Local Enterprise Agencies in Britain.

The insertion of private sector actors into the delivery and formulation of public policy is clearly apparent in Wales. Taking Cardiff and Vale Enterprise (CAVE) as an example it is clear that government policies to encourage business are increasingly delivered by private sector or private sector dominated bodies in Wales. In its 1991 annual it lists amongst its achievements "successfully tendered to South Glamorgan TEC to deliver enterprise counselling and training to all new firms and to completely manage the Enterprise Allowance Scheme", "achieved an average letting rate of 95 per cent throughout the 150 small units managed on behalf of Cardiff City and South Glamorgan County Councils" and "successfully moved 61 firms out of the Cardiff Bay Development Area" (Cardiff and Vale Enterprise 1992); all functions with a considerable impact on public policy.

In evidence to the Welsh Affairs Committee in its investigation of local enterprise agencies and employment creation a Welsh Office official said "the Government firmly takes the view that the ideal arrangement is one under which public funds are used for pump-priming with a clear intention that the private sector should pick up this operation and provide on a continuing long term basis, the financial resources that successful Enterprise Agencies will require... It is important from the Government's point of view that there should be adequate pump-priming input form the private sector [in addition to the public sector] but that Local Enterprise agencies are consciously planned to stand on their own feet within a period of five years (Q49 HC 502 Session 1985-86). The specialist adviser to the Welsh Affairs Committee drew attention to the way LEAs "emphasise the importance of private sector involvement and funding, with the private sector component providing approachability for the client, understanding of his interests..." (Welsh Affairs Committee E 1986 HC 502 Vol. 2 Evidence p27 Session 1985-86). It would seem therefore that a process of quasi-privatisation of the Government's enterprise culture policies has taken place. This is the case also in Wales. In the same Welsh Affairs Committee Report a Welsh Office official says that only a minor difference in funding arrangements of LEAs in Wales "is the only extent to which there will be a geographical difference" (Q27 HC 502 Session 1985-86).

Conclusion

In his oral evidence to the Welsh Affairs Committee inquiry into inward investment Peter Walker quoted a passage from a speech by Michael Heseltine which stated "Throughout the United Kingdom we shall pursue the policies that Peter Walker is pursuing in Wales" (Q1060 HC 86 Volume 2 Evidence Session 1988-89). These words appear true even if not in the sense that Heseltine intended. Many of the policies carried out by the Welsh Office have been similar in intent and implementation to policies carried out elsewhere in the United Kingdom. In areas such as inward investment other regions have adopted similar strategies of regional co-operation (though not always with the same degree of success). In other areas, such as the inculcation of enterprise as a spur to economic growth little distinguished government policies in Wales from government policies elsewhere. In Wales, as in England, the contribution of the private sector was emphasised and the intervention of public agencies was downgraded. Wherever possible, the private sector was encouraged to take a leading role in delivering functions that had once been chiefly the responsibility of public or local government bodies. Co-operation between the public and private sectors was evident, but this was less the unique 'positive partnership'

114

that Hunt and Walker had spoken of as Welsh Secretaries but the familiar process, repeated in England and Scotland of private interests in the shape of TEC boards or Local Economic Agencies playing a larger role in the determination of economic policies.

It is perhaps difficult to see how economic polices in Wales could have been conducted otherwise. The Welsh Office and bodies such as the Welsh Development Agency lack the institutional autonomy to pursue policies that fundamentally change economic conditions within Wales. It is thus incorrect to speak as some have done of Wales during the 1980s being "an enclave of relative Keynesianism in a Britain where the Government's monetary economics exposed companies which could not compete, and then refused to intervene to help them" (Barrie Clement 6-6-1991) as the basis of Keynesianism is the ability to manage the level of demand in the economy. The Welsh Office has negligible powers at best to vary the level of government spending, let alone the level of aggregate expenditure in the Welsh economy. Some of the debate concerning the 'exceptionalism' of government policies in Wales during the 1980s suffered from a weak understanding of political or economic concepts. This is a point I shall return to in chapter 7.

In this chapter I have looked at policies that had as their aim, the regeneration of the Welsh economy as a whole. In the next chapter, I look at how policies to regenerate smaller areas, chiefly urban areas, have been applied in Wales during the 1980s and 1990s.

6 Urban policy in Wales

Introduction

Urban policy had a high profile during the 1980s. Sporadic riots during the decade meant that several British inner cities were regarded as battlefields. For the urban left of the early 1980s, urban areas were also political battlefields, sites of opposition to central government and its economic and social policies (Stoker 1988 chapter 9). Finally, for Mrs Thatcher after the 1987 election, they were citadels of socialism and economic failure (the two were maybe not distinguished in her mind) which had to be tackled by means of displacing the 'dependency culture' with the revitalising 'enterprise culture'. Wales too saw a new focus on urban issues by the government. The regeneration of Cardiff Bay and the Valleys Initiative in particular were given a high profile. It has been claimed that these and other examples of urban policy in Wales are characterised by a high degree of government intervention, and unlike some examples in England, a great deal of co-operation between central government and local authorities as well as the enthusiastic involvement of the private and voluntary sectors.

To try to evaluate these claims of interventionism, co-operation and partnership (and their uniqueness) I will, in this chapter, examine some aspects of urban development policy in Wales during the 1980s and early 1990s. I examine the Urban Programme in Wales, the regeneration of Cardiff Bay and the work of the Cardiff Bay Development Corporation, the only Urban Development Corporation in Wales. Finally, I look at a policy closely connected with urban policy, housing policy. I begin, however, by examining urban policy in England during the 1980s.

Urban regeneration policy in England and Wales since 1979

Urban policy during the 1980s in Britain has been characterised by an enhanced emphasis on economic regeneration of the inner cities, the diminution of the role of local authorities in urban regeneration and an enhanced role for business and commercial interests as part of the enterprise revolution (Deakin and Edwards 1993).

The emphasis on economic regeneration being a vital component of urban policy was first made by the Labour Government in its White Paper 'Policy for the Inner Cities' (Cmnd 6845 1977). It spoke of a need to strengthen "the economies of the inner areas and the prospects of their residents" (Cmnd 6845 p25) and to do this

> it is vital to preserve the basic firms and businesses which at present exist in the inner areas ...

> indigenous growth needs to be cultivated by facilitating the expansion of local firms.

> New sites and premises ... are needed in order to attract suitable manufacturing, service and office firms to settle within the cities.

> (Cmnd 6845 p27).

A central role for the private sector was assumed in urban regeneration but the White Paper in addition to speaking of the need to "stimulate investment by the private sector, by firms and individuals, in industry, in commerce and in housing" (Cmnd 6845 p39) also asserted that "Local Authorities are the natural agencies to tackle inner area problems" (Cmnd 1685 p31). Innovations in urban policy after the election of the Conservative government in 1979 shifted policy away from a partnership between central and local government, increasingly to a partnership between central government and business interests, excluding or reducing the role of local authorities. Urban Development Grant, introduced in 1982, for example was offered to development projects that had been designed collaboratively by local authorities and the private sector and its aim was "to act as a stimulus to the economic regeneration of our urban areas ... real economic growth and development cannot be sustained without the close involvement of the private sector" (Department of the Environment 1982, i). Urban Development Grant was also "designed to lever significant private sector investment into the inner cities, providing the minimum public sector contribution necessary to enable development projects which might otherwise not go ahead to do so" (Department of the Environment 1982, ii). Urban Regeneration Grant introduced in 1987, bypassed local authorities altogether, being paid directly to private developers. In 1988, Urban Development Grant, Derelict Land Grant and Urban Regeneration Grant were replaced by a new grant, City Grant, that was also payable directly to private developers. The role of local authorities in urban regeneration had been truncated from leading players (1977) to partners with the private sector (1982) to virtual bystanders (1988).

Another part of the process of excluding local authorities was the creation of Urban Development Corporations (UDCs). These were given powers to acquire, hold, manage and dispose of land in its area, grant planning permission for developments in its area and provide various forms of grants and financial aid to developers, all functions at one stage normally vested with local authorities. Urban Development Corporation boards are appointed by the Secretary of State for the Environment in England and contain a majority of business representatives. Local authority representatives are normally restricted to a small minority on the board.

The government also encouraged the private sector to become involved in urban policy in other ways. Business in the Community (BiC) was established in 1981 after a conference organised by the Department of the Environment. BiC had the aim of creating Local Enterprise Agencies in all major cities. Local Enterprise Agencies (see chapter 5 above) are collaborations between the private and public sector, led by local business, providing business counselling, training and other support services (Deakin and Edwards 1993 p31). Business in the Community and Local Enterprise Agencies are another aspect of the enterprise culture in the service of urban regeneration.

Government initiatives on urban policy have sometimes seemed piecemeal (Audit Commission counted 34 inner cities policies and programmes (Audit Commission 1990) but the Government believes it has a clear strategy for the regeneration of the inner cities. This strategy is (triumphally) outlined in "Action for Cities" (Cabinet Office 1988). In this document Mrs. Thatcher condemns local authorities for their "civic hostility to enterprise" (Cabinet Office 1988 foreword) and describes the results of previous urban policies in many cities thus: "All too many have had their problems intensified by misguided post-war planning and development which had the best of intentions but the direst results for people living there" (Cabinet Office 1988 Foreword). The above analysis of urban problems points to a clear and radical approach. It "does not mean leaving it all to the local authorities which for many years were allowed to decide the priorities and be the main channel for finance" (Cabinet Office 1988 p5) . Instead, the solution lies in "Pooling the resources of the private and public sectors" (Cabinet Office 1988 p4). Obstacles to business must be removed and a "direct approach" is needed to achieve this. The "direct approach" is the hallmark of the Urban Development Corporations whose "special executive powers enable them to cut through red tape and press on with action". Such bodies with such powers "are a prime example of the Government's determination to take effective action to encourage business and new investment" (Cabinet Office 1988 p4). Government, but especially local government, should get out of the way of business as "Businessmen know better than local councils what it is that new businesses need most to prosper and expand" (Cabinet Office 1988 p6).

Action for Cities states baldly many features that have come to be hallmarks of urban regeneration policy in England. Firstly, there is a concentration on small discrete areas, the derelict areas of inner cities. Secondly, the problems of inner cities are seen in economic terms (or at least to stem from economic decline). Revitalising the economies of the inner cities is the key to doing something about those inner cities (the task Mrs. Thatcher set herself after the 1987 election). Urban problems are now problems of urban regeneration rather than urban deprivation. The attraction of economic activity into these areas is the solution to urban problems, not improved service provision of welfare, education or training. Thirdly, the private sector, it is assumed, is most capable of restoring prosperity to the inner cities. Local authorities, it is believed, are often ineffective and may be a positive hindrance to the fulfilment of economic prosperity in inner cities. The role of local authorities should be excluded as far as possible and the role of government (both local and central government) is to 'enable' the private sector to realise the economic opportunities that exist in the inner cities. Thus, although partnership is a key concept in much of the discussion surrounding urban regeneration it is a partnership where central government has prescribed that business should play a major, often dominant, role and local government's role should be restricted to a subordinate, supportive role. This is the central government's understanding of partnership.

Urban policy in Wales since 1979

Wales provides an interesting stage to examine these trends in urban regeneration policy more closely. Wales offers many examples of urban regeneration policy. Also, some have claimed that urban policy in Wales displays some important differences from England. Norman Lewis, for example, claims that Wales displays a degree of co-operation not seen generally in England, "Welsh politics seems very much more consensual and networked than has been the general fashion elsewhere in Britain in recent years (Lewis 1992 p18) and that "The significance of the Welsh experience will not be lost on those who see advantages in regional solutions and in integrated planning involving a wide range of interested parties" (Lewis 1992 p6).

Wales provides numerous examples of industrial and urban dereliction. The coal and steel industries left slag heaps and spoil heaps in their wake. The decline of these industries in turn has created areas of high unemployment and deprivation. Policies to restore the environment in localities despoiled by industry and regenerate the economies of localities damaged by economic change are a necessity in Wales. Urban policies in Wales are administered by the Welsh Office and Wales specific bodies such as the Welsh Development Agency and the Land Authority for Wales are also involved in urban policy. The institutional capacity for specifically Welsh initiatives in urban policy would appear to exist. The Audit Commission (1990 para 49), contrasts Wales (and Scotland) favourably with England in terms of the environment in which urban policy takes place. In Wales local authorities liaise with the Welsh Office on most matters of urban policy whereas in England, different aspects of urban policy are controlled by the Department of Employment, the Department of Trade and Industry and the Department of the Environment. The responsibility for several different aspects of urban policy 'under one roof' in Wales, thanks to the multi-functional nature of the Welsh Office, may explain why certain features of urban policy in England are absent in Wales. City Action Teams and Inner City Task Forces, composed of civil servants from the various government departments involved and private sector secondees, are a feature (and result) of the complex 'patchwork quilt' of urban policy in England (see Audit Commission 1990) but absent in Wales. In this section I examine to what extent urban policies operated within Wales by the Welsh Office but also applied in England have diverged in practice from England.

Urban Programme in England and Wales

The Urban Programme has come increasingly to emphasise economic projects and correspondingly gives lower priority to social schemes. The Audit Commission (Audit Commission 1990 p66) highlights this shift in central government thinking by quoting passages from central government documents concerned with urban policy:

> The Secretary of State may ... pay grants ... to local authorities who in his opinion are required in the exercise of any of their functions to incur expenditure by reason of the existence in any urban area of special social need.

Local Government Grants (Social Need) Act 1969

> The Government have now decided to recast the Urban Programme and to extend it to cover industrial, environmental and recreational provision as well as specifically social projects.

Policy for the Inner Cities' White Paper 1977

The Role of the Urban Programme is to encourage local authorities to develop a co-ordinated approach and an action programme to tackle the problems of their inner areas; to work with the private and voluntary sectors; to involve with other agencies including central Government Departments; to promote and encourage economic activity, enterprise and private investment...

Urban Programme Ministerial Guidelines 1985

In 1969, policy was targeted at 'social need' and specifically economic objectives were scarcely mentioned. By 1977 however, urban problems were seen to be caused (in part at least) by declining local economies, and regenerating local economies become a priority. By 1985, economic objectives had come to the fore of the Urban Programme and 'social need' was a subsidiary goal. At its inception in 1978 it emphasised social renewal and gave a relatively low priority to economic (or environmental) regeneration.

The Urban Programme in Wales has not been immune from this process. The Urban Programme 1992/93 Circular to local authorities (Welsh Office Circular 25/91) describes the aims of the Urban programme as contributing "to the regeneration of deprived areas by creating healthy local economies" and states that "the main emphasis will be on sharply targeted economic and environmental projects. Social projects will also be eligible, although priority will be given to those which contribute to a well-targeted strategy". The document also states that at least half of the resources available should go to economic regeneration and only some 20 per cent should be devoted to social projects, the remainder being devoted to environmental improvement. Finally, the document emphasises that local authorities are to play an enabling role in Urban Programme projects as successful projects should "demonstrate partnership with other agencies, including the private and voluntary sectors, in preparing and delivering the strategy".

A degree of centralisation of the Urban Programme has been achieved by the Welsh Office awarding funds to strategies that it considers merit special funding. This is akin to City Challenge operated by the Department of the Environment in England. Competition for Urban Programme resources between authorities are to become a more prominent feature of the Urban Programme in Wales as in 1994-5 and 1995-6 up to thirty per cent of Urban Programme resources will be committed in this way (Cm 2215 para 7.08).

Although City Grants are not operated in Wales, Urban Investment Grant which is operated by the Welsh Office in Wales operates in a similar fashion. Introduced in 1988, like City Grant, Urban Investment Grant is payable directly to private developers and the role of local authorities is effectively marginalised. The type of scheme eligible for UIG includes "residential schemes and office, factory, retail and commercial developments" (Cm 1516 para 9.22). Like the City Grant Scheme operated by the Department of the Environment, UIG has, as its principal objective "to encourage private sector development on derelict or run-down sites to assist the economic regeneration and environmental improvement of deprived urban areas ..." (Cm 1516 para 9.20) and emphasises, as one measure of achievement, the leverage ratio of public to private funds attracted to a project.

Urban Policy in Wales (as in England) still sees a role for local authorities however. Section 33 of the Local Government and Housing Act 1989 makes consideration of promoting local economic development a function of local authorities. Since 1992-1993 all local authorities, and not just designated districts, have been able to establish commercial and industrial improvement and renewal areas where they may provide grants to encourage small businesses to upgrade premises, and create or safeguard jobs. The 'enabling role' of the local authority, supporting business and enterprise, is encouraged by central government in Wales as in England. The Vale of Glamorgan's Economic Development Strategy Statement for 1992/3 for example states that, in the 1990s, the role of promoting economic development, "will increasingly develop into more of an enabler function, providing the infrastructural and strategic framework within which the public and private components of the industry can co-ordinate their investment and marketing plans. The highest priority should be placed on further encouraging and sustaining private enterprise" (Vale of Glamorgan Borough Council 1992 p21).

Thus, the Urban Programme in Wales shares many of the same assumptions as the Urban Programme in England. During the 1980s the role of local authorities in the process of regeneration was recast and reduced to that of enablers. Central government saw enterprise and business as the salvation of urban areas and altered its policies to foster enterprise. The role of local authorities was to 'enable' business in the task of economic regeneration of urban areas, and urban problems were seen primarily in economic terms.

Cardiff Bay Development Corporation

In the previous section it was shown that the main current of urban policy in Wales has been similar to that seen in England. In England, Urban Development Corporations were seen as the 'flagship' of what the Government was doing for the inner cities (Cabinet Office 1988). In Wales too, a great deal of publicity and money has been invested in the one Urban Development Corporation there, the Cardiff Bay Development Corporation (CBDC). As befitting a flagship, the claims surrounding, and the ambitions of, the Cardiff Bay Development

Corporation are hardly modest. Its objective is to "co-ordinate the redevelopment of 2,700 acres of South Cardiff" (CBDC September 1991), an area that comprises one sixth of Cardiff, creating "a superlative maritime city which will stand comparison with any such city in the world" (CBDC September 1991) and "establish the area as a centre of excellence and innovation in the field of urban regeneration" (CBDC September 1991). The Regeneration Strategy to achieve these objectives is equally bold and ambitious. At its heart is a scheme to build a 3/4 mile long barrage, impounding the waters of the Taff and Ely rivers to create a 500 acre inner lake and eight miles of waterfront development. The strategy aims to build 6,000 new homes (including a quarter for rent and low cost purchase), 4 million square feet of office space and six million square feet of industrial floor space, create over 30,000 new jobs and attract up to £2 billion in total investment (Cardiff Bay Development Corporation September 1991). The claims made by the Cardiff Bay Development Corporation have been bold as well. In its marketing literature it describes Cardiff Bay as "Europe's Most Exciting Waterfront Development" (*Western Mail* 30-6-1992) and the process involved in the development of Cardiff Bay is claimed to be either unique or at least exceptional. In evidence to the Welsh Affairs Committee, its Chairman, Geoffrey Inkin, declared that CBDC was "... still the lead example in the country of partnership between local authorities and development corporations... It is very much an exercise in partnership" (HC 259 Session 1992-93 WAC Q149). Even opponents of government urban policy generally have looked favourably on Cardiff Bay Development Corporation. Jim Cousins, Labour MP for Newcastle upon Tyne Central, accused the government of failing to help Tyne and Wear Development Corporation and claimed that the Welsh Office was generous in its aid towards the regeneration of Cardiff. He said "It is one thing to be told we have a non-interventionist government and these are matters that ought to be left to the private market. It is quite another thing to be told that that is the policy in Newcastle while a quite different policy can operate in Cardiff as a result of the initiative of the Secretary of State for Wales" (Quoted in *Western Mail* 22-7-88). Norman Lewis commends CBDC for its emphasis on involving the local communities living in the Bay in the formulation of the Corporation's regeneration policies (Lewis 1992 p18).

To judge these claims it is necessary to examine the Regeneration Strategy, the assumptions underlying the Regeneration Strategy and the implementation of that strategy. Does the strategy emphasise economic regeneration as the solution and what assistance does it give to the existing communities in the area? Also, is the process of regeneration in Cardiff Bay characterised by 'partnership' to an unique or exceptional degree?

Partnership: local authorities

Local authority co-operation with other bodies including the private sector need not seem a great surprise in the case of the local authorities in South Cardiff and Cardiff Bay Development Corporation. Local Authorities in South Cardiff, South Glamorgan County Council, Cardiff City Council and the Vale of Glamorgan Borough Council had displayed a willingness to work with the private sector to the benefit of Cardiff before the creation of Cardiff Bay Development Corporation. In partnership with Tarmac, South Glamorgan County Council regenerated 133 acres of redundant dockland, including the 43 acres of Bute East Dock (now renamed Atlantic Wharf). As a mark of confidence in the regeneration of Cardiff Bay, South Glamorgan County Council located its new County Headquarters there. The Association of County Councils awarded Atlantic Wharf its centenary award for the most successful urban environmental scheme in England and Wales in 1989. Michael Boyce, then chief executive of South Glamorgan County Council, claimed that Atlantic Wharf was held up as the model way in which a Conservative government could work with a Labour controlled county council and the private sector (Cardiff Bay Barrage Bill Evidence to Select Committee 7-2-1990). In the area of the Bay covered by the Vale of Glamorgan, Crest Nicholson, a private property company, created a marina with housing and retail premises in conjunction with the Borough Council. This is testimony to the fact that local authorities were not neglecting Cardiff Bay even before the advent of CBDC. The "civic hostility to enterprise" (Cabinet Office 1988 Foreword) that had blighted inner cities according to Margaret Thatcher was not present in Cardiff. In terms of the provision of infrastructure the local authorities had also played an active supportive role, the sort of role praised by the Audit Commission (1990). Work on the Peripheral Distributor Road to link South Cardiff directly to the M4 motorway was begun by South Glamorgan County Council before the creation of the Development Corporation and the local authorities had also examined public transport to the Bay before the establishment of the CBDC. In their response to the Cardiff Bay Development Strategy,the Cardiff City District Labour Party and South Glamorgan County Labour Party stated (Cardiff City District Labour Party and South Glamorgan County Labour Party no date p1): "It is a fact that Labour began the development of the Bay area ... We approach the Bay Development from a position of strength, not one of weakness; with a clear record of commitment to economic regeneration...".

Local authority co-operation with CBDC itself is not surprising as it was South Glamorgan County Council which called for the creation of an urban development corporation to regenerate the bay area of Cardiff in the first place. A report by South Glamorgan County Council published in September 1986 proposed "that a single-purpose body should be charged with securing the regeneration of South Cardiff and that that body should be an urban development corporation" (SGCC 1986 p.3).

Such a proposal by the county council may at first sight have appeared as surrender to the centralising forces of central government and the abandonment of a role for democratically elected local government in the process of regeneration. However, SGCC's proposal has hallmarks of what has sometimes been called the Welsh form of attack namely 'getting your concession in first'. Further on (SGCC 1986 p6) the SGCC report states:-

"The County Council has the necessary political commitment, the resources, the statutory powers, and an appropriately qualified and enthusiastic staff to undertake that single purpose role itself and is willing to do.

The County Council, which has the merit of being a democratically elected body responsive to the interests of the County as a whole and to the local community in particular, would wish to be the single purpose body charged with securing the future of South Cardiff.

Nevertheless, the County Council understands that a local authority led initiative may not be universally acceptable and recognises that if this is the case, some form of urban development corporation established under the Local Government Planning and Land Act 1980 might be appropriate."

South Glamorgan County Council's response cannot be termed 'resignation' as its own proposals envisaged a substantial role for itself and other local authorities in the regeneration of South Cardiff. The need for an urban development corporation that usurps all powers to itself is disputed as the local players are already actively and positively involved in the process of regeneration and are not hindering that process as has been allegedly the case elsewhere. The report states (SGCC 1986 p7):

"It [South Cardiff] is not an area of massive dereliction. Nor is it an area whose regeneration has been held back by endless squabbling between the public authorities in the area.

On the contrary, the existing agencies in South Cardiff – the County Council, Cardiff City Council, Vale of Glamorgan Borough Council, the Land Authority for Wales and the major land owner in the area, Associated British Ports – are all committed to the regeneration and redevelopment of the area.

The County Council would not wish to see the creation of an urban development corporation that excluded either local authorities and other existing local agencies from the opportunity to shape the direction of development of the area, or in which the voice and wishes of the large and existing local community would not be represented.

Accordingly, the County Council prefers the formation of an urban development corporation that brings together and uses, rather than displaces the powers, duties and functions of the public bodies already in the area."

The County Council also proposed an active local authority representative component on the board of the urban development corporation as this would ensure the fulfilment of its aims (SGCC 1986 p13).

Nicholas Edwards, Secretary of State for Wales in 1986, acknowledged the co-operation of local authorities in regenerating South Cardiff when announcing the creation of the Cardiff Bay Development Corporation. In the House of Commons he said:

"The situation is unique. The unity of central government, the local authorities and the political parties is unique ... Because I am anxious not to create a large bureaucratic body and as the local authorities are involving themselves so completely in the corporation's work I have decided that the corporation should not be given all the development control functions that are given to the UDCs in England".

(Parliamentary Debates House of Commons Official Report Fourth Standing Committee on Statutory Instruments Session 1986-87. Cardiff Bay Development Corporation (Area and Constitution) Order 1987).

Also, unlike the situation in some areas where an Urban Development Corporation was imposed (for a discussion of London Docklands see Deakin and Edwards 1993 Chapter 6), political opposition was largely absent. Whilst the Cardiff City Labour Party can hardly be described as having enthusiastically called for the UDC they accepted from the start that "the Bay Development is here to stay" and rejected "any response which says that the Bay must be stopped and the Development handed over to democratically elected Councils, any suggestions of non-co-operation, as unrealistic" (Cardiff City District Labour Party no date p1). Again in pragmatic fashion the Cardiff City Labour Party accommodated itself to the existence of CBDC and sought to imprint its goals on the regeneration process in Cardiff. "The Bay is here, and despite our dislike of and hostility to aspects of its existence, we have to work with it and try to benefit the people of Cardiff. The fact that we have representatives on its board and some planning powers is cause for some hope of maintaining an influence. But the influence of constructive engagement should not be underestimated" (Cardiff City District Labour Party no date p12).

Such co-operation from local authorities and local political parties has brought its reward in one important and unique respect. Cardiff Bay is unique amongst urban development corporations in that planning powers remain with the local authorities and have not been vested in the board of the UDC (CBDC Annual Report and Accounts 1988-89). This is strong evidence for claiming that Cardiff Bay Development Corporation was at least established with the co-operation of the local authorities involved.

South Glamorgan County Council in its proposal for the creation of an UDC in south Cardiff had insisted that a substantial local authority component should sit on its board (SGCC 1986 p13). In the event five Councillors (out of a total board membership of 13) sit on the board, drawn from South Glamorgan County Council (2), Cardiff City Council (2), and Vale of Glamorgan Borough Council (1). It is argued that this gives some measure of local authority control over the actions of the development corporation, makes it more accountable to the local authorities in the area, and, indirectly, more accountable to the inhabitants of the area. The Labour Party document too notes that the presence of (Labour) councillors on the board can provide a measure of influence over the strategy of the development corporation (Cardiff City District Labour party no date p12). However, it should not be imagined that local authority representation on the board of CBDC is unique. All Urban Development Corporations, thus far, have had provision for local authority representatives to sit on their boards, albeit as a minority on the board (as is the case with the board of CBDC), although in the case of London Docklands some local authorities have refused to take up the seats offered to them on the board. It is interesting to ask whether the co-operative stance of the local authorities towards CBDC has led to local authority representatives having influence over the policies of CBDC.

Much controversy surrounds the role of local councillors on the board of CBDC. Opponents of the Development Corporation claim that the councillors on the board have been ineffective and have even been compromised by their membership of the corporation's board. This is the view of the Cardiff Resident's Against the Barrage organisation (CRAB). For them, far from the inserting some measure of democratic control into the deliberations of CBDC, councillor representatives on the development corporation's board emasculate democratic control by co-opting or compromising influential local councillors such as Jack Brooks, Labour leader of SGCC, or Paddy Kitson, chair of SGCC Economic Development Committee, who agree with the basic strategy of the development corporation and are unlikely to oppose its policies. In a press release (CRAB 15-4-1991) CRAB declared that

"... the actions and attitudes of some leading Councillors who have promoted the proposed Barrage whilst accepting money from the Cardiff Bay Development Corporation ... suggests to us unscrupulous practice and shameful behaviour. After all, how can you act in an open minded way if you are on the promoters payroll. Such Councillors, who are members of CBDC, are not allowed to discuss the business of their meetings with their fellow councillors. Is this Democracy?"

A more positive view of the influence of councillors on the board of CBDC was given in an interview with an official of Cardiff City Labour Party. Far from being poodles of the CBDC, this informant described local councillor members as being able to sometimes dominate proceedings and even "run rings round" other board members and board officials. One instance where such influence was successful it is claimed was in the matter of a proposal to site a City Technology College in Cardiff Bay. This had the enthusiastic backing of the Welsh Secretary, Peter Walker, and some members of the CBDC board. However, local authority members vetoed the idea. In particular it is claimed that one member (Lord Jack Brooks) responded to the Welsh Secretary's suggestion for a CTC by saying "No [expletive deleted] way" (private interview with a senior official of Cardiff City Labour Party). A CTC has not been built in Cardiff Bay.

However influential local authority board members are, the composition of development corporation boards dilutes local authority control over regeneration policies and injects an explicit business orientation into the formulation of policies to tackle urban problems. As a Cardiff City Council official said to me "A manager from Woolworth's may know a lot about retailing but may know very little about urban regeneration".

Whatever their role on the board, the appointment of local authority representatives to the development corporation board has itself become a political issue. The Welsh Secretary has interfered with the process of selection of councillors to sit on the development corporation's board. For example, Cardiff City Councillors understood Peter Walker to have given local authorities an assurance that the Welsh Secretary would not interfere with the selection of councillors to sit on the board. At the time of this assurance, the composition of Cardiff City Council was evenly divided between Labour and the Conservatives and one councillor from each party was nominated to the board by the Council. However, following the death of the Conservative Councillor on the board, Councillor Ron Watkiss, the Labour Party, which by this time had overall control of the City Council, nominated a Labour Councillor, Councillor Mungham. His appointment was vetoed by Peter Walker's successor, David Hunt, and Hunt instead appointed another Conservative, Councillor Jeff Sainsbury. The Labour group considered this to be political interference and the breaking of a promise by the Welsh Secretary (interview with Cardiff City Labour Party official).

Liaison with local authorities

It is inevitable that Cardiff Bay Development Corporation and the local authorities in Cardiff Bay should have extensive dealings with each other. Regeneration has diverse consequences on housing, local transport, refuse, leisure and amenity and many other local authority services. The local authorities have a store of accumulated knowledge of the area and expertise in the field of administering urban areas. The City Council for example assisted the

Development Corporation in the preparation of two Area Planning Briefs, for the Bay area. Given that, in the case of Cardiff, it is the local authorities and not the development corporation which have responsibility for planning, it is inevitable that these interactions are liable to be more extensive than is the case with other urban development corporations. Often such dealings are specific to one area or one area of policy and may be ad hoc and irregular as a result. However, both Cardiff City Council and South Glamorgan have liaison committees which meet regularly with CBDC board members and officials, supplemented by regular meetings between senior members of the councils and senior CBDC board members. Both the City Council and the County Council therefore have the ability to make their views known to the Development Corporation. As South Glamorgan County Council note however (letter to myself 4-2-1992), although there are opportunities for the County Council to make its views known "they are not always accepted".

There have also been complaints from some quarters about the attitude of CBDC towards consultation with the local authorities. Councillor Sue Essex, chair of planning in Cardiff City Council who sits on the liaison committee described consultation with CBDC as "minimal" and claimed its attitude was "basically wrong" (South Wales Echo 19-5-89). Substantiating this claim she said "I only happened to catch a glance of the Core area development plan by chance when I visited CBDC chairman Geoffrey Inkin's office on a completely different matter" (South Wales Echo 19-5-89).

On specific issues where the City Council have been involved the behaviour of CBDC has given rise to much annoyance. One major issue has been the Ferry Road rubbish tip which is the main rubbish site for the city. CBDC have made several proposals over what to do with this site, including, initially, excavating all the refuse (some 3 million tones it has been estimated) and moving it by train to another site in Bedfordshire (South Wales Echo 17-4-1991). This scheme has been abandoned but the issue of where the city's rubbish will be dumped in future remains controversial. CBDC's single minded focus on the economic regeneration of the bay area (the reason for its creation) may mean that it neglects wider social interests and the wider geographical context of Cardiff as a whole.

Another example of the development corporation's failure to consult with local authorities in the area was its proposal to remove a traveller's site (about which it did not inform the County council which has an obligation to find sites for such people) without any suggestion as to where a new site for travellers might be provided (Cardiff City District Labour Party and South Glamorgan County Labour Party no date p8).

However, the clearest example of poor relations between the Development Corporation and the City Council was the Council's decision to petition against the building of the barrage in December 1991. Labour Councillors felt that this was the only means to make the development corporation discuss the city council's fears over the barrage seriously. Such a confrontational stance was not new however. The Labour controlled City Council proposed to issue a petition in July 1991 when the government barrage bill contained no special provisions to safeguard home owners that might be affected by raised groundwater levels. Leader of the City Council, Councillor John Phillips, who is also a member of the CBDC board, claimed that the only way to influence what went on was to issue a petition against the bill (South Wales Echo 4-7-91).

Partnership: local communities

Cardiff Bay Development Corporation emphasised its commitment to supporting the local community early on. In its Summary of the Regeneration Strategy CBDC states that "Throughout the Strategy Report there is a continuous thread of reference to the need of the present community within the Bay: be it housing, employment, social support or leisure facilities. The Corporation is firmly committed to the important principle that regeneration of the Bay area must be achieved by a wide mix of developments in parallel with realistic and durable enhancement of the community itself" (CBDC Cardiff Bay Regeneration Strategy: The Summary 1988 Preface). CBDC also committed itself to consultation with the local communities, enabling local people to identify their needs and solutions. CBDC declared that:

The 'Community Development' approach should aim to make local people better able to identify their needs and priorities and produce programmes of action. CBDC should establish systematic means of consultation and of producing, appraising, monitoring and evaluating proposals. CBDC will need to work with old and new communities, major employers, elected representatives, leaders in local life, local authorities, statutory bodies, voluntary organisations and specific interest groups.

The procedures and responsibilities must be formalised, straightforward, equitable and unambiguous. Crucial areas of attention will be access to education, business opportunities, employment and skill training, and community involvement in improving housing and the environment"
(CBDC 1988 p23).

Housing

As stated above, part of the CBDC's commitment to the inhabitants of Cardiff Bay concerned housing. In the original regeneration Strategy prepared by Llewelyn Davies (1987) a case is explicitly made for a role for the public sector for housing provision in the Bay: "Any suggestion that housing can be left to market forces working entirely through private capital fails to recognise that the Bay is part of Cardiff and cannot therefore be isolated from the general housing provision in the city. To do so would be seen as socially irresponsible and politically unacceptable, and would have a marked negative impact on public opinion. Moreover, since the future shape of the Bay's population will be largely determined by the pattern of housing, the participation of the Development Corporation in the creation of a housing strategy, in collaboration with others would be a major factor in creating a balanced community" (Llewelyn Davies Planning 1987 p89). CBDC has responded to this statement by giving a firm commitment to the retention of existing housing stock in the Regeneration Strategy and offers support to housing authorities to improve the residential environment, housing stock and management (CBDC 1988 p26). In the Regeneration Strategy, a target of six thousand new homes in the development area is mentioned, approximately 75 per cent of which should be for sale (CBDC 1988 p26). About a quarter of these new homes, it is suggested could be a mix of rental and social housing for lower income, disabled or other groups (CBDC March 1989 p5). The involvement of housing associations in the provision of social housing in Cardiff Bay is emphasised (CBDC 1988 p26). Here, as elsewhere in England and Wales, the formerly predominant role of local authorities in the provision of social housing has been usurped by housing associations in accordance with government policy (see below).

Progress has been made on the provision of social housing in Cardiff Bay. In July 1991 a £37 million scheme to build 840 homes for low rents between 1991 and 1995 was announced by Housing for Wales and the Cardiff Bay Development Corporation (Housing for Wales Press Release 30-7-1991). Around 70 per cent of the costs were to come from Housing for Wales and around 30 per cent from the private sector. Cardiff Bay Development Corporation's main contribution to the provision of social housing was the transfer of four sites, free of charge, to housing associations for four of the fourteen developments. (The total value of the land donated to the Moors Housing Association during 1990-91 by CBDC was almost £2.5 million (CBDC Annual report and Accounts 1991 p25)). Half of the homes built will go to people on Cardiff City Council waiting lists and others will be allocated to others put forward by the housing associations concerned (Cardiff Independent Advertising Feature 25 December 1991). Thus, social housing in Cardiff Bay may not make as much of an impression on the housing and homeless problem in Cardiff as is possible. The Cardiff City District Labour Party criticised CBDC for allocating only a quarter of the proposed housing for social housing, claiming that a half of the new housing should be social housing if the housing need in Cardiff was to be properly addressed (Cardiff City District Labour Party no date p7).

Cardiff Bay is an area of high and high long term unemployment (Senior Training Group no date Section 5:1). A reduction in the level of unemployment through finding work for more of the present inhabitants would be a substantial benefit to the local community. It has been alleged that, in London Docklands for example, local people did not benefit from the developments taking place in Docklands and that many remained without work despite the level of investment in the area (Evidence to Employment Committee HC 327 Session 1987-1988 Evidence by Newham, Tower Hamlets, Southwark). The provision of training in the Bay is the task of the Senior Training Group. This Group was formed in 1988 and represented in 1990 Cardiff Bay Development Corporation, Cardiff City Council, Confederation of British Industry, Department of Employment, South Glamorgan County Council, Training Agency, Vale of Glamorgan Borough Council, Wales Trade Union Congress and the Welsh Development Agency. It acknowledged the importance of reducing unemployment in the bay area for the Regeneration Strategy to succeed, stating that "It is also critical to the success of the Regeneration Strategy that local people, especially from those areas of South Cardiff with traditionally high levels of unemployment, should be able to take full advantage of the new opportunities" (Senior Training Group Section 1:5 no date).

The Senior Training Group made a number of proposals in its strategy document for training and employment in the bay. Some of these emphasised consultation and co-operation with local community groups and also acknowledge that more would have to be done to attract women, racial minorities, and those who had become disillusioned through participation in training schemes that did not lead to work in the past. In this concern for how discrimination can affect the operations of the market the STG's strategy showed a broader appreciation of the realities of urban deprivation and urban regeneration than documents such as Action for Cities for example had displayed. The free market is not by itself a solution to the problems of inner city residents. The distribution of the rewards of a market led regeneration do not go automatically to the poor and unemployed in a deprived area. Issues such as skills, training, child care and discrimination must be addressed to ensure that the poor benefit from the process of regeneration (Deakin and Edwards 1993 p7).

The Senior Training Group addressed these issues by acquiring information on the impact that the development of Cardiff Bay would make on the training needs of South Glamorgan (Senior Training Group no date para 1.8), developing links with local community representatives such as Cardiff Inner City Initiative, improving access to information about training available within the Bay and encouraging all employers in the County to formulate and publicise Equal Opportunities policies.

Again the efforts of CBDC and others were helped by the fact that these problems were already being addressed within the Bay area. Fullemploy, a national organisation with the aim of eliminating the gap between the levels of unemployment of minority ethnic communities and the majority population already had a business training, advice and support centre in the Bay. Cardiff Inner City Initiative already ran a number of training centres and a Job Club and the Employment Service Inner City Team was already based there as well. CBDC with other organisations, has enabled these organisations to expand their efforts. A monthly newsletter is published by Fullemploy Wales for the Cardiff Bay area, with the sponsorship, amongst others, of CBDC. This publicises job and training opportunities within the Bay, especially for members of ethnic minorities in the area. An attempt to 'reach out' to communities disadvantaged by the job market is made.

However, no compulsion such as setting ethnic job quotas in contracts is made. The strategy attempts to persuade business into employing more people from ethnic minorities. The Development Corporation's attitude to equal opportunities is a long way from the 'contract compliance' strategies used by certain Labour local authorities in the early 1980s (Eisenschitz and Gough 1993 pp81-82).

CBDC's efforts to promote training and employment in the Bay area have for most of its existence been directed towards the skills needed by the construction industry. A training centre in the Bay is sponsored by CBDC (amongst others) and run by Mowlem Training. The training centre has won the approval of the Wales TUC for example (*Western Mail* 21-7-1992). Linked to the provision of training is the Bay's Construction Training Charter which urges employers to invest in training to produce a skilled local workforce. Attempts have been made to encourage contractors working in the Bay to employ local people. Of the 227 jobs building the Butetown link road, 123 jobs were filled by local people (*Western Mail* 21-7-1992).

This theme of encouraging business to invest in the skills of the local workforce and employ local workers is also repeated in the Bay Business Charter launched in April 1993. The Business Charter also commits its signatories to an equal opportunities policy. It is to an examination of the involvement of local business in the regeneration strategy that I now turn.

Partnership: business

The Development Corporation has made great efforts to foster close links with the local business community in Cardiff Bay. Local business is represented by the Cardiff Bay Business Forum, founded in June 1991. Its chief officers have sought to develop a close relationship and understanding with the Development Corporation (private interview). This partnership was cemented in 1993 with the publication of the Bay Business Charter. Before its launch, Alun Michael MP, vice president of the Business Forum, stated that "Partnership – and a dynamic partnership at that – between business, the community and the public bodies is the only way in which we can make the most of this once-and-for-all opportunity for the redevelopment of South Cardiff" (CBBF Forum News March 1993 p3). CBDC receives advice and proposals form the Business Forum on its development proposals, which it considers before undertaking development. The Business Forum gave the development corporation a number of suggestions for its Inner Harbour development plans. A CBDC official responded:

We are looking very seriously at these helpful contributions, some of which we accept in principal [sic] and will work closely with the Forum to implement... The important thing is that the development of close working partnerships at every level will speed the programme of bringing benefits for all those involved in the Inner Harbour project ... We will only achieve our infrastructure and project targets if our partners share our strategic aims and see the advantages to themselves of whole hearted participation (CBBF Forum News March 1993 p5).

This response, though positive, is in some respects an exhortation to 'share the dream' rather than engage in a real dialogue where the views of local businesses and local people are received with an open mind by the development corporation.

The marketing officer of a large property developer at the heart of the Bay talked of CBDC having made blunders and being 'unduly insensitive' (interview with myself). He claimed that the property developers he worked for (the largest in the Bay besides CBDC itself) had had only formal dealings with the Development Corporation and the informal meetings that could lubricate a partnership had not yet taken place (December 1992). Particular criticism of the Development Corporation focused on the Dormant/Vibrant campaign by CBDC to counterpoint their success with the failure of past efforts at regeneration in Cardiff Bay. This, he said, had annoyed many involved in the regeneration of Cardiff Bay, and their handling of planning issues such as Ferry Road rubbish tip, might actually, he said, deter rather than attract investment.

Cardiff Bay Business Forum, has also found occasional difficulties in its dealings with the development corporation. On some issues which CBBF raised with the development corporation, such as parking in the bay, CBDC implemented the Forum's proposals "even if it did take an extra push" (CBBF Forum News June 1993 p2). However, on other issues CBBF, speaks of confusion within CBDC over issues such as marketing (CBBF Forum News April 1993 p2) and on others of being ignored or left in the dark by CBDC

(CBBF Forum News June 1993 p1, p2). A forum official was also candid about the failings of some aspects (and personnel) of CBDC. Initial publicity by the development corporation was described as 'crap' and the climate for consultation was said to have improved after the development corporation appointed a new chief executive (private interview with CBBF official). The Business Forum has on occasion and on some issues acted as a lobbyist promoting the interests of its members, and seeking to impress CBDC of their views. The Forum's campaign over company relocations and for a Relocations Charter by the Development Corporation is an example of the Forum adopting a more detached role form the Development Corporation (CBBF Forum News March 1993 p7; interview with CBBF official).

Cardiff Bay Business Charter

The Cardiff Bay Business Charter, launched in April 1993, attempts to foster co-operation between the businesses within Cardiff Bay and public organisations with responsibility for the economy of the Bay such as CBDC. Stressing links with the development corporation, the charter states that "it is essential for the Corporation and local businesses to work in unison now and to forward-plan [sic] for the future (CBBF April 1993 p2). However, the charter also emphasises, in true Samuel Smiles fashion, the benefits of self-help. Eisenschitz and Gough (1993 pp10-11) describe how a 'bootstraps strategy' has become common in local economic policy. Local actors develop links amongst themselves to benefit their locality. Thus, the charter emphasises "the mutual advantage of joint working..." (CBBF Cardiff Bay Business Charter: An Opportunity for Partnership April 1993 p2), stresses how "the prompt sharing of information, and voluntary commitments, can go a long way towards ensuring that local businesses play a part in, and directly benefit from, regeneration in the Bay" (CBBF 1993 p2), and focuses on how companies can contribute to the work of voluntary and other organisations in the Bay. Thus the charter states that "Many statutory and voluntary institutions and groups act to support and sustain social services in the Bay. Increasingly, the burden falls on the local community and enormous effort is freely and willingly given by voluntary organisations and community groups in the Bay. Many companies have a long tradition of providing support to charitable activity in the educational, social welfare and cultural field... The task is to support community development initiatives which strengthen community skills and expertise in the delivery of voluntary services – supporting local people with personnel, equipment, material resources, but, most of all with expertise and knowledge" (CBBF April 1993 p10). One example of this work would be the Forum's support (with other organisations) for the landscaping of a school in Butetown (CBBF Forum News May 1993 p3).

Community links

The Development Corporation and other organisations involved in the regeneration of Cardiff Bay have emphasised the need to involve, support and foster the community in the development strategy. Cardiff Bay Development Corporation for example, employs four community development officers, two with specific responsibilities for areas of the Bay, and two with responsibility for grants to local community groups and employment and training issues. The Development Corporation also provided subsidised offices for fourteen local community groups, including Bay Community Radio, Somali Women's Advice Centre and the Butetown Carnival Committee, within Cardiff Bay (CBBF Forum News June 1993 p3) and sponsored free air time for local charities on local radio (CBBF Forum News April 1993 p7). During 1990-91 some £300,000 was made available for grants under the CBDC's Community Initiatives programme and between 1988-1991 about £1 million was donated to local organisations in the Bay area (CBDC Annual Report and Accounts 1991/2). Cardiff Bay Development Corporation has made an effort to support local community initiatives which support existing communities.

Another aspect of its community work however, seems to be more closely tied in with its marketing objectives as well promoting community links within Cardiff Bay. The series of 'Bay days', jazz festivals in the bay, firework displays, horticulture shows and street carnivals are partly about making Cardiff Bay a joyful, entertaining place to local communities in Cardiff Bay and beyond, but is also designed to promote the new image of the bay (and of the development corporation and its strategy, critics have claimed (CRAB officials)).

Consultation on the regeneration strategy

CBDC's Regeneration Strategy is certainly ambitious. To ensure its success many groups had to be convinced of its viability in order to invest in Cardiff Bay or co-operate with CBDC in its activities. In order to try to secure this, CBDC engaged in a programme of presentations and discussions during May to October 1988 after the Regeneration Strategy had been unveiled. Six exhibitions were staged during this period and altogether 81 formal presentations were given to groups as diverse as the Nature Conservancy Council, Bute Town Historic Rail Society and the St Peter's Women's Fellowship (CBDC March 1989 pp9-11). Many informal presentations were also given and written responses to the Regeneration Strategy from organisations such as the local authorities, Associated British Ports and a lecturer in urban design were received (CBDC March 1989 p11). It is fair to say that considerable efforts were made to persuade local inhabitants, local authorities and business people of the merits of the

Regeneration Strategy. An official from the Cardiff City Labour Party acknowledged that CBDC did give a number of good presentations to explain its regeneration strategy to local community groups and initially at any rate was keen to consult with the local community (private interview with Cardiff City Labour party official).

Nevertheless, when the Royal Society for the Protection of Birds (RSPB) hired MORI in March 1992 to find the opinions of the citizens of Cardiff on the Regeneration Strategy, it was found that only 69 per cent were aware of proposals to construct a barrage (a key and controversial part of the regeneration strategy) and only 33 per cent considered the barrage a good idea (48 per cent felt they did not know enough to judge the merits of the barrage scheme) (information given by RSPB). Fears over groundwater, pollution and concern over its effects on wildlife were commonly mentioned. The Development Corporation's consultation process had not achieved all that the Corporation had hoped. Towards those that were opposed to its strategy, comments by CBDC officials sometimes betrayed a sense of exasperation. Michael Boyce, then chief executive of South Glamorgan County Council, now chief executive of CBDC and a long time proponent of the barrage, said "Nobody wants a barrage which would poison fish, generate algae and cause flooding. Nobody in their right minds would build a barrage like that. All our reports say this will not happen...We are willing to meet anyone to discuss the effect of the barrage on the city. But the barrage itself will be built" (Western Mail 15-9-1988). Geoffrey Inkin, chairman of CBDC brushed aside concerns about the effects of the barrage on wildlife by saying "As for the SSSI [Site of Special Scientific Interest], I'm not convinced it should ever have been designated – and I'm an active conservationist" (Cardiff Telegraph 3-3-1990). Barry Lane, the first chief executive of CBDC, described opponents of the barrage proposals in a forthright manner "What is the consortium? It is not elected as they are self appointed representatives. You will find that they are all unemployed people who spend their lives fighting development. They are cynical and I detest cynicism. I want to be positive. They are mad, absolutely mad. Do they really think they can create a social empire?" (*Western Mail* 15-9-88).

The Regeneration Strategy

In some respects consultation over the Regeneration Strategy by CBDC with the local authorities, local communities and local businesses concerned has been an improvement over attempts at consultation by other urban development corporations in their areas. However, the nature of the Regeneration Strategy itself remains to be investigated. Did it emphasise physical regeneration and property led growth or has there been an attempt to respond to wider social and environmental concerns by CBDC? If there has been such an attempt to respond to such concerns how successful have these attempts been? It is to an examination of these questions that we now turn.

The Preface of CBDC's Summary of the Cardiff Bay Regeneration Strategy (CBDC 1988 Preface) begins "Shortly after the establishment of the Cardiff Bay Development Corporation (CBDC) and the appointment of the board in April 1987, it was decided that the regeneration of Cardiff Bay should be undertaken against a far sighted strategy, prepared after much research, consultation and thought, rather than solely against the imperative of the market". Later on in the summary CBDC states that "The Strategy defines a blueprint for achieving a superb and varied urban area. The challenge is now to manage development successfully to this end, fighting off those many types of schemes readily on offer which are however not of the quality to produce the environment that is desirable and achievable" (CBDC 1988 p27). This statement would appear to eschew an exclusive reliance on market forces to achieve the goal of regeneration of Cardiff Bay. In its summary of the Regeneration Strategy, CBDC describes the Strategy as "comprising many policies and proposals designed to perform in a cohesive and integrated manner to provide a framework for the achievement of the objectives of CBDC" (CBDC 1988 p2). These objectives are listed (CBDC 1988 p2) as

a) Promote development which provides a superb environment in which people will want to live, work and play.
b) Achieve the highest standard of design and quality in all types of investment.
c) Re-unite the city centre of Cardiff with its waterfront.
d) Bring forward a mix of development which will create a wide range of job opportunities and will reflect the hopes and aspirations of the communities in the area.
e) Stimulate residential development which provides houses for a cross section of the population.
f) Establish the area as a recognised centre of excellence and innovation in the field of urban regeneration.
g) substantial progress is expected within ten years and the maximum leverage on private sector investment is a prime requirement

The objectives of CBDC combine explicitly commercial aims such as obtaining "the maximum leverage ratio as a prime requirement" with objectives geared towards improving the lot of local inhabitants such as creating job opportunities which "reflect the hopes and aspirations of the communities of the area" and providing housing for "a cross section of the population". On the face of it therefore, it would appear that CBDC is indeed mindful of the needs of local inhabitants and is aware that physical regeneration alone will not bring them prosperity. Indeed, the Regeneration Strategy prepared for the Development Corporation by Llewelyn Davies Planning Consultants states that it provides a "framework within which the twin strands of economic expansion and social concern can work together to the benefit of each" (Llewelyn Davies Planning 1987 p5)

However, for the Regeneration Strategy to work a substantial increase in property values is necessary. The aim of increasing property values within and attracting private investment into the Bay area is at the heart of the Regeneration Strategy. This is reflected in the centrepiece of the regeneration strategy, the barrage and the 500 acre fresh water lake created by the impounding of the Taff and Ely rivers. The purpose of this "high profile high cost strategy involving a series of strategic infrastructural and flagship investments" is "to restructure aspects in the economic base of the city region, resulting in a major growth centre" (CBDC 1988 p4).

The justification for the barrage and the cost involved is primarily economic. It has been claimed that the barrage will put Cardiff Bay on the map in terms of attracting commerce and industry (Llewelyn Davies Planning 1987 p29). Without the Barrage and the man-made lake, business will stay away it is argued. A consultant's report prepared for the Welsh Secretary, Nicholas Edwards, in May 1986 claimed that "The creation of a lake together with a good shore environment and an insistence on quality will guarantee development and development value" (Jones Lang Wootton May 1986 Conclusion).

Three questions emerge from this discussion. Firstly, are the promoters of the Regeneration Strategy correct in believing that their favoured strategy will yield the returns they predict? Secondly, even if the promoters are correct in their economic assumptions will the regeneration Strategy create jobs that can be filled by the local communities? Lastly, are these economic gains achieved at a wider cost to the community or the environment? I shall deal with these questions in turn.

The confidence with which the Jones Lang Wootton report makes its predictions seems at odds with the admission, also contained in the report that "we are required to fast track the study and to reach conclusions and judgements within a period of four months. It was therefore accepted that much of the analysis would, of necessity, be fairly superficial and that our conclusions would be preliminary". Also, whereas later reports claim to predict future levels of investment in the Bay to quite astonishing degrees of accuracy, this initial report had, at least some measure of humility. On leverage ratios it admitted that "All too often such estimates are perforce inexact" (Jones Lang Wootton May 1986 p12) and discussing land values if a barrage was built it conceded that "Valuation is not an exact science, particularly in those circumstances where it is necessary to make a range of assumptions about the likely type, quality, and level of uses which would be attracted to the Cardiff Waterfront following the construction of the barrage" (Jones Lang Wootton May 1986). A report prepared by Roger Tym and Partners et al in 1990 also notes (in the appendix) that "... it is recognised that the residual valuation method has to be treated with caution as the resultant figures are sensitive to changes in the variables that make up the appraisal" (Roger Tym et al 1990 p40 appendix).

Other economic assessments lack this degree of humility. An economic appraisal prepared by Peat Marwick Mclintock (Peat Marwick Mclintock April 1989) confidently predicts that 22,150 (net) direct jobs would be created if the barrage were built but only 12,700 net direct jobs if the development went ahead without the barrage. In terms of the leverage ratio, a measure of success close to the government's heart, the predicted difference is equally stark. With the barrage the leverage ratio is 1:8.9; without the barrage the leverage ratio falls to 1:4.6. The Peat Marwick Mclintock report concludes "a high level of public expenditure on the barrage, site preparation and environmental upgrading is essential if the area is to complete successfully with alternative locations ..." (Peat Marwick McLintock 1989).

However, some of the assumptions made by CBDC's consultants in preparing their projections appear unrealistic with hindsight. The Roger Tym and Partners report (Cardiff Bay Barrage: Planning Update and Economic Appraisal Statement) prepared in January 1990 assumed "that during the period of development there will be a stable to gently improving UK economy and a stable national and international property market"! The report used 1990 rent figures for its valuation of commercial property, ignoring the possibility of a fall in those rental values (which subsequently took place). The report also used estimated the cost of building the barrage at £126 million; by 1992 the estimated cost of constructing the barrage had risen to £152 million. Finally, the report claimed that the development of high value projects on the Ferry Road site was a prerequisite of successful regeneration. Due to the problems with clearing the rubbish tip at Ferry Road, by 1992 Ferry Road was not intended for high value uses.

In any case, CBDC has not relied on dry and dusty numerical appraisals of the Regeneration Strategy to justify its case. The Cardiff Bay Inner Harbour Final Report contains such gems (of near poetry) as "Like a flower blossoming after a long winter, Cardiff bay offers a wealth of opportunity for development" or, a crowning hyperbole, "The destination is no longer a foreign shore but a quality environment, a quality of life that offers Cardiff and Wales a capital city of which to be proud, to live in, to work in, to enjoy – A City of Man" (CBDC Inner Harbour Final Report 1990). An extract from Roger Tym *et al*'s report for CBDC in January 1990 (Roger Tym *et al.* January 1990 Section 1.6) relies on impressions rather than facts to make its case:

The central question, however, is how much investment is necessary to reform the image – what is the threshold that has to be passed before the world perceives that a fundamental change has indeed taken place in the Bay area? Is the threshold the creation of a new water area, alive with boats and sailing, a new international destination with broad vistas; or a small enclosed water space with development crowding into it, and the mud beyond?

Unsurprisingly, given this loaded introduction the report concludes that "There is no doubt that the updated Regeneration Strategy requires the Inland Bay to create the environment for successful development and the implementation of the Corporation's objectives for the whole of the Bay related area" (Roger Tym and Partners 1990 Section 4.6).

The economic case for the Regeneration Strategy and the Barrage in particular have come into question. In evidence to the Select Committee investigating the case for the Barrage, councillor Sue Essex, chair of planning for Cardiff City Council said that the claim the Barrage was essential was 'nonsense'. Cardiff, she said, was already attracting investment without the barrage and the Barrage would force many existing employers in the Bay to move and might therefore threaten jobs (Councillor Essex Evidence to House of Commons Select Committee 28-2-1990). Jonathan Morris, a lecturer at the Cardiff Business School, also drew attention to the risk posed to employment posed by relocating the existing firms in Cardiff Bay. In addition, Jonathan Morris queried the job creation figures given by CBDC's consultants. Creating commercial floorspace was no guarantee he said that jobs would fill that floorspace, especially given the scale of other developments in Cardiff and South Wales. Finally, Jonathan Morris stated that there was no guarantee that the new jobs created in Cardiff Bay could be filled by the existing inhabitants of Cardiff Bay (Jonathan Morris Evidence to Select Committee 29-3-1990). Finally, in evidence before the select committee on private bills, Mr John Bowers, a reader in Applied Economics at the University of Leeds, claimed that the case made in the consultants' reports was 'implausible' (John Bowers evidence to Select Committee March 1990). He found that for the consultants' estimate of the rise in land values following the construction of the barrage to be correct, people in houses around the bay would have to be willing to pay £2,017 a year for the privilege of living by a lake rather than a tidal estuary. Like other critics of the Barrage scheme, he claimed that the consultants had not allowed for the displacement of economic activities from elsewhere in Cardiff, South Wales or the UK and that most developments were not in any case barrage dependent.

Jacqueline Mallender, a former Treasury economist, examined the economic case for the Barrage, on behalf of the Royal Society for the Protection of Birds (who oppose the construction of a barrage) in the summer of 1992. This found several flaws in the case for the Barrage. Firstly, the capital costs associated with the construction of the barrage had risen substantially since the consultants made their case in 1990 (Jacqueline Mallender/RSPB 1992 paras 2.8-9). Secondly, the projected returns from developing the Ferry Road site had had to be sharply reduced (Jacqueline Mallender/RSPB 1992 para 2.15). The decline in property values in Cardiff since 1990 (Jacqueline Mallender/RSPB 1992 para 2.25) also weakened the case for the Barrage development. The growth values contained in the consultants' appraisal was "significantly higher than that experienced anywhere else in the UK over a similar extended period (Jacqueline Mallender/RSPB 1992 para 3.30) without any justification for this assumption (Jacqueline Mallender/RSPB 1992 para 3.31). Instead of yielding a large positive value as the consultants had claimed, Jacqueline Mallender found that the net present value of the Barrage scheme was a large loss of £110 million (Jacqueline Mallender/RSPB 1992 para 2.27). She also found flaws in the assumptions and methods of the consultants' appraisal of the scheme. Other schemes had either not been considered at all, or had not been considered seriously (Jacqueline Mallender/RSPB 1992 paras 3.10-12). Other developments in the Bay area, such as the Peripheral Distributor Road were assumed to have little effect on development "whereas the change of outlook (the creation of the harbour)" was assumed to have a major effect (Jacqueline Mallender/RSPB 1992 para 3.13). Lastly, the analysis behind the estimate of the value of the bird feeding ground that would be lost (the environmental cost of the Barrage scheme) was, according to Ms Mallender "neither appropriate, nor adequate as a measure of the costs" (Jacqueline Mallender/RSPB 1992 para 3.22). This is important, she argued, as "a realistic assessment of environmental loss could fully offset a realistic assessment of betterment" (Jacqueline Mallender/RSPB 1992 para 3.25).

Jacqueline Mallender concluded that "the economic case for the barrage has not been made. The revisions to costs and benefits since March 1990 undermine the economic case. Furthermore, there are fundamental problems with the approach used to make the economic case which render the appraisal invalid" (Jacqueline Mallender/RSPB 1992 para 4.4).

Thus, the benefits projected to accrue from the Regeneration Strategy have been called into question. However, the costs in terms of loss of employment to the existing workforce through relocations has also been cited as a significant cost of the Regeneration Strategy. This will be evaluated below. Finally, the claim that the economic regeneration of the Bay has subordinated other interests, particularly the environmental costs of the Regeneration Strategy must be examined.

If the projections of investment and job creation in the Bay after the building of the Barrage may be optimistic, concern has also been expressed about the effects of the Regeneration Strategy on jobs already in the Bay. In particular, there has been concern that the Development Corporation's relocation policy may drive some existing firms in the Bay out of business (Cardiff City District Labour Party and South Glamorgan County Labour Party no date p8). In a question to CBDC chairman, Sir Geoffrey Inkin, Cardiff MP Jon Jones said "those companies who are no longer in existence will be in no state to exploit the recovery and to some extent quite a number of small and medium sized companies are not in existence now as a result of your [CBDC's] activities" (Welsh Affairs Committee HC 259 Session 1992-1993 Q211).

The Development Corporation has shown some awareness of the problems of existing firms in the Bay. In 1988 CBDC declared: "The existing industries in the Bay need to be protected and nurtured as the economy changes. The current industrial improvement area policies should be supported by upgrading access, services and environment... a wide range of types of sites and premises should be made available in association with the industrial development strategy to allow local firms to expand and move as necessary. This will be particularly important in relocating those industries that need to move for reasons of site assembly, environmental impact, or infrastructure development ... a process of close liaison with the industrial and commercial communities, and the handling of each move individually is necessary to maintain the enterprises and jobs and avoid misunderstanding, blight or loss of confidence. This process should be conducted on an integrated basis with the work of the local authorities and local development agencies in the industrial sector and with the business community generally (CBDC 1988 p21).

However, there is some evidence to indicate that these good intentions by CBDC have not always been fulfilled. A report prepared by Cardiff and Vale Enterprise, found that of 112 businesses relocated, fifty remained in South Glamorgan, ten had moved elsewhere and the remainder had ceased trading, merged or been taken over (quoted in *Western Mail* 10-7-1991). The report warned: "There are many problems still to be addressed, not least the timing of relocation in relation to availability of suitable premises which needs to tied in to compensation negotiations. There is no longer the urgency from CBDC either to encourage potential relocatees to come forward or to negotiate with those who do so of their own accord. Taking this into account and the current economic climate, it is possible that the relocations strategy will grind to a halt unless some stimulus is found (quoted in *Western Mail* 10-7-1991). An academic study by Imrie and Thomas (1992) found that the companies in part of the Bay were left in a state of confusion and uncertainty by the Development Corporation over relocation and compensation and offered unsuitable, undeveloped alternative sites at often higher rents to the ones they were currently paying. The study concludes: "The experience of the firms in CR [a part of Cardiff Bay] clearly suggest that CBDC's strategy is poorly focused on the particular needs of the local business community. While CBDC has devised a plan for the regeneration of CR, evidence from our interviews suggests that the Development Corporation has systematically failed to provide a co-ordinated or coherent relocation package to enable the firms to be placed in similar circumstances elsewhere. In particular, firms are being forced to move to higher cost locations, while the only sites on offer by CBDC are unserviced and undeveloped. Furthermore, CBDC has failed to provide any time scale to enable the firms to plan their relocation, and negotiations have generally been adversarial in tone. This has been compounded by CBDC's refusal to subsidise rents or grant compensations comparable to the market valuations which firms will face elsewhere" (Imrie and Thomas 1992 p223).

Thus, in terms of preserving existing jobs (which are mainly filled by the local community in the Bay, the record of the Development Corporation has been flawed in some respects. This may have very important implications for who eventually benefits form the regeneration strategy. The economic regeneration of the Bay may leave some people as poor as before, and by eroding the manufacturing base of south Cardiff and South Glamorgan, may actually leave some even poorer than before.

Cardiff Bay Development Corporation's Regeneration Strategy was originally intended to balance the needs of economic regeneration with other interests. However, it has been claimed by environmental groups that, whatever the economic realities of the Regeneration Strategy, it imposes a great cost on the environment.

A consortium of environmental groups led by the Royal Society for the Protection of Birds (RSPB no date p6) point out that the Taff/Ely Estuary was notified as a Site of Special Scientific Interest in 1980 because its mudflats provide feeding grounds for many thousands of wading birds and has the highest density of wading birds of any site in the Severn Estuary. Although the Taff/Ely Estuary comprises only 1.6 per cent of the area of the Severn Estuary it supports ten per cent of the bird life there.

The Nature Conservancy Council in a petition against the Barrage bill in 1989 (Nature Conservancy Council Petition Cardiff Bay Barrage Bill House of Commons Session 1988-89) claimed that under the Convention on Wetlands of International Importance, especially Waterfowl Habitat, adopted at Ramsar in 1971 the Government is bound to protect sites such as the mudflats at Cardiff Bay. In addition the NCC petition (p5) pointed out that the European

144

Communities Council Directive (79/409) on the Conservation of Wild Birds obliged the British Government to take measures to protect the habitats of rare or migratory species. One of the measures has included the proposed designation of the Severn Estuary as a Special Protection Area, which would limit the scope of development in the Severn Estuary, including Cardiff Bay.

The Government's response to these issues was to exclude Cardiff Bay from the proposed Severn Estuary Special Protection Area. The Government's reasoning is contained in a letter from the Welsh secretary to the Royal Society for the Protection of Birds in November 1991 (Secretary of State for Wales Designation of the Lower Severn Estuary 4-11-1991). In this letter the Secretary of State for Wales said:

> ... member states enjoy a certain margin of discretion in selecting the most suitable territories to be classified as SPAs... Cardiff Bay is located near the heart of the City in an area surrounded by poor environment and dereliction.

> There is a clear and urgent public interest in the much needed regeneration of the area, for economic, social and environmental reasons, which the Cardiff Bay Barrage Bill is intended to promote, for example the economic appraisal of the Barrage Strategy estimates that some 25,000 new jobs would be created...

> We have concluded that the potential loss of the bay as a habitat would not be incompatible with the need to preserve, maintain or re-establish sufficient diversity and area of habitats for wild birds... the wider environmental improvements for residents of the area together with the economic regeneration which will ensue are so important as to outweigh the ecological interest in this case.

Thus the Regeneration Strategy is prepared to subordinate ecological considerations to the needs of economic regeneration. However, environmental and residents groups have claimed that the environmental costs associated with the Barrage and the Regeneration Strategy are higher than just the loss of bird feeding grounds. In particular, Cardiff Residents Against the Barrage have warned that the construction of the Barrage could lead to raised groundwater levels and dampness and even flooding of basements in some houses, an increased risk of flooding in south Cardiff, and the attraction of nuisance midges into the area. The National Rivers Authority in December 1991 warned that the water quality in the lake would be low, subject to algal growths and midges and would require extensive remedial measures (National Rivers Authority Welsh Region December 1991). CBDC's own environmental assessment conducted by the Environmental Advisory Unit based at Liverpool University stated that "Many of the feasibility studies show that there is a distinct possibility that lake water quality will be poor, particularly in the first few years. This may well lead to the development of nuisance algal growths and midge populations. Such problems will certainly detract from the landscape value and are likely to be perceived as undesirable by lake users and people who live in lakeside houses. Remedial measures will probably limit these problems and maintain the landscape value. The turbid water of the Bay without a barrage could be perceived as a similar problem, but we suggest that does not necessarily detract from the landscape because it is a natural feature" (Environmental Advisory Unit February 1989 p48).

Thus the case for the barrage being an attractive feature to lake side users, home buyers and inward investors rests ultimately on a value judgement of what is aesthetically pleasing. For the Development Corporation, economic considerations seem to have overridden wider environmental considerations as another passage from the Environmental Assessment report makes clear: "This report only addresses the environmental impact as outlined in the Parliamentary Bill. The impacts of alternative project options were not included in our terms of reference. Possible alternatives to the proposed barrage did not fulfil the objectives of the Promoters, or were rejected on economic grounds. They have not therefore been subject to a full environmental assessment, although it appears that some alternatives would offer fewer environmental costs and more environmental benefits than the proposed scheme" (Environmental Advisory Unit February 1989 p73).

These conclusions rather belie Nicholas Edwards', former Secretary of State for Wales, words to Cardiff 2000, a civic society, in 1988: "Now whatever else may be said about the plans to construct a barrage and redevelop the huge derelict areas of South Cardiff, they are not frivolous. Very few schemes of urban renewal anywhere in the world have been so carefully researched; and an enormous amount of effort has been and is being put into the preparatory work, and not least into the studies of the environmental and ecological implications (*South Wales Echo* 30-4-1988).

Uniqueness of CBDC's experience

As I have shown, ambitious claims have been made about Cardiff Bay Development Corporation and the regeneration of Cardiff Bay. Not least of these claims is that the experience of CBDC is 'unique' and that as one of its aims states, the regeneration of Cardiff Bay as a "centre of excellence and innovation in the field of urban regeneration" (CBDC 1988). Although it is not possible to examine these claims thoroughly it is possible to compare the experience of Cardiff Bay with the record of other areas with Urban Development Corporations. Fortunately, the Employment Select Committee of the House of

Commons undertook a major investigation of urban development corporations in 1988 and it is this source which is used to make comparisons with the experience of Cardiff Bay Development Corporation. Comparisons are made in a number of areas, including the nature of the regeneration strategies adopted, policies towards jobs and training, inclusion of racial minorities in the regeneration process and consultation between the development corporations and all those concerned with the regeneration of their areas.

1 The scope of the Regeneration Strategy

In contrast to the London Docklands Development Corporation (Employment Committee HC 327-1 Session 1987-88 Q459), the Cardiff Bay Development Corporation did not see its role solely in terms of physical regeneration supported by the activities of property developers. Rather its Regeneration Strategy explicitly eschewed relying "solely against the imperative of the market" (CBDC 1988 Foreword). and instead adopted a "far-sighted strategy, prepared after much research, consultation and thought (CBDC March 1988 Foreword). The Regeneration Strategy also spoke of the need to place community development at the heart of the regeneration of Cardiff Bay. LDDC however, in 1987 and after six years of existence spoke of its mission in terms of "the primary task laid on us through the Act and Government Directives to us is to do with the physical regeneration of Docklands (LDDC Q459 Employment Committee The Employment Effects of UDCs Session 1987-88). The Public Accounts Committee also concluded that LDDC had paid too little attention to social and other needs of people living there. The Department of the Environment concurred with the PAC's report and stated that "securing the provision of housing and social facilities is part of the regeneration task "(quoted in National Audit Office 1993 para 2.17). In terms of considering social issues in its regeneration strategy and not seeing regeneration solely in terms of physical regeneration, CBDC compares well with London Docklands Development Corporation.

Also, CBDC has made much of its planning approach to regeneration, as opposed to the more *laisser-faire* approach of London Docklands for example. Geoffrey Inkin, chairman of CBDC has claimed that this planning approach to regeneration as opposed to a market led approach has led to CBDC's regeneration strategy being able to weather the 1990-92 recession better than some other development projects; "...(W)e deliberately decided on a planning led basis as opposed to a market led basis...we have planned right; we are producing the infrastructure; we are committed to environmental improvements through landscaping. As that is achieved, then we can encourage the market to take advantage of our public investment" (Western Mail 30-6-1992). Some elements of the Regeneration Strategy have won the commendation of persons with

147

experience of urban regeneration projects. The marketing director of Capital Waterside (private interview), the property development arm of Associated British Ports in Cardiff Bay, praised the urban planning contained in the Regeneration Strategy and supported CBDC's claim that "an overall urban design concept of vision and strength has been produced and illustrated" (CBDC 1988 p6). Here too, it would seem that CBDC compares favourably with London Docklands Development Corporation.

2 Jobs/training

Cardiff Bay Development Corporation has also appeared to pay greater attention to training local inhabitants for the jobs that regeneration will create. CBDC developed close links with training bodies in its area early on and one of its first measures was to commission a skills audit of the existing population (Senior Training group no date). In conjunction with other bodies it has established a well-regarded construction training centre in Cardiff Bay and encouraged contractors to hire local labour. Here too, the record of CBDC compares favourably with that of LDDC which took six years to establish formal links with the Manpower Services Commission. No training centre for construction skills existed in Docklands after that time and a report by Peat Marwick and McClintock criticised the training efforts of LDDC (Evidence of Newham Community College, Manpower Services Commission and Construction Industry Training Board – Third Report of Employment Committee The Employment Effects of Urban Development Corporations Session 1987-88 Volume 2). However, some criticisms such as the claims that jobs had been lost (needlessly) due to the Corporation's policy on relocating existing firms had a more familiar ring (Employment Committee 327-1 para 57, 327-2 Q684, Q845, Q605). Also, the claim that many of the jobs established in Docklands were simply 'transfers' from other parts of London (or further afield) has some applicability in the case of Cardiff Bay as well. Two of the largest employers attracted to Cardiff Bay, the Welsh Health Common Services Authority and NCM Insurance were previously based elsewhere in Cardiff. Whilst it is true these jobs might have gone elsewhere in Wales or even the United Kingdom and have not been lost to Cardiff and Wales entirely, they are not 'new' jobs to Cardiff or South Wales.

More generally, the employment forecasts of CBDC have come in for criticism (Jonathan Morris Evidence to Cardiff Bay Barrage Select Committee March 1990 for example). These projections appear to be based on the capacity of the commercial floor space projected for Cardiff Bay rather than any realistic projection of demand for labour. An estimate of the employment capacity of a development is not the same as an estimate of the labour that will be created by a development. This is echoed in reports on other UDC's. The NAO in 1993 for example found that corporations had interpreted key output measures differently and until output measures were standardised "it was difficult to arrive at consistent measures of UDCs' performance or to make valid comparisons" (NAO 1993 para 2.11).

3 Ethnic minorities

Cardiff Bay Development Corporation has shown an awareness of the problems of ethnic minorities living in Cardiff Bay, and again in conjunction with others has tried to involve members of ethnic minorities in training programmes, employment opportunities and community development schemes. The Commission for Racial Equality and the Tower Hamlets Association for Racial Equality (THARE) were bitterly critical of LDDC's approach to ethnic minorities (HC 327-II Employment Committee The Employment Effects of Urban Development Corporations Volume 2 Session 1987-1988).

4 Consultation

CBDC, unlike some other urban development corporations, especially LDDC, quickly established formal mechanisms for consulting local authorities. Whilst these mechanisms have not created complete unity and agreement of purpose, they are widely felt to have been beneficial for all concerned. CBDC has also consulted widely with many community groups and with some groups such as the group representing local business it has also established formal consultation procedures. LDDC was criticised for its failure to establish consultative mechanisms with its local authorities (Evidence of Bishop of Stepney, Docklands Consultative Committee, Docklands Forum, Southwark Borough Council, Newham Borough Council, Third Report Employment Committee The Employment Effects of Urban Development Corporations Volume 2 HC 327 Session 1987-1988).

Thus, on some measures CBDC's practices are an improvement on those of LDDC (and also the Merseyside Development Corporation). This may indicate that the urban development corporation model could be implemented with greater sensitivity in Wales, possibly due to a greater degree of consensus as to the aims and methods of regeneration and a climate of compromise between central government, local government and other interested parties. However, it is also possible that the comparatively harmonious experience of CBDC (by no means completely harmonious) is not unique to Wales and the CBDC. The Trafford Park and Birmingham Heartlands UDCs were also established with local authority and a wide measure of local cross-party support (Deakin and

Edwards 1993). By 1987, even LDDC was addressing the need for closer consultation with local authorities and claiming some success in this regard (Employment Committee 1987-1988 Vol. 2 Evidence Q654, Evidence p188). Some of CBDC's comparatively harmonious activities may be due to the passage of time eroding some of the opposition to the UDC concept, and UDCs gradually learning form previous mistakes (Judge, Local Economy May 1989; Atkinson and Moon 1994) as well as a relatively consensual elite political culture in Cardiff that is hardly unique to the city or to Wales generally.

Housing

Poor housing, housing lacking in basic amenities, or housing problems such as overcrowding, or even homelessness are some of the ingredients of urban problems in Britain. Housing policy can therefore play an important role in relieving urban problems and in urban regeneration.

In some respects housing problems in Wales are especially severe. Thirty-eight per cent of dwellings in Wales were built before 1919 whereas in England only some 27 per cent were built before 1919 (Cm 1516 The Government's Expenditure Plans para 8.18). Also, 7.2 per cent of the Welsh housing stock is unfit as compared to 4.8 per cent of the English housing stock and 4.3 per cent of housing in Wales lacks basic amenities as against 2.5 per cent of housing in England (Shelter Cymru October 1992).

Housing in Wales is also an interesting area of study as it is an area of policy where Welsh institutions have apparently gained greater autonomy from England in recent years. Since April 1989 housing policy in Wales has been the responsibility of Housing for Wales, which took over the Welsh responsibilities of the London-based Housing Corporation. At the same time the Welsh Federation of Housing Associations also acquired independence from its English sister organisation. The devolution of administrative responsibility has, it is claimed, brought with it benefits for housing policy in Wales. Mr Allen, chairman of Housing for Wales, said before the Welsh Affairs Select Committee:

> Prior to the Housing Act 1988 the housing corporation carried out its function for the whole of England, Scotland and Wales. Wales was administered through a regional office. It had no board structure, but had one board member who sat on the board of the Housing Corporation. Undoubtedly very strong benefits have emerged from the ability in Wales to have its own organisation, both in terms of the board being representative of the various parts of Wales, the board being able to direct its attention specifically to the particular problems of Wales which are in many ways

quite different from some of the problems of industrial England, particularly the south-east of England, and it also provides a much firmer and more direct interface with the housing association movement in Wales and with the local authorities and all other interested parties in Wales

(Welsh Affairs Committee HC 259 Session 1992-1993 Q403).

To what degree has this process of institutional differentiation led to differences in housing policy? There are clearly some differences between housing policies in Wales and in the rest of the United Kingdom. Housing Action Trusts have not been applied to Wales. Housing Associations in Wales also can perform one function which English housing associations are not permitted to do. Welsh Office Circular 30\86 permits housing associations to build high quality homes for 'key workers' in addition to their function of providing low cost, affordable social housing. This provision was seen as important in attracting inward investors into Wales, by offering senior management in inward investing firms a high quality of life in addition to the other benefits Wales can offer inward investors. Housing policy in Wales has, then been bent to serve wider policies such as the attraction of inward investment.

Though these differences may be indicative of some autonomy they are somewhat peripheral to the main thrust of housing policy. Broadly, housing policy since 1979 in Britain has had two main goals. Firstly the extension of home ownership, particularly through the right to buy scheme, has been a significant aim. Secondly, the provision of low cost social housing for those too poor to purchase their own homes has been an area that has seen many changes as the government sought to reduce the role of local authorities as providers of social housing. Does housing policy in Wales differ in these areas from housing policy in England?

In 'Housing in Wales: An Agenda for Action' published by the Welsh Office in November 1991 the Government set out its housing philosophy and policies for Wales. Here the privatist philosophy of Government policy with regard to housing policy was made explicit. The document stated that:

The philosophy underpinning the Government's housing policy rests firmly on the belief that housing is first and foremost a matter of the private sector. The success of the private housing market means that most people, most of the time, will be able to house themselves, and that the State only needs to intervene where people cannot otherwise afford a decent home. Owner occupation stands at the centre of the Government's housing philosophy

(Welsh Office 1991 p5).

The central role of home ownership in the Government's thinking is repeated elsewhere. One of the chief goals of the housing programme in Wales is "encouraging home ownership" according to the Welsh Office's report on the Government's Expenditure plans 1993-94 to 1995-96 (Cm 2215). In "Housing in Wales" the goal is described as "to spread home ownership through the Right to Buy and the Rents to Mortgages scheme and other action by ensuring an adequate supply of land for housing". "Housing in Wales" even mentions an explicit target "to encourage home ownership for the vast majority of people in Wales, so that around 80 per cent of households can achieve owner occupation by the turn of the century" (Welsh Office 1991 p14). (In 1991 the level stood at 72 per cent having risen from 59 per cent in 1979).

One of the means by which home ownership has been extended in Wales as elsewhere in the UK has been through the Right to Buy scheme introduced in 1980. Nearly 97,000 local authority, housing association and new town dwellings have been sold under Right To Buy or on voluntary terms since 1979 (Cm 2215 para 6.07). Indeed Right to buy sales since 1979 account for almost half of the increase in the proportion of home owners in Wales since that year (Welsh Office November 1991).

Table 6:1
Sales of Local Authority, New Town and Housing Association Dwellings
1987-88 to 1992-93

	Year				
	87-88	88-89	90-91	91-92	92-93
Local Authority & New Town	6253	10946	11729	5002	3541
Housing Associations	414	399	205	419	355

Source: Cm 2215

The Welsh Office has not merely followed central government policy in terms of its housing policy. In pursuit of its objective of extending home ownership the Welsh Office has been in the forefront of devising new schemes to enable public sector tenants to become home-owners.

Peter Walker, whilst Welsh Secretary, lobbied Whitehall to adopt a scheme whereby public sector tenants could become part owners of the homes they rented (Walker 1991 pp214-5). A flexi-ownership scheme of this type now exists for Development Board for Rural Wales properties and by the end of 1992 65 properties had been sold in this way (some 8 per cent of the eligible stock) (Cm 2215 para 6.08). With the enactment of the Housing and Urban Development Act in 1993, this policy, pioneered in Wales, was extended to other public sector tenants in the United Kingdom.

Wales has not only been at the forefront of the campaign to extend home ownership, it has also experienced, especially during the early 1990s some of the costs of a push to extend home ownership. Mortgage repossession orders made in Wales in 1991 totalled 3958, a rise of over 50 per cent on the previous year (Hansard 13-2-92). Homelessness has also risen in Wales. At the end of 1991 1214 homeless households were living in temporary accommodation in Wales. This represents a 103 per cent increase over the preceding decade (Shelter Cymru October 1992 p2). Also in 1991, 24,025 people were accepted as homeless according to Welsh Office statistics, an increase of 63 per cent over the decade (Shelter Wales 1992 p1).

Thus, far from being non-Thatcherite, housing policy in Wales was enthusiastically in favour of extending a property owning democracy and used what autonomy it had to pursue this aim. I now turn to examine the role of the Welsh Office in the provision of social housing.

Social housing

The provision of social housing has also undergone a process of change during the 1980s. During the 1970s, local authorities were the main providers of low cost housing for low income households which could not afford to purchase. However, during the 1980s the role of local authorities was redefined in social housing (as in other areas) to that of 'enablers', commissioning others (housing associations) to provide services that they would previously have provided themselves. The role of local authorities declined and the role of the voluntary and private sector correspondingly rose.

The document 'Housing in Wales: Agenda for Action' contains the Welsh Office's thinking on the role of local authorities in the provision of social housing. It declared "The role of the local authority will be that of the enabler. Housing authorities are used to the distinction between purchasing and providing which is now being introduced progressively for health and personal social services..." (Welsh Office November 1991 p3).

The reliance on the private and voluntary sector and the exclusion of local authorities from providing social housing has had a significant effect on social housing in Wales during the 1980s. Firstly, there has been a dramatic decline in the number of social housing unites built. Table 6:2 illustrates this:

Table 6:2
Housing Public Sector Completions by Year

Year	Local Authority	Housing Association	Other	Total
1975	7332	275	629	8336
1976	6864	182	608	7654
1977	6575	388	328	7291
1978	4111	1072	364	5547
1979	3010	1016	325	4351
1980	3493	917	211	4621
1981	3370	540	166	4076
1982	1771	794	109	2674
1983	1543	529	195	2267
1984	1997	593	155	2745
1985	992	607	83	1682
1986	744	534	126	1404
1987	810	467	2	1279
1988	793	708	1	1502
1989	566	1642	6	2214
1990	608	1653	–	2261
1991	418	2446	–	2864
1992	133	2497	–	2630

Source: Digest of Welsh Statistics No.39

The table clearly demonstrates the decline in council building. It also shows, that for most of the period, housing associations were unable to make anything but a small impact on housing need in Wales.

Only since the late 1980s have housing associations made a significant impact in terms of social housing provision. In addition, the rate of new building is insufficient to replace social housing lost through right to buy legislation. Between 1980 and 1991, 87,398 council houses were sold but only 17,108 council houses built and 11,417 housing association homes built (Shelter Cymru October 1992 p2).

Housing for Wales finances the bulk of the housing association schemes in Wales through the provision of Housing Association Grant to registered housing associations. The sums spent distributed as Housing Association Grant by Housing for Wales are given in Table 6:3.

Again, in keeping with the ideology of the Conservative government, there is an increasing emphasis on the attraction of private sector monies to supplement government provision. The encouragement of private sector monies to housing

154

Table 6:3
Housing Association Grant Spent by Tai Cymru (Housing Corporation for Wales) 1986/87 to 1991/92 £M

1986/87	1987/88	1988/89	1989/90	1990/91	1991/92
51.8	64.45	72.89	90.42	115.98	131.74

Source: Tai Cymru Investment Policies and Plans 1992/93

Table 6:4
Private Finance Supplementing Housing for Wales Programmes £M

1987/88	1988/89	1989/90	1990/91	1991/92
7.8	7.5	22.0	33.0	53.0

Source: Government Expenditure Plans for Wales 1993/4 to 1995/6 Cm 2215

association social housing schemes was enshrined in the 1988 Housing Act and the funds coming from private sources increased after this time (Table 6:4).

Again, the Welsh Office has been at the forefront of involving the private sector in public policy. Mr Peat, chief executive of Housing for Wales, said before the Welsh Affairs Select Committee (Welsh Affairs Committee HC 259 Session 1992-1993 Q438)

> What is happening both in England and Wales is that we make a grant of only a proportion of project cost. The housing association is then required to borrow the balance of the funding in the private sector. That policy applies in England as it does in Wales. We have been perhaps a little faster out of the starting blocks and we are now at a point where virtually all, certainly 98 per cent which is our target figure, of schemes are on this mixed funding basis. It substantially expands the amount of housing we are getting from the quantum of public resources provided, because we put in a grant of 67 per cent on average, so we are getting half as much again from the public money because of this policy.

Whilst Housing for Wales states that this private sector involvement has the laudable aim of increasing the number of affordable homes that can be built with any given level of government funding, it does not mention that rents charged rise in order to generate a sufficient return to attract private sector capital. Shelter Wales (October 1992 p3) found that average council house rents in Wales in 1992 were £26.44 whereas average housing association rents in 1992 were £38.78. Local Authority rent rise for 1992/93 were projected to average 8.5 per cent whereas housing association rents had risen on average by 14 per cent (Shelter Cymru 1992 p3). Raising the cost of social housing could defeat the whole purpose of building 'affordable' social housing for low income families.

Thus in terms of securing a greater role for the private and voluntary sector in public policy and reducing the role of local authorities in particular, housing policy in Wales would appear to be consistent with developments elsewhere in the United Kingdom. Privatisation and centralisation appeared to be the hallmarks of housing policy in Wales during the 1980s.

This centralising tendency does not seem to have yet run its course. In a discussion document issued in June 1992 Tai Cymru called for a "fundamental reappraisal of the framework in which housing is being developed and managed by housing associations in Wales" (Tai Cymru 1992 p.1). What this document suggested was that Tai Cymru should normally decide what designs could be used, should deal with only a small number of housing associations (about ten in place of the 36 that currently dealt with it) and that projects should normally be between 50 and 200 units in order to reap economies of scale. A spokesman for the Housing associations movement in Wales described this as the death of the housing association movement in Wales. Langstaff has argued that similar trends in England have "progressively eroded the autonomous, self-governing nature of housing associations – turning them into hired agents of central government, operating as branch offices of the Corporation" (Langstaff 1992 pp42-43). Certainly, the proposals would mean that housing associations could not respond so sensitively and imaginatively to local needs if they were to go through. The degree of oversight which Tai Cymru would exercise over these supposedly autonomous bodies is clear when the document further states that in order to monitor progress against cash allocations with each housing association Tai Cymru proposes "the use of compatible computer software for programme management in all developing associations and a modem link to Housing for Wales" (Tai Cymru 1992 pp 7-8). The Welsh Federation of Housing Associations commented "This on-line electronic monitoring is an arrangement which could be expected between the head office of a company and its branches, but it is an unusual and rather disturbing requirement between a government agency and fully autonomous and independent organisations" (Welsh Federation of Housing Associations July 1992 p8). The move to fewer associations charged with building also has parallels with fears in England that the diversity that was held to be one of the advantages of housing associations over council housing may be about to be eroded. The WFHA claimed that these proposals appeared to owe "more to the administrative convenience of Tai Cymru than any genuine wish to improve the effectiveness of the housing association movement in Wales" (Welsh Federation of Housing Associations July 1992 p1).

Thus, in the area of social housing policy, policy in Wales has closely mirrored developments in England, and on occasion, it would seem, moved further towards involving the private sector than has so far been the case in England. Institutional autonomy and administrative devolution does not ensure that a different policy will be pursued in Wales.

Conclusion

In this chapter I have studied the Urban Programme in Wales, the activities of Cardiff Bay Development Corporation, and housing policy in Wales. In these policy areas the role of local authorities have been reduced as in urban regeneration policy or marginalised altogether as is the case in the provision of social housing. Non-departmental public bodies, institutions of central government, such as urban development corporations or housing corporations have played an increasing role in the provision of local public services. Also starkly apparent has been an increasing emphasis on the role of the private sector in urban regeneration and the provision of social housing. Public bodies, both central and local, increasingly play the role of 'enablers', commissioning the private sector to provide public services or more generally, adjusting their activities to support the needs of business. This emphasis on the use of market mechanisms and a subsidiary role for the public sector, especially local authorities, echoes the findings of the previous chapter which looked at economic policies in Wales. This emphasis is also consistent with the characteristics of Thatcherism offered in Chapter 4.

In the concluding chapter I examine what lessons these findings have for studies of government and policy-making in Wales.

7 Conclusion:
Thatcherism and Welsh politics

"To write a book about Scottish nationalism ... or Welsh nationalism... is to focus upon only one part of the United Kingdom... Similarly to write a book about the Scottish political system ... is to assume what remains to be proven, namely the things differentiating Scotland are politically more important than what Scotland and England have in common, such as government by Westminster. It is more accurate to speak about British government in Scotland or British government in Wales, *leaving open to empirical investigation whether and in what ways, politics in one part of the United Kingdom differs from another...*

(McAllister and Rose 1984 p8 my emphasis)

"Attention is drawn away from personalities and burning issues of the moment towards longer trends and the role of the structural characteristics of the system of territorial politics in shaping current issues and responses"

(Rhodes and Wright 1987 p3)

In this book I have attempted to study the nature of politics and policy-making in Wales, looking in particular at the claim that there were significant differences between politics and policy-making in Wales and England since 1979. As I showed in the first chapter, such claims have gained wide currency in recent years both from politicians and academics and may even have become the conventional wisdom regarding Welsh politics during this period. If true, this account of significant deviation from the Thatcherite norm in terms of an important policy area such as local economic policy and urban regeneration policy (where successive Conservative governments have invested a good deal of time, resources and legislation in trying to impose their will on recalcitrant local authorities) would hold important lessons about the distribution of power within the unitary British state. Some commentators spoke almost of the jacobinism of Thatcherism as it attempted to turn (all of) Britain into an enterprise culture, and remove the last pockets of resistance to this project in the inner cities, Scotland, Wales and the North of England. Policy deviation in Wales could mean that parts of central government in the United Kingdom, a whole department even, could under exceptional circumstances be colonised by actors with different policy agendas who could then implement their policies relatively undisturbed even from a dynamic Prime Minister such as Mrs Thatcher.

However, as a previous study of territorial politics in the United Kingdom reminds us, it is necessary for political scientists to critically examine claims about a Scottish or Welsh political system or a Welsh economic miracle. Such a critical examiniation can only be an empirical examination. This was the nature of this book. In evaluating this evidence it is also necessary to use concepts clearly. It is my view that those who have described a Wales where the Welsh Office was able to pursue policies at variance from Thatcherism have misunderstood the nature of government in Wales and the nature of Thatcherism. In this chapter I will outline my understanding of these concepts and what light they cast on politics and policy-making in Wales since 1979.

Welsh exceptionalism

The claim to Welsh exceptionalism contains many elements. Proponents of Welsh exceptionalism have pointed to the growth of the Welsh Office and various government bodies in Wales as providing the capacity to implement policies that were distinctive or unique to Wales. Proponents have also claimed that there is a Welsh political culture or a Welsh way of doing things that emphasises co-operation, consensus, and partnership (if not collectivism). Welsh political and governmental institutions and the actors within them, are supposed to be suffused with these values and this makes for co-operation, partnership and government intervention. Similar actors or institutions in England, where these values are absent or, at any rate weaker, must compete against an ethic of enterprise and laisser-faire held by some dominant actors or institutions. Lastly, some proponents of Welsh exceptionalism point to the individual contributions of successive Secretaries of State for Wales during this period. Policies applied in Wales were different from policies applied in England precisely because Peter Walker and David Hunt wanted them to be different. Two prominent advocates of this view have been Walker and Hunt themselves!

What some have regarded as insitutions of Welsh government and even the expression of the Welsh people for national freedom (Osmond 1992) are in fact institutions of British government operating within Wales administering policies decided outside Wales. The Welsh Office, headed by the Secretary of State for Wales is a relatively small Whitehall department, with insufficient resources to initiate separate policies in many areas of policy. The Secretary of State himself is a fairly junior Cabinet minster, who need not have any close connection with Wales itself. The constitutional position of the Welsh Office and the Welsh Secretary is identical to that of any other central government ministry or minister. They are accountable to Parliament at Westminster not to a Welsh assembly or some 'Wales only' body. Whilst Parliament contains some committees which have special responsibility for scrutinising government activity in Wales, the Welsh Affairs Committee, the Welsh Grand Committee and the Welsh Standing Committee are all committees of the House of Commons, and derive their authority from the conventions of the British political process not from some exclusively Welsh basis. Whilst the Welsh Office, the Welsh Development Agency and the other public bodies under the authority of the Welsh Office administer policies in Wales they do not do so because they possess a Welsh mandate. In this respect they are no different from other institutions of central government operating in Wales without specifically Welsh responsibilities such as Companies House in Cardiff or the Vehicle Licensing Agency in Swansea.

The capacity that the Welsh Office and the Secretary of State for Wales possess to develop policies for Wales is subject to tight constraints imposed by the British constitutional framework. Where an issue is central to the central government's strategy or general ideology it is unlikely that significant deviations can be tolerated by central government. Local economic policy, urban regeneration policy, and housing policy since 1979 have been areas which the government has seen as central to its strategy both of creating an enterprise culture and a property owning democracy and of reducing the role of groups opposed to this strategy. It seems difficult to construct a case arguing why central government should have allowed policies at variance with its fundamental goals to have been pursued in Wales when it pursued this strategy so vigorously in England.

One element in such an argument would presumably be the distinctive political culture of Wales with its alleged emphasis on co-operation, consensus and even collectivism. However, to believe that a distinct political culture can overcome or re-shape policy initiatives from central government is to ignore the record of urban policy in Scotland in the 1980s and into the 1990s. Scotland has many of the same elements of distinctiveness, a separate Scottish Office, a separate sense of identity, and a record of support for the party of the left in national politics which might indicate a collectivist political culture. In addition, some ambitious

160

urban renewal schemes such as the Glasgow Eastern Area Renewal Project have taken place in Scotland and the Scottish Office has an active record in urban policy through its new towns programme. However, by the late 1980s urban policy in Scotland had come to share many of the characteristics of English 'Thatcherite' urban policy as Midwinter et al. note:

> Urban regeneration policy has thus moved a long way since the vision of integrated urban renewal, involving central-local partnership and a simultaneous attack on physical, social and economic ills. In the new dispensation, economic development is seen primarily as the task of the private sector, albeit with generous public subsidies, distributed by central government or its successor organisation. Its focus is on areas of maximum market potential, mainly commercial and service activities in the urban centres. The problems of deprived communities are now conceptualised as a 'social' issue, to be handled by the social security system and by local authorities, on a strictly limited resource base.

> There is nothing specifically Scottish about this. Despite the existence of the Scottish Office and the Scottish Development Agency, policy in Scotland has followed the same broad lines as that in England, albeit with institutional modifications. The tradition of integrated regional planning and public sector leadership in urban development which was characteristic of Scotland for much of the post-Second World War period has largely disappeared in favour of a more fragmented approach and the encouragement of private initiative. This again reflects the influence of the New Conservatism rather than any Scottish factor.

(Midwinter, Keating and Mitchell 1991 pp193-4).

In any case, it is difficult to define Welsh political culture precisely. Support for the Labour Party need not indicate support for collectivism; it may simply be the product of inertia (Miller 1984) or result from a sense of Welsh identity with little specific ideological baggage attached to it (Balsom et al. 1983). Elite opinion might be different in any case, and might either support the main thrust of government policy or might see the role of local authorities in Wales as co-operating with central government to secure what advantages it can for its area. Some evidence for this might be the work of the Institute for Welsh Affairs and particularly its report, "Wales 2010: Creating our future" (Institute of Welsh Affairs 1993). This report was written by a team of twenty people from "the larger corporations, small businesses, professional firms and the fields of education, health and agriculture" (IoWA 1993 p3). This report placed great reliance on developing an enterprise culture in Wales; on the Welsh Office, the Welsh Development agency, TECs, the universities in Wales and other public bodies refocusing their activities to support the enterprises in Wales; and on the use of private sector venture capital (including even the possible use of foreign banks) to support businesses in Wales. At least some people (in the self-appointed) Welsh elite are prepared to accommodate themselves to or enthusiastically endorse the ideological assumptions of Thatcherism. A relative absence of central-local conflict in Wales might not be indicative of non-Thatcherite policies applied in Wales, policies more amenable to Welsh political culture, but might instead reveal that leading figures in local government, the trade unions and business in Wales were prepared to go along with a Thatcherite policy if they saw they might gain some benefits from it. It is important to remember that a policy of consensus does not of itself suggest the nature of that consensus.

The final element of the Welsh exceptionalism thesis is the character of the Welsh Secretary himself. As we have seen above, Peter Walker and David Hunt were both keen to suggest that they were implementing interventionist strategies with an active role for government. This was taken to be a deviation from Thatcherism and its adherence to neo-liberal laisser-faire economics. However, this is to understand how Thatcherism worked in practice. 'Real-existing Thatcherism' was, as we saw in chapters five and six very interventionist. The activities of the urban development corporations, Training and Enterprise Councils, the reform of urban grants, the attraction of inward investment all involved a great investment of government resources. However, intervention by Conservative governments since 1979 has promoted the needs of business and an enterprise culture, downgraded the role of local authorities and has assumed that social problems such as unemployment can be solved by simply regenerating the economies of urban and other deprived areas. As Batley noted, the real question has not concerned intervention per se but "what sort of intervention, under whose control and for whose ends?" (Batley 1989 p180).

In addition, in some cases where government in Wales was interventionist, this was a result less of the personal clout of Peter Walker or David Hunt than the force of policy inertia. The successful land reclamation programme of the Welsh Development Agency was inherited form previous governments and the impetus for this policy originates from the Aberfan Disaster in Wales in 1966; the attraction of inward investment was a goal of the Development Corporation for Wales created as far back as 1958. These policies have survived through 1979 but, in some cases, have been re-shaped by Thatcherism to emphasis the needs of business or the contribution that the private sector can make to fulfilling goals such as land reclamation.

In his autobiography, Peter Walker makes much of the improved performance of the Welsh economy during the late 1980s as evidence of the success of his strategy (Walker 1991 p212). As I showed in chapter five, accounts of the 'welsh economic miracle' may have been exaggerated. The performance of the Welsh

162

economy viewed form a longer perspective was not exceptional and, in any case, considerable economic problems remained. Without an economic miracle there is little need to look for policies that created such a miracle!

Finally, if non-Thatcherite policies were applied in Wales solely because the Secretary of State did not favour Thatcherite policies then the conditions for Welsh exceptionalism seem precarious indeed. The Welsh Secretary is appointed by the Prime Minister with, apparently, little concern for the wishes of Wales. The appointment of John Redwood as Welsh Secretary in 1993 and William Hague in 1995 seemed to owe more to the desire of the Prime Minister to balance the left wing and right wing of the Conservative Party around the Cabinet table rather than reflecting a desire to maintain Wales as a relative haven of 'wet' Conservatism.

Conclusion: the territorial politics approach

What is needed to understand government in Wales today is a perspective which draws attention away from singular events such as alleged economic miracles or the role of personalities and instead concentrates on the structures of government as a factor in determining policies in Wales. Such an approach is offered by territorial politics. In this account, the power of the centre is such that it can ensure compliance by local actors in policies that it considers to be important. Economic policy, urban regeneration policy and housing policies were all deemed important by Mrs Thatcher during the 1980s as they promoted an enterprise culture and a property owning democracy and weakened the role of bureaucratic local government with its 'civic hostility to enterprise'. Central government had invested too much money, effort and prestige in these policies and the goals they were designed to achieve to see these policies undermined in part of the United Kingdom. The autonomy of the Welsh Office is constrained by the ideology and aims of the centre.

The Welsh Office has some room for autonomy, however, under certain circumstances. Where conditions are unique to Wales or the consequences of government policy can be restricted to Wales (avoiding spillover effects or accusations of territorial bias) then the Secretary of Wales may have a relatively free hand to address Welsh issues. An obvious example of such a policy area is that of the Welsh language and in 1993 a new Welsh Language Act was passed by the Conservative government. In other areas, the Welsh Office may have the power to adapt policies to meet particular Welsh circumstances. The history of the Valleys and their decline has created a situation which is distinctive (though hardly unique) and the Welsh Secretary can alter priorities to reflect particular Welsh conditions.

The Welsh Office may have some degree of autonomy in specialised policy areas of interest mainly to professional groups with a relatively low political salience. The Welsh Mental Handicap Strategy developed by the Welsh Office was innovative but was peripheral to most people's concerns. Other areas where the Secretary of State for Wales enjoys a degree of autonomy are areas where there is a history of separate policy-making in Wales. Unlike Scotland, Wales lacks a history of administrative autonomy but the history of distinctive education policy in Wales goes back over a century and the Secretary of State for Wales has been able to create a national curriculum for Wales with little interference from the centre.

However, for the most part, the role of the Welsh Office was, as it was for Kellas and Madgwick "the humdrum business of implementing policies decided elsewhere and introducing modest variations where they can suit the needs and idiosyncracies of [Wales]" (Kellas and Madgwick 1982 p29). For those who have talked of Welsh exceptionalism such a conclusion seems surprising. As I showed in chapter 2 Welsh political life does display some differences. There is a nationalist movement that has enjoyed a degree of electoral success. The major political parties operate separate organisations in Wales which publish Welsh manifestoes and hold Welsh conferences. Local government in Wales is represented by all-Wales organisations. There are a variety of Welsh economic, social, cultural and political pressure groups – everything from the Welsh TUC to *Cymdeithas Yr Iaith Gymraeg* to *Urdd Gobaith Cymru* (a Welsh youth organisation) – placing demands on government in Wales. It would seem fair to speak of a Welsh arena of British politics, a space where British political issues are coloured by the circumstances and sentiments of Wales.

The Welsh Office is not, however, free to respond to these demands as it wishes. The main source of policy ideas for the Welsh Office is not Wales itself but the centre, the Cabinet, the Prime Minister, Whitehall and Westminster. In this sense it is a central department, implementing the policies decided by the Cabinet and overseeing the activities of local authorities in Wales from a centre perspective. More occasionally, the Welsh Office acts as a spokesman for Welsh interests in Whitehall (or Brussels). An earlier study of the Welsh Office by Madgwick and James (1979) written shortly after Mrs Thatcher's first election victory in 1979 claimed that in the favourable climate of nationalist demands and the devolution debate of the 1970s "Welsh government was edged along the scale from agency towards autonomy" (Madgwick and James 1979 p1). The conclusion I draw from my research is that, although the Welsh Office has grown as an administrative machine since 1979, it has travelled only a very little way further along the scale towards autonomy.

164

Bibliography

Adamson, D L 1991 *Class, Ideology & the Nation: A Theory of Welsh Nationalism* University of Wales Press 1991

Agnew, J 1987 *Place and Politics: The Geographical Mediation of State and Society* Allen and Unwin London

Aitchison J, Carter H, 1986 Language Areas and Language Change in Wales 1961-1981 in I Hume, W T R Pryce (eds) *The Welsh and Their Country* Gomer Press Llandysul Dyfed

Anderson B, 1983 *Imagined Communities: Reflections on the Origin and Spread of Nationalism* Verso

Atkinson R abd Moon D, 1994 *Urban Policy in Britain: The City, the State and the Market* Macmillan London

Bacon R and Eltis W (1976) *Britain's Economic Problem: Too Few Producers* Macmillan London

Balsom D, 1983 *An Analysis of Recent Voting Patterns in Wales with particular reference to Socio-economic factors derived from the Census in Wales* University of Wales Ph.D. Thesis (unpublished)

Balsom D, 1985 The Three Wales Model in J Osmond (ed) *The National Question Again: Welsh Political Identity in the 1980s* Gomer press Llandysul Dyfed

Balsom D, (no date) Introduction in *The 1987 General Election in Wales* Welsh Political Archive Aberystwyth

Balsom D, Madgwick P J, Van Mechelen D P, 1982 *The Political Consequences of Welsh Identity* Centre for the Study of Public Policy Strathclyde Glasgow

Balsom D, Madgwick P J, Van Mechelen D P, 1983 The Red and the Green: Patterns of Partisan Choice in Wales *British Journal of Political Science* XIII pp299-326

Balsom D, Madgwick P J, Van Mechelen D, Miller W L, Brand J A, Jordan M, 1982 *Democratic or Violent Protest? Attitudes Towards Direct Action in Scotland and Wales.* Centre of the Study of Public Policy University of Strathclyde

Batley R, (1989) London Docklands: An Analysis of Power Relations between UDCs and Local Government *Public Administration* vol. 67 pp. 167-187

BBC Cymru/Wales *General Election 1992 Results* BBC Cymru Wales Cardiff

BBC 2, 23 November 1989 *The Welsh Office: 25 Years*

Bennie L and Mitchell J (1994) *Thatcherism and the Scottish Question* Paper for Elections, public opinion and parties in Britain Conference, Political Studies Association, Cardiff

Birch A H, 1977 *Political Integration and Disintegration in the British Isles* Allen and Unwin London

Beer W, 1980 *The Unexpected Rebellion: Ethnic activism in Contemporary France* New York University press New York

Bogdanor V, 1979 *Devolution* Oxford University Press Oxford

Bradbury J, (1993) *Bringing the State Back In and Interpretations of British Politics Since the First World War*, paper to the Political Studies Association Annual Conference Leicester

Brittan S, (1983) *The Role and Limits of Government* Temple-Smith London

Budge, I and Urwin D 1966 *Scottish Political Behaviour: A Case Study in British Homogeneity* Longmans London

Bulpitt J, 1983 *Territory and Power in the United Kingdom. An Interpretation* Manchester University press Manchester

Bulpitt J, 1986 The discipline of the New Democracy: Mrs Thatcher's Domestic Statecraft *Political Studies* 34:1 (1985) pp. 19-39

Bulpitt J, 1989, 'Walking Back to Happiness? Conservative party Governments and Elected Local Authorities in the 1980s' in Crouch C. and Marquand D (eds.) 1989 *The New Centralism: Britain Out of Step in Europe?* Basil Blackwell: Oxford

Butt Philip A, 1975 *The Welsh Question: Nationalism in Welsh Politics 1945-1970* University of Wales Press Cardiff

Cabinet Office, 1988 *Action for Cities* Cabinet Office

Cardiff and Vale Enterprise (CAVE) *1992 Annual Reports and Accounts 1991-1992* Cardiff and Vale Enterprise Cardiff

Cardiff Bay Business Forum 1992 *Cardiff Bay Business Charter* Cardiff Bay Business Forum Cardiff

Cardiff Bay Development Corporation 1989 *Annual Report and Accounts 1988-89* Cardiff Bay Development Corporation Cardiff

Cardiff Bay Development Corporation *1992 Annual Report and Accounts 1991-92* Cardiff Bay Development Corporation Cardiff

Cardiff Bay Development Corporation 1990 *Inner Harbour Final Report* Cardiff Bay Development Corporation Cardiff

Cardiff Bay Development Corporation, 1988 *Cardiff Bay Regeneration Strategy: The Summary* Cardiff Bay Development Corporation Cardiff

Cardiff Bay Development Corporation, 1989 *The Regeneration Strategy – Response by the Board Following Presentations and Discussions* Cardiff Bay Development Corporation Cardiff

Cardiff City District Labour Party, no date *What Will Be Our Response to the Cardiff Bay Development Strategy* Cardiff City District Labour Party Cardiff

Cardiff City District Labour Party, South Glamorgan County Labour Party no date *Cardiff Bay Development Strategy. A Response* Cardiff City District Labour Party Cardiff

Cardiff Residents Against the Barrage *Press Release 15 April 1991*

Carter H, Thomas J S, 1969 The Referendum on the Sunday Opening of Licensed Premises in Wales as a Criterion of a Culture Region *Regional Studies* III pp61-71

Central Statistical Office, 1993 *Regional Trends number 28* Central Statistical Office

Central Statistical Office, 1994 *Regional Trends number 29* Central Statistical Office

Centre for Local Economic Strategies, 1992 *Reforming the TECs: Towards a New Training Strategy Final Report* of CLES TEC/LEC Monitoring Project CLES Manchester

Civil Service Department, 1993 *Public Bodies* HMSO London

Claval P (1980) Centre/Periphery and Space: Models of Political Geography in J Gottman (ed.) *Centre and Periphery* Sage Publications London

Cole D, 1990 Introduction in D cole (ed) *The New Wales* University of Wales Press Cardiff

Conservative Central Office Wales, 1992 *The Dragon Awakes* Conservative Central Office Wales Cardiff

Cooke P, Morgan K, 1991 *Learning Through Networking: Regional Innovations and the Lessons of Baden Wurttemberg* Regional Industrial Research Cardiff

Crewe I, 1979 The Voting Surveyed in *The Times Guide to the House of Commons May 1979* Times Books London

Crewe I, (1983) The electorate: partisan dealignment ten years on *West European Politics* vol. 6 pp183-215

Crewe I, (1988) Has the Electorate become Thatcherite? in Skidelsky R (ed.) *Thatcherism* Chatto and Windus London

Crossman R H S, 1976 *The Crossman Diaries: Condensed Version* Methuen Books London

Council of Wales and Monmouthshire *Third Memorandum on its Activities: Report of the Administration Panel* Cmnd.53 HMSO London

Davies D P, 1990 A Time of Paradoxes among the Faiths in D Cole (ed) *The New Wales* University of Wales Press Cardiff

Dahrendorf R (1988) *A Sociologist's View of Thatcherism* in R. Skidelaky (ed) Thatcherism Chatter and Winder London

Davies, G T, 1983 The Role of Broadcasting in the Referendum in D Foulkes, J B Jones, R A Wilford (eds) The Welsh Veto: *The Wales Act 1978 & The Referendum*

Davies G, Thomas I, 1976 *Overseas Investment in Wales* Christopher Davies Swansea

R Denniston and M Linklater, (1992) *Anatomy of Scotland: how Scotland works* (Edinburgh: Chambers)

Deutsch K, 1966 *Nationalism and Social Communication* New York

Deakin N, Edwards J, 1993 *The Enterprise Culture and the Inner City* Routledge London

Department of the Environment 1977 *Policy for the Inner Cities* Cmnd 6845 HMSO London

Duncan S and Goodwin m, (1988) *The Local State and Uneven Development* Polity Press Cambridge

Eisenschitz A, Gough J, 1993 *The Politics of Local Economic Policy: The Problems and Possibilities of Local Initiative* Macmillan London

Ellis E L (1972) *The University College of Wales, Aberystwyth 1872-1972* University of Wales Press Cardiff

Emmerich M, Peck J, 1993 Training and Enterprise Councils: Time for Change *Local Economy* vol VIII pp 4-21

Environmental Advisory Unit, 1989 *Cardiff Bay Barrage Environmental Assessment* Environmental Advisory Unit Liverpool

Evans N, (1983) *Interpreting the Industrialisation of Wales: Internal colony, Imperial Node or Uneven Development* Paper presented to the British Sociological Association Annual Conference Cardiff

Gaffikin F, Morrissey M, 1990 *Northern Ireland: The Thatcher Years* Zed Books London

Gamble A, (1988) *The Free Economy and the Strong State: The Politics of Thatcherism* Macmillan: London

Gamble A, 1993 Territorial Politics in P Dunleavy, A Gamble, I Holliday, G Peele (eds) *Developments in British Politics 4*, Macmillan London

George K D, Mainwaring L, 1988 Introduction in K D George, L Mainwaring *The Welsh Economy* University of Wales Press Cardiff

Gottman J, 1980 Confronting Centre and Periphery in J Gottman (ed) *Centre and Periphery* Sage Publications Beverley Hills

Gowan I, 1970 Government in Wales in the Twentieth Century in J A Andrews (ed) *Welsh Studies in Public Law* University of Wales Press Cardiff

Greenwood J, Wison D, 1989 *Public Administration in Britain Today* (second edition) Unwin Hyman London

Hechter M, 1975 *Internal Colonialism: The Celtic Fringe in British National Development, 1536-1966* Routledge and Kegan Paul London

Hill S, Morris J, Economist Intelligence Unit, 1991 *Wales* Economist Intelligence Unit London

Hill S, Munday M, 1991 The Determinants of inward investment: a Welsh analysis *Applied Economics* vol XXIII pp 1761-1769

Hill S, Munday M, 1992 Foreign Direct Investment in Wales *Local Economy* vol VI pp21-34

House of Commons Welsh Grand Committee 16 December 1964 *Functions of the Secretary of State for Wales and Constitutional Changes in Wales* Parl Debates 16 December 1964 col3-52 Session 1964-65 vol V

House of Commons Employment Committee 1988 HC 327-I *The Employment Effects of Urban Development Corporations* Employment Committee Third Report HMSO London

House of Commons Employment Committee 1988 HC 327-II *The Employment Effects of Urban Development Corporations* Employment Committee Third Report Minutes of Evidence HMSO London

House of Commons National Audit Office 1991 HC 664 *Creating and Safeguarding Jobs in Wales* HMSO London

House of Commons National Audit Office 1993 HC 898 *The Achievement of the Second and Third Generation Urban Development Corporations* HMSO London

House of Commons Public Accounts Committee Fifth Report *Creating and Safeguarding Jobs in Wales* Committee of Public Accounts Fifth Report HMSO London

House of Commons Committee of Public Accounts, 1993 HC 353 *Welsh Development Agency Accounts 1991-92* Committee of Public Accounts Forty-Seventh Report HMSO London

House of Commons Fourth Standing Committee on Statutory Instruments 1987 *Cardiff Bay Development Corporation (Area and Constitution) Order* 1987

House of Commons Parliamentary Debates 28 November 1991 *Welsh Development Agency Bill* Vol 199 col 1093-1161 Session 1991-92

House of Commons Welsh Affairs Committee 1986 HC 502-II *Enterprise Agencies and Job Creation Minutes of Evidence* HMSO London

House of Commons Welsh Affairs Committee 1988 HC 86-I *Inward Investment into Wales and its Interaction with Regional and EEC Policies* First Report HMSO London

House of Commons Welsh Affairs Committee 1988 HC 86-II *Inward Investment into Wales and its Interaction with Regional and EEC Policies First Report Minutes of Evidence* HMSO London

House of Commons Welsh Affairs Committee, 1993 HC 259-I *The Work of the Welsh Office* Welsh Affairs Committee First *Report* HMSO London

House of Commons Welsh Affairs Committee, 1993 HC 259-II *The Work of the Welsh Office* Welsh Affairs Committee First Report *Minutes of Evidence* HMSO London

Housing for Wales 30 July 1991 *Press Release* Housing for Wales Cardiff

Housing for Wales 1992 Investment Policies and Plans 1992/93 Housing for Wales Cardiff

Housing for Wales 1992 *Improving the Effectiveness of Housing Association Development* and Management Housing for Wales Cardiff

Imrie R, Thomas H, 1992 The Wrong Side of the Tracks: A case study of local economic regeneration in Britain *Policy and Politics* Vol XX pp 213-226

Inglehart R, (1977) *The Silent Revolution: Changing Values and Political Styles Among Western Publics* Princeton University Press New Jersey

Institute of Welsh Affairs (1993) *Wales 2010: Creating our future* Institute of Welsh Affairs Cardiff

Jenkins D, 1993 *The Response of the Wales TUC to the Opportunities and Challenges of Inward Investment* in Welsh Economic Review Special Issue: Inward Investment in Wales

Jessop B, Bonnett K, Bromley S and Ling T (1988) *Thatcherism: A Tale of Two Nations* Polity Press Oxford

Jones J B and Wilford R A, (1983) Implications: Two Salient Ismes in D Foulkes, J Barry Jones and R A Walford (eds) *The Welsh Veto: The Wales Act 1978 & The Referendum* University of Wales Press Cardiff

Jones J B, 1988 The Development of Welsh Territorial Institutions: Modernization Theory Revisited *Contemporary Wales* II pp47-62

Jones B 1975 *Etholiadau Seneddol yng Nghymru 1900-1975/Parliamentary Elections in Wales 1900-1975* Y Lolfa Talybont

Jones Lang Wootton 1986 *South Cardiff Waterfront: Preliminary Development Appraisal*

Judge D, 1989 Urban Development Corporations: Parliamentary Pointers Towards Assessment *Local Economy* vol IV pp 57-66

Kavanagh D, (1987) *Thatcherism and British Politics: The End of Consensus?* Oxford University Press Oxford

Kellas J G, 1989 (Fourth Edition) *The Scottish Political System* Cambridge University Press Cambridge

Kellas J G, Madgwick, 1982 Territorial Ministries: the Scottish and Welsh

Offices in P J Madgwick, R Rose (eds) *The Territorial Dimension in United Kingdom Politics* Macmillan London

Kilbrandon 1973, *Royal Commission on the Constitution* HMSO London

Lambert J and Rees G (1981) Nationalism as Legitimation? Notes Towards a political economy of regional development in South Wales in M Marlowe (ed.) *New Perspectives in urban change and conflict* Heinemann London

Langstaff M, 1992 Housing Associations: A move to centre stage in J Birchall (ed) *Housing Policy in the 1990s* Routledge London

Lewis N, 1992 *Inner City Regeneration: The Demise of Regional and Local Government* Open University Press Buckingham

Lipset S M, Rokkan S, 1967 Cleavage structures, party systems and voter alignments in S M Lipset, S Rokkan *Party Systems and Voter Alignments* New York Free Press New York

Llywelyn Davies Planning 1987 *Cardiff Bay Regeneration Strategy* Llywelyn Davies Planning Cardiff

Lovering J, 1983 Uneven Development in Wales: The Changing Role of the British State in G Williams (ed) *Crisis of Economy and Ideology* University of Wales Press Cardiff

Madgwick P J, Griffiths N, Walker V, 1973 *The Politics of Rural Wales: A study of Cardiganshire* Hutchinson London

Madgwick P J, James M, 1979 *Government by Consultation: The Case of Wales* Centre for the Study of Public Policy Glasgow

Madgwick P J, Rose R, 1982 *The Territorial Dimension in United Kingdom Politics* Macmillan London

Mallender J, RSPB 1992 *Report on the Economic Case for the Proposed Development of a Barrage at Cardiff Bay*, RSPB

Marquand D, 1988 *The Unprincipled Society: New Demands and Old Politics* Fontana Press London

Marsh D, and Rhodes R A W (1992) Thatcherism: An implementation Perspective in Marsh D and Rhodes R A W (eds.) *Implementing Thatcherite Policies: Audit of an Era* Open University Press Milton Keynes

Marx K, Engels F, 1975 *Manifesto of the Communist Party* Foreign Language Press Peking

McAllister I and Rose R (1984) *The Nationwide Competition for Votes* Frances Pinter London

McCrone D, 1992 *Understanding Scotland: The sociology of a stateless nation* Routledge London

McKenna C J, 1988 The Overall Level of Activity in K D George, L Mainwaring (eds) *The Welsh Economy* University of Wales Press Cardiff

Meny Y, Wright V, 1985 Introduction in Y Meny and V Wright *Centre Periphery Relations in Western Europe* Allen and Unwin London

Midwinter A, Keating M, Mitchell J, 1991 *Politics and Public Policy in Scotland* Macmillan London

Miller W L, 1983 The denationalisation of British politics: the re-emergence of the periphery *West European Politics* VI pp 103-129

Minchinton W E (1969) *Industrial South Wales: 1750-1914* Frank Cass London

Morgan P, 1986 Keeping the Legends Alive in T Curtis (ed) *Wales: The Imagined Nation* Poetry Wales Press Bridgend

Morgan K O, 1980 *Wales in British Politics 1868-1922* (Third Edition) University of Wales Press Cardiff

Morgan K O, 1981 *Rebirth of a Nation: Wales 1880-1980* Oxford University Press Oxford

Morgan R, Cardiff: 1994 *Half-and-half a Capital* Gomer Press Llandysul Dyfed

Morris J, 1986 *The Matter of Wales: Epic Views of a Small Country* Penguin London

Morris J, Wilkinson B, 1989 *Divided Wales A Report for HTV Wales*

Mr Lightman's Lecture 22 October 1987 *The Welsh Office: Little whitehall or large local authority* UWIST/RIPA

Moore C, 1988 Enterprise Agencies: Privatisation or Partnership? *Local Economy* vol III pp21-29

Munday M, 1990 *Japanese Manufacturing Investment in Wales* University of Wales Press Cardiff

Nairn T, 1977 *The Break-up of Britain: crisis and neo-nationalism* New Left Books London

National Rivers Authority Wales Region, 1991 *Cardiff Bay Barrage: The NRA's Position*

Nature Conservancy Council 1988 *Petition of the Nature Conservancy Council* Cardiff Bay Barrage Bill House of Lords

Osmond J, 1974 *The Centralist Enemy* Christopher Davies Llandybie (Dyfed)

Osmond J, 1978 *Creative Conflict: The Politics of Welsh Devolution* Routledge & Kegan Paul London

Osmond J, 1983 The Referendum and the English Language Press in D Foulkes, J B Jones, R A Wilford (eds) The Welsh Veto: *The Wales Act 1978 and the Referendum* University of Wales Press Cardiff

Osmond J, (1985) Coping with a Dual Identity in J Osmond (ed) *The National Question Again: Welsh Political Identity in the 1980s* Gower Press Nordgend Dyfed

Osmond J, 1992 *The Democratic Challenge* Gomer Press Llandysul Dyfed

Peat Marwick McLintock, 1989 *Cardiff Bay Development Corporation Updated Economic Appraisal of the Barrage Strategy*

Pubier P G J, (1967) *Political Representation and Elections in Britain* George Allen and Unwin London

Randall P J, 1972 Wales in the Structure of Central Government *Public Administration* L pp 353-372

Rees G, Thomas M, 1994 Inward Investment, Labour Market Adjustment and Skills Development: Recent Experience in South Wales *Local Economy* vol IX pp 48-61

Rees I B, 1971 *Government by Community* Charles Knight London

Royal Society for the Protection of Birds, no date *The Case Against the Taff/Ely* Barrage

Rhodes R A W (1985) *Intergovernmental Relations in the United Kingdom* in Y Meny and V Wright (eds.0 *Centre-periphery relations in Western Europe* George Allen and Unwin London

Rhodes R A W, 1988 *Beyond Westminster and Whitehall: The Sub-Central Government of Britain* Unwin Hyman London

Rhodes R A W, 1987 Territorial Politics in the United Kingdom: the Politics of Change, Conflict and Contradiction in R A W Rhodes And V Wright (eds) *Tensions in the Territorial Politics of Western Europe* Frank Cass London

Rhodes R A W, Wright V, 1987 Introduction in R A W Rhodes and V Wright (eds) *Tensions in the Territorial Politics of Western Europe* Frank Cass London

Riddell P (1985) *The Thatcher Government* Basil Blackwell Oxford

Riddell P (1991) *The Thatcher Era and its Legacy* Basil Blackwell Oxford

Roger Tym and Partners, Conran Roche, Chesterton, peat Marwick McLintock 1990 *Cardiff Bay Barrage: Planning Update and Economic Appraisal* Statement

Rokkan S, Urwin D, 1982 Introduction: Centres and Peripheries in Western Europe in S Rokkan and D Urwin (eds) *The Politics of Territorial Identity – studies in European Regionalism* Sage Publications London

Rokkan S, Urwin D, 1983 *Economy, Territory, Identity – The Politics of West European Peripheries* Sage Publications London

Rose R, 1976 The United Kingdom as a Multi-National State in R Rose (ed) *Studies in British Politics: a reader in political sociology* Macmillan London

Rose R, 1982 *Understanding the United Kingdom: The Territorial Dimension in Government* Longman London

Rose R, 1984 *Understanding Big Government: The programme Approach* Sage Publications London

Rose R, 1987 *Ministers and Ministries: A Functional Analysis* Clarendon Press Oxford

Rowlands E, 1972 The Politics of Regional Administration: The Establishment of the Welsh Office *Public Administration* L pp 333-351

Senior Training Group, no date *A Strategy for Training and Employment in South Glamorgan* Senior Training Group Cardiff

Sharpe L J, 1987 The West European State: The Territorial Dimension in R A W

Rhodes and V Wright (eds) *Tensions in the Territorial Politics of Western Europe* Frank Cass London

Shelter Cymru 1992 *Housing in Wales: The Facts* Shelter Cymru Swansea

South Glamorgan County Council, 1986 *The Regeneration of South Cardiff – Proposals for an Urban Development Corporation* South Glamorgan County Council Cardiff

Stoker G, 1988 *The Politics of Local Government* Macmillan Education

Thomas Skinner Directories, 1991 *Willings Press Guide* Thomas Skinner Directories East Grinstead

Smith A D (1981) *The Ethnic Revival in the Modern World* Cambridge University press Cambridge

Smith D, 1984 *Wales! Wales?* Allen and Unwin London

Smith J B, 1978 James Griffiths: an appreciation in *James Griffiths and his Times* Labour Party Wales

Tarrow S G, 1977 *Between Centre and Periphery: Grassroots Politicians in Italy and France* Yale University Press New Haven

Thomas B, 1962 Preface in B Thomas (ed) *The Welsh Economy: Studies in Expansion* University of Wales Press Cardiff

Thomas D, 1991 *The Welsh Economy: Current Circumstances and Future Prospects* University of Wales Press Cardiff

Thomas D, 1993 Wales: Image and Reality in *Parliamentary Brief* August/September 1993 pp 15-18

Thomas D, 1994 Wales in 1991: An Economic Survey in *Contemporary Wales* VI pp 137-198

Thomas D, Day G, 1992 Rural Wales: Problems, Policies and Prospects *Welsh Economic Review* vol V

Thomas I, 1980 *The Creation of the Welsh Office: conflicting Purposes in Institutional Change* Centre for the Study of Public Policy Strathclyde Glasgow

Thomas I, 1987 Giving Direction to the Welsh Office in R Rose *Ministers and Ministries: A Functional Analysis* Clarendon Press Oxford

Thomas N, 1991 *The Welsh Extremist: Modern Welsh Politics, Literature and Society* (new edition) Y Lolfa Talybont Dyfed

Tunstall J, 1983 *The Media in Britain* Constable London

Urwin D W, (1982) Territorial Structures and Political Developments in the United Kingdom in S Rokkan and D Urwin (eds.) *The Politics of Territorial Identity: Studies in European Regionalism* Sage Publications London

Urwin D W, (1985) The Price of a Kingdom: Territory, Identity and the Centro-Periphery Dimension in Western Europe in Y Meng and V Wright (eds) *Centro-Periphery Relations in Western Europe* George Allen and Unwin London

Vale of Glamorgan Borough Council 1992 *Vale of Glamorgan Economic Development Strategy 1992/93*

Wales TUC, 1992 *Low Pay in Wales – A Tory Trademark*, Wales TUC Cardiff

Walker P, 1988, Wales: An Economy on the Move *Welsh Economic Review* vol I pp4-8

Walker P, 1991 *Staying Power* Bloomsbury London

Watson M (ed), 1990 *Contemporary Minority Nationalism* Routledge London

Welsh Development Agency, 1992, *Welsh Development Agency Report & Accounts 1991-92*, Welsh Development Agency Cardiff

Welsh Development Agency, 1993 *Welsh Development Agency Report & Accounts 1992-1993* Welsh Development Agency Cardiff

Welsh Federation of Housing Associations 1992 *Improving the Effectiveness of Housing Association and Management: Response from the Federation's National Council* Welsh Federation of Housing Association Cardiff

Welsh Office 1991 *Circular 25/91*

Welsh Office, 1992 *Welsh Economic Trends/Tueddiadau'r Economi* no. 13 HMSO Cardiff

Welsh Office, 1993 *Welsh Economic Trends Tueddiadau'r Economi* no. 14 HMSO Cardiff

Welsh Office, 1991 *Housing in Wales: An Agenda for Action* Welsh Office Cardiff

Welsh Office, 1991 *The Government's Expenditure Plans 1991-92 to 1993-94: A Report by the Welsh Office* Cm 1516 HMSO London

Welsh Office, 1992 *The Government's Expenditure Plans 1992-93 to 1994-95: A Report by the Welsh Office Cm 1916* HMSO Cardiff

Welsh Office, 1993 *The Government's Expenditure Plans 1993-94 to 1995-96:* A Report by the Welsh Office Cm 2215 HMSO Cardiff

Welsh Office, 1994 *The Government's Expenditure Plans 1994-95 to 1996-97 A Report By the Welsh Office* Cm2515 HMSO Cardiff

Welsh Office, 1993 *Digest of Welsh Statistics* number 39, HMSO Cardiff

Williams C (ed), 1982 *National Separatism* University of Wales Press Cardiff

Williams D, 1950 *Modern Wales* John Murray London

Williams G A, 1985 *When Was Wales?* Penguin London

Williams G, 1991 *The Welsh and their Religion* University of Wales Press Cardiff

Other Sources

Cardiff Bay Barrage Bill Select Committee 1990 Minutes of Evidence

Economist

Forum News Cardiff Bay Business Forum

Independent

Independent on Sunday

Invest in Britain Bureau: Annual Reports

Liverpool Daily Post

South Wales Echo

Wales Yearbook edited by Denis Balsom 1991, 1992, 1994 HTV Wales Cardiff

Western Mail

Index

Modernisation theories, 3; 4
monetarism, 67; 69
Montesquieu, 2
Moors Housing Association, 131
Morgannwg, Iolo, 31
Morris, John, 51
Morris, Jonathan, 141; 148
Mowlem Training, 133
Mungham, Councillor, 128
Myth (making), 23; 24

National Audit Office, 99
national government environment, 18
National Health Service Trusts, 62
National Rivers Authority, 145
Nature Conservancy Council, 136; 144
Newport, 90
Northern Development Company, 95
North Wales Liberal Federation, 47
Northern Ireland Office, 59
Northern Ireland, 5; 6; 21

Operation WIZARD, 63; 64; 103;

Peat Marwick McLintock, 140
Peat, Mr, 155
Penyberth, 33
Peripheral Distributor Raod, 124; 129
Phillips, councillor, 130
Plaid Cymru, 7; 10; 38; 39; 51
Point of Ayr Colliery, 58
Policy for the Inner Cities (Cmnd 6845), 117; 120
Postmaterialism, 9
Pred, 3
President of Board of Trade,58

Radio Cymru, 26; 37
Ramsar, 144
Redwood, John, 54; 56; 163
Regional Selective Assistance, 90; 99; 100
Rhondda by-election, 7
Rhone Alpes, 64, 111
Right to Buy, 152
Roberts, Eigra Lewis, 42
Roberts, Kate, 42
Roger Tym and partners, 140
Rowlands, Edward, 57
Royal Society for the Protection of Birds (RSPB), 137, 142; 144; 145
Rugby, 42
Runciman, Walter, 47

Sabbatarianism, 27; 29
Sainsbury, Councillor, 128
Scottish Development Agency, 161
Scottish National Party, 7; 8; 51
Scottish Office, 6; 59; 161
Senior Training Group, 132
Severn Estuary Special Protection Area, 145
ShelterWales/Cymru, 150; 153; 155; 156
Sianel Pedwar Cymru (Channel Four Wales), 26; 37; 42
Small firms Merit Award for Research and Technology (SMART), 111
Somali Women's Advice Centre, 136
Source Wales Initiative, 111
South Glamorgan County Council, 124; 125; 127; 129
South Glamorgan County Labour Party, 124
South Glamorgan, 79; 91; 92
South Pembrokeshire, 82

St Peter's Women's Fellowship,
136,
Steel-making, 34
Stormont, 6; 8
Support for Products Under
Research, 111
Switzerland, 87

Taliesin, 36
Taylor, Teddy, 55
Team Wales, 93; 94
Temperance, 27; 29
Thatcherism, 18; 67-75, 159
Thomas, Alfred, 46
Thomas, Dafydd-Elis, 20
Thomas, Peter, 53; 55
Thomas, R S. 42
Tonypandy, 24
Toyota, 95
Trafford Park Development
Corporation, 149
Training Agency, 72
Training and Enterprise Councils
(TECs), 54; 12; 107; 113
Training Enterprise and Education
Department, 106
Treaty (Act) of Union, 6
Trustee Savings Bank, 90
Tlyweryn, 48
Tsuda Plastic Industry Company
Limited, 96
Tynged yr Iaith (Fate of the
Language), 7

Un Nos Ola Leuad (One Moonlit
Night), 42
Union-State, 6
Unitary state, 1
United States of America, 86
University of Wales, 29; 30
Urban Development Corporations,
116; 118
Urban Development Corporations,
72; 73
Urban Development Grant, 117; 120
Urban Investment Grant, 121
Urban Programme (in Wales), 121
Urban Regeneration Grant, 117; 118
Urdd Gobaith Cymru, 164

Vale of Glamorgan Borough
Council, 122; 124; 125
Valleys Initiative, 116
Valleys Initiative, 83
Vehicle licensing Agency, 160

Wales 2010, 161
Wales and Berwick Act, 46
Wales CBI, 94; 98
Wales Council for Voluntary Action,
108
Wales European Centre, 65; 111
Wales Health Common Services
Authority, 62
Wales Tourist Board, 60
Wales TUC, 94
Wales: The Way Ahead, 50
Walker, Peter, 20; 54; 57; 63; 64;
78; 93; 102; 109; 114; 128; 160;
162
Walters, Donald, 108
Watkin, Tudor, 49
Watkins, Councillor, 128
Weber, Max, 3
Welsh Affairs Select Committee, 53;
57; 58
Welsh Board of Agriculture, 46
Welsh Board of Health, 46
Welsh Board of the Department of
Education, 46; 47
Welsh Consultative Council on
Local Government, 54; 61

Welsh Consumers Council, 63
Welsh Development Agency
   (WDA), 19; 40; 41; 52; 63; 65;
   83; 89; 91; 92; 93; 94; 95; 97; 99;
   101103; 111; 120; 160;
Welsh Federation of Housing
   Associations, 156
Welsh Intermediate Education Act
   (1889), 30;46.
Welsh Language Act (1967), 7; 25
Welsh Language Act (1993), 25
Welsh Mental Handicap Strategy,
   58; 164
Welsh National Insurance

Commission, 46; 47
Welsh Office, 6; 19; 20; 41; 48-52;
   57; 58; 83; 97; 106; 160; 163; 164
Welsh Property Venture, 102
Welsh Sunday Closing Act, 29; 46
West Glamorgan, 79; 91; 92
Winvest, 96
Wrexham Maelor Borough Council,
   96

Y Cymro, 36
Y Traethodydd, 36
Youth Training, 107